STORMCHASERS

STORMCHASERS

The Hurricane Hunters
and Their Fateful Flight
into Hurricane Janet

DAVID TOOMEY

W. W. Norton & Company
New York   London

For information about permission to reproduce selections
from this book, write to Permissions, W. W. Norton &
Company, Inc., 500 Fifth Avenue, New York, NY 10110

The text of this book is composed in New Baskerville with
the display set in Bell Italic and Kenyan Coffee Book
Composition by Julia Druskin
Manufacturing by The Courier Companies, Inc.
Book design by Dana Sloan
Production manager: Amanda Morrison

Library of Congress Cataloging-in-Publication Data

Toomey, David M.
    Stormchasers : the Hurricane Hunters and their fateful
flight into Hurricane Janet / by David Toomey.
      p.   cm.
    Includes bibliographical references.
    ISBN 0-393-02000-2
      1. United States. Navy. Weather Reconnaissance
Squadron, Four (VW4)—History. 2. Hurricane Janet,
1955. 3. Hurricanes—Research—United States. I. Title.

VG94.6.W43 T66 2002
551.55'2'072073—dc21
                                        2002016601

W. W. Norton & Company, Inc., 500 Fifth Avenue,
New York, N.Y. 10110
www.wwnorton.com

W. W. Norton & Company Ltd., Castle House, 75/76 Wells
Street, London W1T 3QT

1 2 3 4 5 6 7 8 9 0

for my mother and father

The essence of the difference between meteorology and most sciences is the fact that meteorology studies a system that cannot be controlled by man. No adequate laboratory has ever been devised to simulate the atmosphere itself for study of the weather. Laboratory methods are useful for certain small-scale determinations; but in general the meteorologist must search for idealized processes that he considers "most likely" to occur, in lieu of controlled experiment in the laboratory. If the first selected ideal process fails to produce results that are in fair correlation with observations, he simply drops that concept and searches for another.

—*Handbook of Meteorology*, p. 315

It may happen that small differences in the initial conditions produce very great ones in the final phenomena. A small error in the former will produce an enormous error in the latter. Prediction becomes impossible. . . .

—Jules Henri Poincare,
Science and Method

Contents

Acknowledgments

Many people contributed to this book, some in ways they may not realize. I want to express appreciation to Captain Ron Price and the staff of the Mid-Atlantic Air Museum in Reading, Pennsylvania, for allowing me aboard an operational P2V Navy Neptune; to Chris Landsea of the National Oceanic and Atmospheric Administration (NOAA) for explaining the phenomena in the hurricane's eye and recommending sources; to Engineer/Meteorologist Daniel Vietor of Unisys Corporation for answering questions on the history of hurricane nomenclature; to Tracie Barnes for engaging me in extensive correspondence on meteorological history and sharing her enviable knowledge of the peculiarities of violent weather; to Katherine Soniat, who as this project was in its early stages, told me hurricane stories of her New Orleans childhood; to Dr. Raphael Alvarado for sharing his insights into Mesoamerican views of hurricanes; to Dr. Mizan Khan for offering background on differential equations and the first electronic computers; and to Añira Dahlstrom for valuable comments on drafts.

The opportunity to meet and learn from the men who flew hurricane reconnaissance was a special pleasure and a privilege, and I am grateful for it. The men whose names follow shared generously their memories of events that transpired nearly half a century ago, and explained technical matters to a novice with patience: Dr. Ken Clift, Bob Fitzsimmons, Charlie Gertz, Donald R. James, Jim Mick, Rene P. Leger, Joseph Pausner Jr., and Dane Youell. This work benefited greatly from the assistance of Bud Shipman, who supplied detailed background and a pilot's insight. I owe thanks to James Meyer for his friendship, and his willingness to explain a great deal to someone who began this work barely knowing the difference between an airman apprentice and a fleet admiral. I am especially indebted to John C. Haynie Jr. and Nancy Windham DeFevers for sharing memories of Grover Windham Jr.

I am grateful to Leslie Haynsworth, my once and future co-author, for offering friendship and perspective; to my editor Angela von der Lippe for taking a chance on the project and for helping me turn facts into narrative; to her assistant Stefanie Diaz for skillfully managing a hundred details of editing and production; and to the capable and resourceful staffs at W. W. Norton. As always, warm thanks to my agent David Hendin.

I am indebted to the staffs of the Navy Department Library in Washington, D.C.; the Jacksonville Public Library in Jacksonville, Florida; the National Museum of Naval Aviation in Pensacola, Florida; Mills Memorial Library of McMaster University in Hamilton, Ontario; the Carol Newman Library of Virginia Tech in Blacksburg, Virginia; and the W.E.B. Du Bois and Physical Sciences Libraries of the University of Massachusetts (Amherst). The authors of the books and articles whose titles appear in the bibliography provided me a wealth of background material, and I refer the interested reader to them for more complete histories of hurricane science and the weather reconnaissance crews of the U.S. Navy and U.S. Air Force.

Of course, any errors of fact are mine alone.

D.T.

Preface

Technology has a way of numbing us to history. It is easy to take for granted the comforts made possible by science and engineering, easy to forget the everyday hardships experienced by the human species during most of its existence. This cultural amnesia is perhaps nowhere more evident than in our relationship with the earth's weather. In an era of satellite images, Doppler radar, computer models, and three-dimensional time-lapsed animations, in an era when anyone with access to cable television or the Internet can learn the five-day forecast for Kansas City or western Zimbabwe, it comes as a mild shock to realize that until the mid nineteenth century there could be no certain knowledge of whether it was raining or snowing at a location even a few miles distant. To be sure, there was a great deal of *uncertain* knowledge. Most preindustrial societies accumulated a wealth of meteorological folk wisdom, and a corresponding appreciation of natural indicators. Mackerel clouds, rings around the moon, red sky at morning—all are traditional and fairly reliable signs of storms. The rippled altocumuli called mackerel clouds often precede steady rain or snow; those "rings" are reflections off cirrostratus clouds that often signal an approaching frontal system; and a "red sky" is made when the clouds of a storm system approaching from the west are illuminated by the rays of the rising sun.

It is true that our present insulation from the natural world has been purchased at the cost of such awareness. But it is also true that we have a tendency to romanticize prehistoric or preindustrial peoples, attributing knowledge of natural forces where there was only rumor and anecdote. For the preindustrial world, reliable weather forecasting was all but nonexistent. A practiced eye could see changes in clouds, and the barometer, in use since the 1660s, could hint at an approaching storm. But most meteorological knowledge was confined to conditions that were local and current. Matters began to improve greatly in the mid nineteenth century, when the telegraph made possible communication between weather stations at great distances. But it was only in the 1930s that the radiosonde allowed meteorologists a glimpse of atmospheric conditions at high altitudes, and only in the last forty years have Earth-orbiting satellites shown us the weather half a world away.

Among the more interesting periods in the history of our understanding of the atmosphere were the 1950s. In some ways, weather prediction was primitive. Graphical representations of weather systems were made with a marker pen on chart paper, and the most elaborate three-dimensional models of hurricanes were a few handfuls of cotton glued together to approximate the familiar anvil shape. Long-range airborne radar would have to wait for the next generation of aircraft, and the first televised picture from a satellite would not appear until 1960. It would be nearly a decade after that before the U.S. Navy would deploy its network of moored oceanic buoys, and forecasters would begin to detect wind speeds with Doppler radar. Although ground-based radar systems existed at some sites along the Atlantic and Gulf Coasts, the great majority of reports of developing storm systems came from ships that happened to be in their vicinity. Most events on the open ocean went unobserved.

Still, the first decade after World War II brought significant developments. Scientists were beginning to discern the outlines of a global history of the atmosphere. In April 1950 a group working at the Institute for Advanced Study in Princeton, New Jersey, used atmospheric equations and a computer called ENIAC to make a fairly accurate forecast. Journalists in particular seemed to regard the subject of meteorology with great optimism. Newspapers were full of stories about coming advances, not simply for weather prediction but for actual control. Articles in popular magazines interviewed scientists who claimed that by the early 1960s, airplanes would seed the clouds, rain would turn deserts to lush cropland, and the winds themselves would be tamed.

In the field, there was a similar sense that meteorology was about to enter a new era. The war had spurred great advances in aeronautics, and its end had left the United States with tremendous material resources, trained pilots, and new technologies. For the first time, it was possible to perform aerial reconnaissance of violent weather. By 1947 the Weather Bureau, in conjunction with the Air Force and Navy, had begun its around-the-clock hurricane warning service. Like upstart empires, two branches of the U.S. military divided the seas. The Air Force's 53rd began to track hurricanes in the Pacific and the West Central Atlantic. The Navy began reconnaissance in the Caribbean, with missions flown from Naval Air Station Jacksonville in Florida. By the early 1950s techniques for reconnoitering storms were well tested and much refined, and by September 1955 some hundreds of flights had been made into and through hurricanes. The men who flew these missions were called the weather reconnaissance squadrons, or, less formally, the Hurricane Hunters.

The establishment of military weather reconnaissance for peaceful purposes was certainly unusual, but it was not unprecedented. The previous century had also seen a nation turn swords to plowshares—or try to. In 1815, when Britain had ended its war with France, Sir John Barrow, second secretary of the Admiralty and founder of the Royal Geographic Society, devised expeditions for British naval officers and ships. They were sent on missions of exploration, their broad purpose to gain scientific knowledge of Arctic regions, their specific purpose to discover a Northwest Passage to the Pacific. From 1815 until 1854, scores of ships were tasked with mapping the frozen archipelagos north of the sixtieth parallel.

The weather reconnaissance crews had much in common with their British forebears. Both had an appreciation of the aesthetic. As the explorers would write of the spectacle of the pale Arctic sun casting long shadows across ice floes, so the Hurricane Hunters would return with descriptions of the awesome walls of clouds surrounding the storm's eye.[1] Moreover, both groups were made possible by particular historical circumstances. Britain's expeditions could have been mounted only during the middle decades of the nineteenth century. A few years earlier the economic resources were lacking, and the nation was at war with France. In the decade that followed, technological advances like wireless radio would make such endeavors seem quaint and quixotic. Likewise, the particular missions of the first Hurricane Hunters could only have

---

1. Like most comparisons between historical periods, this may be pushed only so far. In some sense the British Arctic expeditions were examples of sheer folly, yielding few tangible scientific results and no practical results, at a cost of many lives. By contrast, the weather reconnaissance crews saved thousands of lives and millions of dollars in property, and produced data with which meteorologists developed the first modern theories of hurricane formation. But it is curious that in the 1850s the British populace was captivated by the expeditions. Newspapers printed detailed accounts of preparations and departures; presses were eager to publish journals and accounts of men upon their return. By contrast, few Americans in the 1950s knew the Hurricane Hunters even existed, this despite the fact that their safety depended on them.

taken the shape they did in the 1950s. A decade earlier there had been neither resources nor the knowledge to reconnoiter storms on a regular basis. A decade later improved telemetry and drop-sondes would render low-altitude reconnaissance unnecessary, and weather satellites and computer models would make investigative flights redundant. Finally, the endeavors of both periods were products of a surplus of resources—a situation that generated a kind of expectation and hopefulness. During the mid-Victorian era, what some called the "Age of Improvement," Britain enjoyed an agreeable sense that the world lay at its feet. G. M. Young wrote, "Of all the decades in our history, a wise man would choose the eighteen-fifties to be young in." Similarly, America in the 1950s was a nation of optimists. A Gallup Poll from 1954 reported that only 21 percent of Americans listed "threat of world war" as their greatest worry, and despite complaints about high taxes and high prices, a clear majority believed they were better off than their parents had been.

In mid-September 1955 Americans were mostly comfortable with their place in the world. There were day-to-day concerns of grocery and electric bills. There were larger, national concerns; newspapers reported that President Eisenhower had suffered a heart attack but was improving daily. As always, there was the diversion of sports: The World Series would begin in a few days. It would be the sixth "Subway Series," with the Yankees a strong 13-10 favorite against the Brooklyn Dodgers.

It is tempting to imagine an earlier generation as naïve, and nearly a cliché to speak of any traumatic moment in American history as the "end of innocence." But the men who flew hurricane reconnaissance were not innocent by most senses of the word. Many had served in the war, and many had seen friends die. Of course, they were naïve—as we all are—of the future. Like most Americans in 1955, they probably imagined that the days ahead, except for minor details, would be much like their present. Few could foresee that within the year, Fidel Castro would invade Cuba, and the triumph of democracy would seem far less certain. Fewer still could imagine the tumultuous events that would shape the decades that followed, or the generations that would live through them.

If the men of first weather reconnaissance crews could not imagine us, how might we imagine them? They entered and explored the most powerful storms on Earth in aircraft of World War II vintage. They estimated the drift of their aircraft by looking at windblown waves, and they located the hurricane they were seeking with rudimentary radar systems. They had no computer technology, no global positioning system, no satellite imagery. Often they did not know what lay ahead of them until they saw it through the forward windscreen or felt it when the deck lurched beneath them. And when all is said and done, it may be this willingness to enter the unknown with so much uncertainty that best defines them and their place in history. The weather reconnaissance squadrons of the 1950s were the first crews who flew into hurricanes deliberately and routinely. And they were the last who did so with so little knowledge of where they were going.

⤙

This work declares itself nonfiction. But a few qualifications are in order. I have tried to remain faithful to actual events, the few quotations I have used were reported by reliable sources, and the few thoughts I have attributed to figures are thoughts which I believe would be probable given their role and circumstance. The three passages that are entirely imagined, as the reader will see, are clearly demarcated as such and are limited to one section of the book. These are included insofar as they are the only available means to offer a sense of the experience I wish to represent. Whatever inventions remain are, I hope, reasonable and modest and extrapolations from the known.

A final word. That much of this book focuses on a mission that ended in tragedy should not diminish the remarkable fact that in thirty years of hurricane reconnaissance by the Navy, it was the only time a crew was lost. This fact is in itself a tribute to their peerless professionalism and astonishing skill. It is to those men and women and their memories that this work is dedicated.

Prologue

Guantánamo Bay, October 1999

The sun rises on a wide bay opening into clear waters. There is the papery rustle of palm fronds and the low rhythmic sounds of surf, and scents of hibiscus and ocean. This is a place of warm breezes and bright sunshine. Yet there are ghosts here. It was here, at Guantánamo Bay, that the United States staged its major air operations of the Cold War, and for thirty years the compound has been a kind of Caribbean West Berlin.

The bay has a large port and two large runways on opposite shores. Beyond this, farther inland, are aircraft hangers, runways, and a control tower; in an area to the north is the base from which Naval Air Station Guantánamo Bay conducted its weather reconnaissance operations. Its headquarters are unassuming—a few whitewashed cinderblock buildings arranged around neat courtyards. In one of the buildings is a small room the size of a large closet. It holds a few metal file cabinets, and in a drawer are old records and a short stack of bound publications called "cruisebooks."

Every year, Navy squadrons compose and print informal records of people and events within their ranks. They are of a format like that of any high school yearbook in America—dedications, formal posed photographs of members of organizations, and candid photos. The 1955 cruisebook of Airborne Early Warning Squadron Four devotes page 21 to the six aircraft crews who flew during the 1955 season. There are five group photographs of each crew standing near their aircraft. Near the bottom of the page, where the photograph of Crew Five would be, there is instead a black border framing nine names:

> *Lt. Cmdr. Grover B. Windham, Jr.*
> *LTJG George W. Herlong*
> *LTJG Thomas L. Greaney*
> *LTJG Thomas R. Morgan*
> *LTJG William A. Buck, Jr.*
> *Aviation Mechanic First Class J. P. Windham, Jr.*
> *Aviation Electronics Man First Class Joseph F. Combs*
> *Airman Kenneth L. Clegg*
> *Aviation Electronics Technician Second Class Julius J. Mann*

The cruisebook is in fact dedicated to these men, whom official Navy records show as having died on active duty. They died in a struggle against an enemy that had no ideology, no army. And no pity. They died studying a hurricane.

⤙

Literature is rich with tales of men and violent weather. In most of them—Homer's Odysseus and his sack of winds, Shakespeare's *Tempest*—weather is incidental to plots whose primary focus is some human interaction. There are, however, other narratives—Conrad's short story "Typhoon," London's short story "To Build a Fire"—in which weather is all: setting, plot, even character. These stories in particular possess a theme that seems archetypal: the "man versus nature" conflict so familiar to high school literature classes. Perhaps the flight of Windham and his crew is another. There is something in it that wants to resolve into a clear and simple equation. A profound and deadly encounter. A simple and fatal merger of trajectories.

Imagine a map of the Caribbean, and on that map superimpose two points. Place the first point on the southeast coast of Cuba. Imagine that it represents the point of departure for an aircraft. A single thin line emerges from that point and lengthens, slowly tending southward. Place the second point in the waters near the Lesser Antilles. Imagine that it represents a hurricane's point of origin. From it emerges a second line, tending westward. Imagine unseen forces pushing the lines slightly in one direction, then in another. Suppose that subtle pressures cause them to lose speed at certain moments and to gain speed at others. Finally, imagine that the lines meet, intersecting at a single point over the middle of the map—a place in mid ocean, 200 miles from the nearest coastline. The mind's eye expects a momentary hesitation, a pause. But there is no pause. Instead, the southward-tending line simply ceases, and the westward-tending line continues unperturbed and unslowed. And yet the mind's eye has lost interest in the surviving line. It is fixed on the point of intersection. It cannot resist examining that point for some clue as to its meaning.

Then, as now, one feels an impulse to seek an answer—to try to trace the sequence of cause and effect that led to that moment. Hindsight would seem to make such an endeavor simple. Of course, it does not. Storms themselves are products of innumerable events, the first so small as to be nearly immeasurable—the swirl of water in a tidal pool, the slightest variation in air temperature. Gradually, they grow, causing other, larger phenomena—a warm air current, a cloudburst. These in turn produce events still greater—an area of low pressure, a shift of the jet stream southward. It was such a sequence that produced a tropical depression that would come to be Hurricane Janet, and within her, whatever killed Crew Five. We cannot know what it was—a sudden powerful downdraft, a sheet of rain that flooded an engine, a twisting gust that sheared a wing, or something else entirely. All we can know with certainty is that any specific answer is beyond our reach.

Still, one seeks to explain. Try another path. Expand the map's edges until they frame much of the Western Hemisphere—all of North America, the Atlantic Ocean, the British Isles, Western Europe. Superimpose a single line, allow it to grow and split into two lines, then three. The lines intersect and branch again. Some lines twist and then split apart. A few trace long graceful arcs; others loop back upon themselves; still others simply fade. Before long the map is a great confused network. Imagine now that the tangle of lines and the map itself fade to transparency. Beneath appears another map, of a slightly older vintage. On this map, too, are networks of lines that seem impossibly complex. In a moment this map also fades to transparency to reveal another, and it in turn fades to reveal yet another.

Suppose that a given line on each of the maps represents something—an event, a circumstance, or an action—that led to that morning in September 1955. A line on an older map is a moment in which a man pauses along a roadside to puzzle over trees fallen in a single direction. Another line is a man sitting on a bed of straw in the attic of a French farmhouse, scribbling equations in a notebook. Lines on more recent maps represent other moments, other events. A world war, a commanding general's concern with the forecast for the day of the Normandy Invasion. A national weather bureau. An interservice rivalry. An aircraft developed to detect submarines and brought into service of another sort. Then, a set of resources managed well but managed imperfectly. An underestimation of wind speeds. An aircraft design that accounted for wing loads and stresses of so much and no more. Somehow, these explanations are likewise inadequate.

Try again. Tighten the focus. Shrink the map's borders until they frame only the southeastern part of the United States. Concentrate on a single thin line, beginning near Birmingham, Alabama, in 1921. A boy's decision, at age seventeen, to enroll at Annapolis. Later, as a young man, to enter flight school and gain certification in flying multiengine aircraft. Still later, to accept an assignment to a weather reconnaissance squadron and a promotion to patrol plane commander. Then, on one day in September 1955, to accept the mission into Janet, to choose to fly at such and such an altitude, to glance at the altimeter at this moment and not that one, to ask for recommendations from the navigator, to exit the storm on such and such a heading. Later, to react to an updraft by cutting engine power and giving full left rudder and not by increasing power and maintaining heading. A long chain of decisions—some made with great care and deliberation, others made on split-second instinct using more central nervous system than actual thought, but all forcing a single path through a maze of alternatives. A series of choices, each negating and voiding all that came before, and leading irrevocably to a single moment at which no further choice is possible.

Try once more. This time, disregard history and theories of cause and effect. No maps, no lines. Instead, begin at the place the mission began. Begin at the time the mission began. Begin with what is known.

In late September of 1955 a tropical depression developed into the tenth hurricane of the season. The Naval Air Station Jacksonville responded as per standard procedures. Flight crews were assigned, courses charted, flight rosters posted. The aircraft— P2V Neptunes and WC121N Super Constellations—were checked and fueled. Commander Grover Windham and his eight-man crew were assigned a place in the rotation that had them departing from Guantánamo Bay in a P2V at 6:30 A.M. on September 26. They had every reason to expect a fairly ordinary flight. It would be the fifth reconnaissance of Janet, and every stage of it would be straight out of the manual. They would locate the storm and fly circles inside the eyewall at several altitudes. The onboard aerologist would measure wind velocities and atmospheric pressure. Then, the major work of their mission complete, they would return to base. A reporter and a photographer from the *Toronto Daily Star* were along for the ride, and their presence made for some mild but welcome novelty—the explanation of airsickness bags, the usual question concerning the whereabouts of parachutes, the bemused answer that where they were going parachutes would do little good. Still, it was a decidedly routine mission, as missions into hurricanes go. The whole trip would take perhaps nine hours.

Lieutenant Commander Windham and his crew took off from Naval Air Station Guantánamo Bay, Cuba, at 6:33 A.M. on September 26. They were expected to return at 4:30 that afternoon. At 6:30 P.M. they were considered overdue.

1

Huracan

At the edge of space, hundreds of miles above Earth, so high the curve of the horizon is clearly visible, a few thin wisps are pulled from the thin skein of atmosphere into the emptiness of space, where they are wafted by solar winds and magnetic fields. Call this the exosphere. Miles below, electrical charges move through a dark sky, and meteors leave long streaks through thin, unbreathable air. At still greater depths the air settles into a quiescent layer. This is the stratosphere. And below this, the air thickens further until it meets and pushes against the surfaces of earth and water. Here is endless churning and roiling. The sun heats seas and continents, and the newly warmed air above them expands and rises. Great invisible currents push northward and southward from the equator. Clouds in all varieties—cumulus, cirrocumulus, stratus, altostratus—form, grow, and push against each other, sometimes gently, sometimes with unimaginable violence, releasing their moisture as rain and snow. Eventually they dissipate, leaving air that is rain-washed and clear. Call this the troposphere. This is the place within the atmosphere that gives and sustains life. It is also the place that, suddenly and dispassionately, takes life away.

⤙

It was September 21, a few days before the autumnal equinox. Open ocean, at about 15 degrees north latitude, 200 miles east of Barbados. As usual, the air was warm and calm. By midday the tropic sun had warmed the surface to 80 degrees, until there was little discernable difference between the temperature of one medium and the other. Water temperatures were above 78 to a depth of 200 feet. Were it not for gained speed and a sudden absence of friction, a jumping dolphin would not feel where water ended and air began.

The warmed moisture-laden air rose, and in the space it had vacated, more air was drawn in. The rising air cooled, and when it had cooled enough, its water vapor condensed into small clouds. The clouds, fed by condensation from more rising air, grew larger, spread outward, and then sank. The upwelling continued—rising, condensing, sinking—and the whole process established itself as a cycle. Soon there was a cold and dense mass of air above the water, a few miles across. More air was drawn in, now pulled in a curving path just above the ocean surface. Slowly, the whole mass of air and moisture began to spin.

When adjacent currents of a fluid like water or air are moving in one direction, the faster current will tend to curl around the slower. If the faster current is also the more northern, and both currents are in the Northern Hemisphere, the spin will be counterclockwise. So the clouds pushed by the winds began to stir, and the Coriolis effect gave the spin an extra push. Warm semitropical air from the equator was pulled northward. It moved above the denser colder air. As it rose, it cooled, and the water vapor it carried condensed and fell as rain.

The storm, begun as formless clouds, was developing a shape. Air in streaming currents was pulled inward faster and faster, and some of these currents, long before they reached the center, were slowed and pulled upward, losing their moisture into clouds. The clouds in turn were coalescing into bands and spiral arms, miles long. Still other currents were drawn on a curving path all the way to the clear air at the center, where they continued spiraling, but now ascending too. The air currents began to come faster—20, 30 miles an hour. In the center they spun upward nearly to the upper edge of the troposphere, to 35,000 feet, the moisture within them condensing to form a tower of cumulonimbus clouds. And in the upper troposphere water droplets froze and formed cirrus clouds, and the centrifugal force of their own motion flung them out into the highest reaches of the storm and into the vast ceiling of overcast called the "cloud shield."

The storm was still diffuse. The area of high winds had been nearly 200 miles wide. Its formation entered the final stage. Pressure fell at the storm's eye, and the system contracted and intensified until, in a few hours, it was a mere 30 miles across. It had become a great engine of air, water, and heat. It occupied a volume of space large enough to contain several Everests. And it was growing.

—

In the Coast Guard Air facility at Naval Station San Juan, Puerto Rico, the long-range radar showed a tropical depression in the Atlantic, about 350 miles east-southeast of Martinique. Soon, at weather stations on islands around the Caribbean, a bulletin off the teletypes gave the vital statistics—longitude, latitude, and winds in knots. A few hours later, when the winds reached gale force, 39 miles per hour, she was termed a tropical storm. And at 6:00 A.M. on September 22, long-range radar located the storm at 13°10' north latitude, 57°60' west longitude—east by northeast of

Barbados, moving west at 30 miles per hour. Now she was growing quickly. In a few more hours her winds reached 74 miles an hour, and she had earned a new designation. She was a hurricane, the tenth of the season.

They called her Janet.

⤙

The Caribbean Sea is one million square miles of water, a great roughly oval-shaped expanse whose greatest dimension stretches along the seventeenth parallel for some 1,500 miles. The Caribbean's basins are 16,000 feet deep, as deep as much of the North Atlantic, and its waters are complex and dynamic. The Guiana Current and part of the North Equatorial Current flow from the Atlantic westward past the Lesser Antilles and into the Caribbean at a rate of nearly 20 miles a day. A few hundred miles west, the trade winds push surface waters northward. They are replaced by colder, nutrient-rich water upwelling from depths of 600 feet. Still further west, another current turns north through the Yucatán Strait and into the Gulf of Mexico, where still another channels water eastward toward the Straits of Florida and, finally, back into the Atlantic. The western and southern edges of the Caribbean Sea wash shores in Central and South America. The sea's northernmost boundary is defined by Cuba, Hispaniola (with Haiti and the Dominican Republic), and Puerto Rico. Its eastern edge, the line by which cartographers divide it from the Atlantic, runs through a chain of island sentinels called the Lesser Antilles. The names of these islands are as familiar as they are exotic—St. Croix, Antigua, Martinique.

The easternmost of the islands, and the first to feel the trades, is Barbados. It is a teardrop-shaped speck of land just 9 miles wide. Like its sister islands in the chain, Barbados was formed over millennia by the slow buildup of coral on sedimentary rocks. Its western coast is white sand beaches and turquoise waters; much of the eastern coast, overlooking the dark and turbulent waters of the Atlantic, is limestone cliffs.

On Barbados, it is possible to face east and feel the constant trade winds from the Atlantic, and to turn west and see clouds whose undersides are illuminated by reflected light from the sea. Even in hard times, it is a place of great beauty. But the beauty comes at a price exacted, on average, every twenty years.

The Caribbean is a place used to hurricanes. Since Columbus's voyages, perhaps half a million people have been killed by tropical storms, and most of them have been here. On average 4.6 hurricanes per year have been reported in the North Atlantic and the Caribbean since 1887, when formal meteorological records began. No doubt earlier hurricanes came as regularly, but in the absence of formal records, only the worst were remembered by stories woven into island culture. One of these, the "Great Hurricane of 1780," was probably the most violent storm of the eighteenth century. Estimates of deaths were uncertain as there was no formal census, and communication among the islands was unreliable. But in 1874 Élisée Reclus, in *The Ocean, Atmosphere and Life,* compiled several contemporary accounts and suggested that in all likelihood the storm killed upward of 20,000 people.

Starting from Barbados, where neither trees nor dwellings were left standing, it caused an English fleet anchored off St. Lucia to disappear, and completely ravaged this island, where 6,000 persons were crushed under the ruins. After this, the whirlwind, tending toward Martinique, enveloped a convoy of French transports, and sunk more than 40 ships carrying 4,000 soldiers; on land the towns of St. Pierre and other places were completely razed by the wind, and 9,000 persons perished there. More to the north, Dominique, St. Eustatius, St. Vincent, and Porto Rico were likewise devastated, and most of the vessels which were on the path of the cyclone foundered with all their crews. Beyond Porto Rico the tempest bent to the northeast, toward the Bermudas, and though its violence had gradually diminished, it sunk several warships returning to Europe. At Barbados, where the cyclone had commenced its terrible spiral, the wind was unchained with such fury, that the inhabitants hiding in their cellars did not feel the shocks of the earthquakes which, according to Rodney, accompanied the storm.

Sir George Rodney, admiral in command of a squadron of frigates, wrote, "The strongest buildings and the whole of the houses, most of which were of stone, and remarkable for their solidity, gave way to the fury of the wind, and were torn up to their foundation; all the forts destroyed, and many of the heavy cannon carried upwards of a hundred feet from the first. Had I not been an eyewitness, nothing could have induced me to believe it."

But in 1955 that seemed a distant and irrelevant history. It had been more than fifty years since a hurricane had hit Barbados. Few had even heard of the 1780 storm. Most knew of hurricanes only from rumors, news from other islands, and stories told by old men.

On the southern stretch of Barbados' Atlantic-facing coast was a community called "The Crane." On September 22, 1955, the air temperature at midmorning was in the high eighties. A mostly clear sky, hot sunshine, a few fair-weather cumuli. As usual, the wind was easterly but so gentle that the palm fronds were barely moving. A few hours later the ocean looked different. There was a long low swell, stronger than the normal trade-wind swell, breaking from a different direction. A few fishermen said that a hurricane was out there somewhere. They spoke English with lilting accents; they pronounced the word "huracan."

On the next morning the sky was clear, but the swells rolling in were longer and higher. They broke and crashed with a sound that could be heard a half a mile inland. Hours passed. The sky stayed clear, but the air seemed heavy, and for long moments there was a dead calm. The winds, when they came, were fitful. By afternoon a few wisps of cirri appeared in the southeast. Later they passed quickly overhead, and the clouds in the east grew into a solid bank of cirrostrati.

The fishermen knew the signs. Their luck had ended. It was perhaps a day away. They checked supplies of kerosene and food, filled containers with water. Some squinted at the horizon, examined loose shutters on their houses, and went into tool sheds to find hammer and nails. That evening the sun set among low clouds in the west. It was near the autumnal equinox, and when the moon rose, it was nearly full. After midnight there were breezes, and by then the moon was riding high, shining through clouds. Morning dawned gray. A thin blanket of altostrati stretched from horizon to horizon, and through it the sun was visible as a pale white disk. The wind was blowing from the northeast and gusting to 20 miles an hour. By midmorning fishermen were dragging boats inland, turning them over and tying them down. There was a hard burst of rain. It lasted a few minutes and passed. By late morning the wind was north-northeast, gusting to 35 miles an hour, and the surf was tremendous. The eastern sky was dark, and a few lower scud clouds sped westward against the overcast. There was rain in the distance over the water, and in moments it arrived onshore. Soon the wind blew steadily from the north, nearly 50 miles an hour and increasing. Rain lashed sideways. The air was dark. Power lines fell and occasionally an electric flash threw a weird light. Tree limbs thrashed, the air was full of blown leaves and palm fronds, and people shouted to be heard. They moved into cellars, pulling doors shut over them.

The ocean itself was white with spray—its waves were 20, perhaps 30 feet high, and the air was dark with driven rain. One could not distinguish a horizon; there seemed to be no boundary at all between sea and sky. The water had surged inland perhaps 200 feet, and the entire beach was under water. Soon the seas submerged whole wharves. The sound grew to an unnatural howling that seemed alive and angry, and when the winds seemed to have reached some kind of upper limit of ferocity, when it seemed impossible that they could become stronger, they did exactly that. There were sounds of branches breaking, thuds of debris flung against buildings. There were other, unrecognizable noises. Impossibly, the winds increased again, their pitch gaining so that the air seemed to be tearing at itself. Then, from basements and makeshift shelters the people heard the beginnings of a deep bass rumble like a subway train. The sound grew louder. It was like a hundred freight trains derailing and derailing again, and soon it overwhelmed all other sounds. Its lowest pitch, the deep bass thunder of the crashing seas; its highest pitch, the scream of the wind. Between them and far louder than either was a sound like a sustained chord from a great organ. It could be felt as much as heard. It was as if the atmosphere itself were vibrating.

Time seemed distended, stretched. Just when it seemed possible that the wind would be a permanent condition, its tone changed. The organ note died, the drumming rain ceased. There was only a fitful breeze. The sudden quiet was uncanny.

People ventured outside cautiously and gazed upon a world they did not know. The sky lightened, clouds broke. There was sunshine. But water and mud and debris were everywhere. There were no landmarks. The horizon was lower. It was possible to see great distances, and they realized it was because there was no longer a tree or a shed where it had once been. The land itself was scorched as if a fire had swept across it—trees were stripped of foliage, and where grass had been was only barren earth, the result of salt-water spray and blown sand. Somewhere a dog made a low, mournful sound. The air was clear, but it felt heavy, impending; it seemed hard to breathe. Some people just stood and stared, half in awe, half in shock. Others looked hastily for something—pulling a fallen tree limb away from the wreckage, lifting a small section of wall. Someone thought to look at the ocean. The waves were high, white.

Above there were a few clouds against a circle of blue sky, but on all sides were great curving walls of darker clouds. There was that low sound like distant thunder. The calm lasted for ten minutes before the wind rose and the sky darkened, and again the rain pounded the ground. This time the wind came from the south. The people—again in shelters and basements—heard sounds they did not recognize: the explosive crack of tree trunks splitting, the loud thud of timber, sections of plywood hitting sides of buildings. Again the wind shrieked and increased and lessened and increased again. Again came the bass rumble and the sustained organ note, and again time itself seemed stretched, elongated. Twenty minutes passed. Thirty. The great organ note died, and the steady rumble diminished. Finally, the sky lightened and the wind ceased altogether. The people emerged again, this time to a world altered and ravaged almost beyond recognition.

Across the island an estimated one hundred were dead and thousands homeless. Whole fields of sugarcane had simply been flattened. Damage was in the millions. A meteorologist in the capital city of Bridgetown reported that at about 4 P.M. Janet's winds had reached speeds of 127 miles an hour. No one who had lived through it was surprised.

The earth was scorched, cleansed. Fish were washed onshore in thousands, their eyes popped out from the decrease in pressure. But the destruction had been strangely selective. A single tree would be left standing in the middle of a fallen grove turned to kindling. A few chickens, still alive and scurrying about, were stripped of feathers. A boy's corpse was found, drowned in a lake that had not been there a few hours before. It was as if a great volume of air over the island had been suddenly replaced with weather from some wild and inhospitable planet. For a few hours that strange weather had shrieked and wailed. Then it had simply gone away.

At about the same time Janet swept across Barbados, her southern edge passed over Grenada, 150 miles to the southwest. Matters there were nearly as bad. At least eight were dead. A pilot attempting a landing reported that the airport was covered with debris. All land communication lines were down, and the only reports came from amateur radio operators. They knew that some docks and warehouses were destroyed along the waterfront, and that much of the fishing fleet was destroyed. As to the island's interior they had to guess, but it seemed reasonable to expect that all bridges had been washed away.

Survivors of natural disasters seem to endure similar aftereffects. And while the general profile of symptoms is the same, some of the specifics are different. Many survivors of hurricanes, for instance, develop a phobia that is peculiar but, given the circumstances, understandable. They cannot bear to hear wind. In some ways, it is a very old fear, and it may be rooted in our central nervous system.

Lore of wind runs deep in human culture, and rare is the religion that does not regard wind as a bearer of both life and death. Perhaps it is not surprising that we associate wind with the deity or deities. It is invisible, and it may be gentle as a whisper; it can enter unseen through the crack beneath a door; it can refresh and cool us. But at other times it can rake across a landscape with a fury unmatched by any force on Earth.

Most western cultures arose in areas of relatively benign weather. To be sure, Europe and the Mediterranean peoples knew fierce wind and storm—the Mediterranean *sirocco*, the North African *simoom*, the *sharav* and *khamsin* of Egypt and Israel. But their winds rarely reached velocities much greater than 50 miles an hour, enough to cause a person to seek shelter, but seldom an actual threat to life and limb. Storms fiercer than these were too rare to merit a generic name, and not surprisingly, the sacred texts of cultures that arose in these regions are silent on the subject of truly devastating storms. The religions of the Americas, however, gave more attention to weather. The Navaho, for instance, had enormous knowledge of wind and its various manifestations. But even they did not know hurricanes. In fact, to find mention of hurricanes in sacred texts one must look to parts of the world where such storms arise—specifically, tropical latitudes.[2]

The Aztecs, or Mexica, were a people whose empire, by the close of the fifteenth century, stretched across most of Central America. Theirs was a violent and apocalyptic religion, grounded in beliefs in great cosmic forces and a human existence always having been destroyed or about to be destroyed. Crucial to their relation with their gods was a daily ritual in which four priests held a human sacrifice stretched against a concave stone. A fifth priest cut open the chest with a flint knife. He then reached inside the wound, grasped the heart, and while it was still beating, tore it from the body. In the first decades of the sixteenth century, Spanish conquistadors encountered the Mexica, and it seemed to them obvious that the Mexica religion came from hell, and that its gods were devils. What the Spanish did not understand was that the Mexica were motivated not by inherent cruelty, and that the sacrificed for the most part were willing. The ritual was nothing more and nothing less than their response to the world as they understood it.

The Mexica believed that the apocalypse was preordained. At the world's last act, the appearance of reality would be torn open,

---

2. Four areas in the Northern Hemisphere spawn tropical cyclones: the Gulf of Mexico and the Caribbean Sea, the North Pacific Ocean east of the Philippines, the Pacific Ocean off the west coast of Central America, and the Bay of Bengal and the Arabian Sea. Areas in the Southern Hemisphere that spawn these storms are the South Indian Ocean, and the Pacific Ocean off the northwest and east coasts of Australia. The name *hurricane* refers to a tropical cyclone in the Atlantic or Caribbean. The same phenomena are known as *typhoons* in the Pacific, *cyclones* in the Bay of Bengal and the Arabian Sea, *baguios* in the Philippines, and *willy-nillys* in Australia.

and the last survivors would be attacked by *Tzitzimime*, the monsters of the twilight who await the final hour beneath the western sky. Although the date of the end was fixed, it threatened to arrive sooner. In fact, the existence of the world was continually at risk and required human intervention on a daily basis. The precise means of intervention had been suggested by the most important episode of the creation, the birth of the sun. The myth told that the gods had gathered in the twilight at Teotihuacán. One of their number threw himself into a huge brazier, was killed, and rose from the coals, reborn. He was a newborn sun, but he was motionless. When the other gods recognized that he needed blood to move, they sacrificed themselves. Only then did the sun begin his precession across the sky. Thereafter, men followed the example and fed the sun human blood every day. To the Mexica then, human sacrifice was both a sacred duty and a necessity. Without it, nothing could be born, nothing would endure, and the life of the world would cease.

In fact, the violence of the sacrificial ritual was a reflection of a greater Mexica cosmology. The Mexica believed that the universe had been created five times and destroyed four times. There were five ages, and each age had a name. The name of the second age was "Four Wind." It had lasted for fifty-two years, and at its end men turned into monkeys, and the world was destroyed by hurricanes. Indeed, at least in part, the Mexica's perception of a violent natural world owes something to the hurricane. Their pantheon of ancestors included a god named Tlaloc. He was a deity of growth and rain, forming clouds in mountains, and sending forth rains that nurtured the soil. But he was also fearsome, and he sent out hurricanes.

In 1955 the Mexica had been gone for three hundred years. Still, there was a living religion that spoke specifically of the hurricane. It was a faith with no official sanction. The religion was called Regla de Ocha, or more commonly, Santería, "the way of the saints." Its beginnings could be traced to Africa, specifically, a region on the west coast just north of the equator, an area within the borders of the present-day nations of Benin and Nigeria. For three hundred years, the Spanish and English enslaved the Yoruba people and brought them to the Caribbean to work on the sugar plantations. The Yoruba were baptized by the Roman Catholic Church, and their native practices were suppressed. But like other cults transported from Africa, for example, the voudon of Haiti or the Macumba of Brazil, the Yoruba religion was *syncretic*—that is, it assumed attributes of the culture in which it was practiced.

Santería teaches that there is one Supreme Being, and humans experience the divine most directly through spirits known as *orishas*. Much like Roman Catholic saints, each orisha is associated with a force of nature and has a specific character. The goddess of the wind, fire, and the thunderbolt is Oya. She is easily enraged, and she can create tornadoes and hurricanes.

Santería has numerous rituals—drumming and dancing, food and animal sacrifice, divination with fetishes made of bones or shells, trancelike seizures. All are means to envision an otherwise uncertain future. They are means, we might say, to see the slowly lengthening line on an imaginary map.

From a warm and dry place protected from wind and rain, it is perhaps too easy to dismiss such beliefs as irrational and superstitious. But in severe weather even the most atheistic of seamen have been known to shout at a gale, to curse a god or gods. Perhaps it is a jest, a bit of seafaring theatrics for the benefit of the landlubbers on board. But one suspects there is something more. If most seamen dismiss any idea that a storm is a deity or the agent of a deity, some would allow that it *seems* more alive than do other forces of nature. The novelist Joseph Conrad described a kind of taxonomy of natural disaster: "An earthquake, a landslip, an avalanche, overtake a man incidentally, as it were—without passion. A furious gale attacks him like a personal enemy, tries to grasp his limbs, fastens upon his mind, seeks to rout his very spirit out of him." Indeed, even the most rational of empiricists, the most devout agnostic, will admit that when one is inside a hurricane, it is easy to believe it possesses a conscious malevolence, an actual will.

➳

In September 1955 there were seven weather and seismograph observers on a weather station on Great Swan Island, a speck of land in the western Caribbean. One man stationed there was a U.S. Weather Bureau meteorologist named John Laban. He was expected to take pressure readings, send radiosondes and pilot balloons if he could, and transmit data to the Hurricane Forecast Center in Miami. In fact, Laban had been listening to reports and readying radiosondes. He knew that if Janet continued her course directly westward, there was a good chance at least a part of her fury would be unleashed on the island.

John Laban was trained as a scientist. He could speak knowledgeably about a hurricane's steering levels and high-level divergence. He knew that a hurricane was a phenomenon explained by thermodynamics and climatology. And yet his unconscious had succumbed to a primeval fear that was both more and less than scientific, a kind of premonition.

"I had dreamed two days previously that the storm would hit us," he said. "I had read the message sent to Miami that I was dead."

2

Windham

Grover Windham Jr. was of the generation raised during the Great Depression who came of age on the eve of World War II. He was born in 1921 and raised in Birmingham, Alabama, in a traditional Methodist family. By the time he was eighteen, he was a tall, boyishly handsome young man with dark arched eyebrows. In most photographs he is smiling.

By July 1939 Windham had become a midshipman at the United States Naval Academy. Those who knew him said he liked being the center of attention. On weekends at the academy he always seemed to be accompanied by a female friend, and the prevailing joke was that he waxed the seat covers of his car and deliberately took routes that would allow him to make hard right turns so that his passenger, whoever she happened to be at the time, would find herself pressed against him.

Windham was a senior at Annapolis when he learned of the Japanese attack on the American naval base in Pearl Harbor. He was among some six hundred Annapolis graduates whose senior year would be remembered by that event. Like his classmates, he was eager to serve. In June he shipped out as an ensign on the USS *Portland,* an escort to the carrier *Enterprise.* A few other Academy men were on board, and one of them—John Haynie, also from Alabama—was becoming a good friend.

They would not wait long to see action. It would be known as the Battle of Guadalcanal, a conflict marked by so much confusion and losses so heavy for both sides that one military historian would characterize it as "a bar room brawl in the dark."

The day after the battle, fires were extinguished, survivors were pulled from wreckage, and the surviving ships sought safe harbor. The *Portland* fared better than many, but when a torpedo hit near her stern, twenty men were killed. She anchored at Tulagi for a day. Then, with her remaining crew aboard, she was towed to Sydney, Australia, for repairs. The crew would spend most of December there; the time was relaxed and pleasant. Bing Crosby's "White Christmas" was being played over the armed services stations, and when Windham and Haynie began to hear the song in the Southern Hemisphere's summer, they joked that the only white they could see was their dress uniforms. They were out of the action, at least for a while, and had time for writing and reading letters. At almost every mail call Windham received a few that were perfumed, and the situation was cause for many jibes from shipmates. No one noticed that lately the ensign was giving particular attention to missives from a certain address.

Her name was Nancy McAdams. She was a woman of great charm and southern grace. During the war she studied industrial engineering at the University of Alabama, and after she graduated she went to work at the Goodrich Tire Company. She had met Grover Windham years before, when both were at a church camp in high school. At first, neither had been much impressed with the other. Somehow—it was difficult even for Nancy to say exactly why—she became one of the many women in his magnetic pull. His friends would say that he liked her precisely because unlike the other girls, she was not impressed with him.

When the war ended, they married. And friends said they were a perfect couple. He and Nancy made plans, and there was brief consideration of a civilian career. But Windham enjoyed the status of a naval officer. He liked the sense of mission, the community, and the changing scenery. He decided to make the Navy a permanent part of his life, and soon was assigned to the heavy cruiser USS *Bremerton*, operating out of San Pedro, California. Haynie, who had acted as best man at the wedding, and some other friends bought the couple a Ford convertible as a wedding present, and the newlyweds drove west.

Grover Windham was not the "born pilot" who haunted airfields as a boy and soloed on his sixteenth birthday. In point of fact, during his youth he had never given much thought to flying. But when Windham served on the *Bremerton*, Haynie was in flight training for fighters, and more than once he mentioned to Windham that by most standards it was a better life—more pay, less overseas duty. What made the tours of duty aboard ships more difficult for Windham was that by 1948 he and Nancy had two children—a three-year-old daughter named after her mother and whom they called "Nan," and a newborn son, John, named after Haynie. The deciding factor for Windham was not cramped ship quarters or low pay. It was a fear that his children would grow up barely knowing him.

He entered flight training in January 1948; eighteen months later, in July 1949, when he was twenty-eight, he was made a naval aviator. The change had the desired effect, more or less. Over the next few years many of his assignments had him on the move, but at least they were in the states.

For some months he served as an instructor with the Advanced Training Command in Hutchinson, Kansas, where he was the offi-

cer in charge of what trainees called "charm school." It was a two-
or three-week course for prospective flight and ground school
instructors, and its subjects included speech, techniques of class-
room instruction, and psychology of flight. Everybody said
Windham was a natural for the job.

In the first lesson he conducted for the class he showed up late,
coughed a little, and mumbled an excuse. He said that he was not
really familiar with the subject matter, so they should please bear
with him. He seemed a little nervous, a bit distracted. The junior
officers shifted in their seats. They noticed that his uniform was
wrinkled. He said he was going to show a training film, and they
watched him move to the back of the room where a projector had
been set up. He fumbled about, and seemed to realize that the projector was not loaded. In their seats the junior officers exchanged
glances as if to say, *who is this guy?* All in all, he put on such a good
performance that the class took a full ten minutes to realize they
had witnessed a very effective demonstration of what *not* to do.
Grover Windham had a real stage presence, all the more valued for
its rarity in the military.

On occasion he was handed assignments that took him overseas, away from Nancy and the children. In 1954 he had been on a
Mediterranean cruise for eighteen months, serving as flag secretary to Commander Carrier Division Four. When the tour ended
he put in for a new billet, and it was granted.

For most of that time Nancy and the children stayed with his
parents in Fairfield, Alabama. He arrived at Birmingham Airport,
where his young wife and children met him. As had become his
custom after returning from a tour of duty, he had small packages
for Nan and John, whom they'd begun to call "Buz." There were
embraces, and although Nancy had conscientiously and regularly
enclosed photographs with her letters, he pretended he had not
seen them, and feigned surprise at how much Nan and Buz had
grown.

As they walked toward the car, Nancy asked him if he had received his orders. He smiled a little and said he had orders to Jacksonville. He would be hunting hurricanes. Suddenly she stopped, stood still, and began crying. He held her and looked at her seriously. He said it was the safest job in the Navy. He said that no plane had ever been lost. Besides, missions were flown right out of "Jax," and they lasted for ten or twelve hours at most. He would be home for dinner every night. It was obvious to Nancy that he had prepared this, especially the line about dinner; it was all a regular little speech. Still, it had the right effect. She would remember that statistic and hold it like a talisman. No plane had ever been lost.[3]

Few think clearly about personal risk. If a young man of Windham's generation considered the subject at all, it was with some blend of youthful arrogance, a vague understanding of mathematical odds learned mostly through poker, and perhaps a hint of superstition. In military aviation there were some sets of odds that were generally known. Haynie had chosen fighters because despite the fact that their pilots had a higher mortality rate, he did not want responsibility for the lives of other crewmen. Windham had chosen multiengines for a variety of reasons, one being that they had a better overall survival record. As such, they were the preferred aircraft of men with wives and families.

Certainly Windham had come near death, but perhaps no more or less often than anyone else who had seen combat. And yet a believer in the classical Fates would suspect that they had been at

---

3. It was a half-truth. The whole truth was that no aircraft from VW-4 or its postwar predecessors had been lost in a hurricane. But several crews had been lost during wartime weather reconnaissance, and in 1952 ten crew members of a WB-29 from the Air Force's 54th Weather Reconnaissance Squadron were killed while reconnoitering Typhoon Wilma, then 300 miles east of Leyte in the Philippine Islands.

least tempted. He had survived one of the bloodiest sea battles in the war.

In November of 1942, Japan and the United States were nearly stalemated. Japan had lost seventy-four planes at Santa Cruz. The United States had lost the carrier *Hornet,* and in August its remaining carrier, the *Enterprise,* was badly damaged in the Battle of the Eastern Solomons. The Americans held Guadalcanal's Henderson Field, but they were surrounded by Japanese forces. Both armies were exhausted and quickly running short of supplies. Many on both sides were suffering from malaria. Admiral Isoroku Yamamoto, commander of the Combined Fleet, devised a plan for ending the stalemate. A heavy cruiser and ten destroyers would land and reinforce Japanese troops at Guadalcanal; at the same time, warships would shell Henderson Field. But American code-breakers picked up his orders, and within a day Rear Admiral Richmond Kelly Turner, then deputy in direct command at Guadalcanal, knew their every detail. He ordered a counterstrike, putting Rear Admiral Daniel J. Callaghan in command of five cruisers and eight destroyers. Late on the evening of November 12, 1942, a twenty-one-year-old ensign was stationed in turret number three of one of those cruisers.

Originally, the *Portland* had been assigned duty in the Pacific theater as an escort to the carrier *Enterprise.* But the *Enterprise* required a two-week stand-down to repair bomb damage from the Battle of the Eastern Solomons, and the *Portland* had been reassigned. At the moment she was near the middle of a single column of thirteen vessels in the western Pacific, steaming through the night at 20 knots. The intent was to engage the Japanese. The destroyers *Cushing, Laffey, Sterett,* and *O'Bannon* were leading. They were followed by the light cruiser *Atlanta;* then Callaghan's flagship *San Francisco;* the cruisers *Portland, Helena,* and *Juneau;* and four more destroyers, with the *Fletcher* in the rear. On the bridge of the *Portland* a clock struck midnight, and a watch officer scratched the new date in his deck log: Friday, November 13.

Helena's radar had picked up the Japanese from 12 miles; the groups were moving toward each other at a combined speed of 40 knots. Neither was well prepared for battle. *Atlanta* fired on three destroyers, the *Akatsuki* responded, and fires began on *Atlanta*'s upper decks. Soon her engine room flooded, and she was drifting helplessly. The *Hiei* hit the *Cushing*. The *Laffey* launched several torpedoes at the *Teruzuki*, but they failed to arm, and the *Teruzuki* launched a torpedo in return and blew the *Laffey*'s stern off. Then the *Kirishima* hit the *Laffey*'s boiler room, and Lieutenant Commander Hank ordered his crew to abandon ship. The men began jumping into the water, and in a matter of seconds the *Laffey* exploded, killing those still aboard and many in the water nearby, including Hank. The Japanese *Nagara* hit the *Sterett*'s helm control. The *Sterett* launched a torpedo against the destroyer *Akatsuki*—it struck amidships, and the Japanese ship sank almost immediately. But by then the *Sterett* herself was badly damaged and drifting. *O'Bannon* and *San Francisco* moved into attacking positions. When the disabled *Atlanta* drifted into *San Francisco*'s line of fire, shells from the cruiser struck the ship's superstructure.

It was two in the morning when the crew of the *Portland* felt the ship shudder. They had taken a torpedo hit on the starboard quarter, and twenty men stationed in the stern were killed by the explosion. The gun in the number three turret was locked in train and elevation. The torpedo had struck the inboard propellers and jammed the rudder 5 degrees right. Suddenly the ship was listing about 4 degrees. The crew corrected by shifting ballast, but they could not fix the rudder and they could not steer. As the battle waged in the darkness around them, they had no choice but to steam to starboard in great circles. The crew knew that the prospects for surviving the night were miserable. But the darkness offered some cover, and they still had their guns—or some of them.

On the first circle the watch sighted the battleship *Hiei* illuminated by fires from nearby vessels. The *Portland* launched several salvos, and after a few minutes the crew saw fires aboard and knew they had hit her. It would be a long time until daylight. All they could do was keep steaming in circles, hope no one caught them in crosshairs, and try to hit whatever they could.

A radio officer aboard the *Kirishima* radioed to headquarters at Truk a report of a "severe mixed battle" in which both sides suffered serious losses. From Guadalcanal, troops on both sides had a view. Marine Private Robert Leckie would later describe the scene: "the sea seemed a sheet of polished obsidian on which the warships seem to have been dropped and immobilized, centered amid concentric circles like shock waves that form around a stone dropped in mud."

At 2 A.M. aboard the *Hiei*, Rear Admiral Hiroaki Abe, himself wounded, cancelled the mission and gave orders for his ships to withdraw. Meanwhile, Captain Gilbert C. Hoover aboard the *Helena* was trying to contact anyone senior by radio. He soon realized he was ranking officer, and at 2:26 A.M. he called for the American forces to withdraw. When dawn came, the extent of losses became clear. Two American cruisers and four destroyers had been sunk. More than 1,400 American sailors were dead or missing, two of them admirals.

When that torpedo hit the *Portland*, Ensign Windham had been stationed near the ship's stern. Had the submarine missile exploded 20 feet farther forward, he would have been among those killed.

3

NAS Jax

Even by the modest standards of northern Florida real estate, it had been an unremarkable piece of property. Five square miles of flat and hard-packed sand just south of the Jacksonville city limits, a roughly triangular spit of earth shaped by the confluence of the Ortega and St. Johns Rivers. On the old maps, the small peninsula on its northern shore was labeled Piney Point, another on the southern shore Black Point, but by the 1930s no one—not even the boys who hunted crawfish in the shallows— knew their names.

The U.S. Navy was in need of a southern base to support its growing fleet in the Atlantic and Caribbean and the property south of Jacksonville met the requirements. It was near other inland bases and bases farther north on the coast, and it afforded short flights to points in much of the Caribbean. So in 1939 the land was purchased, brush was cleared, roads and runways were paved. Near them appeared hangers, barracks, and administration buildings. A year later the property was commissioned as Naval Air Station Jacksonville. By the end of World War II more than 11,000 pilots had completed training at a place they called NAS Jax.

After the war, many airbases were summarily closed, but the Jacksonville Chamber of Commerce was convinced that the Navy's presence was crucial to local economic health, and succeeded in having the primary mission of the base changed from training to fleet support. Growth at Jax continued unabated, and in early 1954 the Naval Air Weapons System School was established to train crews in maintenance of air-launched guided missiles and aircraft armament control systems. By 1955 Jax was one of three major fleet bases operating on the East Coast. It was headquarters for 60 percent of the fleet air striking force in the Atlantic, a primary supply base for carriers and patrol bomber operations for NATO commitments in the Mediterranean, and a supply center for all Navy bases in the southeastern United States and much of the Caribbean. It had become the nation's busiest military airport, with more than six hundred takeoffs and landings a day.

The main airstrip stretched west to east, and the main street crossed it, running from the main gate to a pier that extended into the St. Johns River. Just south of that airstrip were four hangars. The crews called them "barns," and most days there were aircraft parked nearby. There was a seaplane ramp to the water to the south. At Jax there was no fence, and every now and then an alligator would crawl right out of the shallows of the St. Johns River and find shade under an aircraft.

There were, of course, amenities. The "Exchange" was sort of a commissary, where Navy personnel and their families could buy merchandise at cost or less. There were facilities for recreation—a ball field, a golf course. There was also a bar on base.

NAS Jax was home of the Navy's Fleet Air Wing Eleven. The wing had administrative control of several squadrons, one of which was Airborne Early Warning Squadron Four, termed in the Navy's shorthand, VW-4.[4] It was the seventh naval aircraft squadron assigned to weather reconnaissance missions, and it had been providing hurricane reconnaissance since 1953. By late 1954 its officer pool had grown to more than forty.

In December 1954, VW-4 administration was changing. Soon it would have a new commander. His name was Edward L. Foster. In civilian life Foster might have been one of those thick-set, dependable men who had a long career in industrial lubricants or a chain of auto parts stores. He was from Chattanooga. He had attended Northwestern University's midshipmen's school, and received his commission as ensign in March of 1941. He had done a tour of duty aboard the USS *Hamilton* and then entered flight training, earning his wings in July of 1943. He served as a flight instructor until December of that year, then held a variety of posts, including operations officer in the Eighth Naval District. In March of 1949 he became executive officer of the reconnaissance or patrol squadron known as VP-3. Foster never saw combat as an aviator, but he had known the terrible responsibility for men killed. A year earlier, on December 17, 1953, one of the squadron's P2V-5s and its crew of nine had crashed on a glacier in Iceland. Rescue teams had only enough time to pull one body from the wreckage before a storm buried the rest under snow and ice. There was a lot about the position that Foster disliked. The worst was telling young women that they had become widows.

On December 15, 1954, the number of VW-4 officers was increased by one—Lieutenant Commander Grover Windham Jr. He would be flying as patrol plane second pilot. To spend a few days in Jacksonville, he and Nancy left the children with her parents in Millport, Alabama. They reported to Jax, and Windham

4. During hurricane season, operational control shifted to Commander, Eastern Sea Frontier, or COMEASTSEAFRON, in New York, which in turn delegated operations control to Officer-in-Charge, Fleet Hurricane Forecast Center, Miami. The center at Miami controlled all hurricane reconnaissance flights.

signed forms at the base and met Foster and administration and flight crews.

When the paperwork was complete, he and Nancy attended to more domestic concerns. Many officers lived with their families on base, where the quarters were inexpensive and fairly comfortable. But Windham had a broad view of the world, and it was his conviction that the military offered only a partial reality. There were other kinds of people, other ways to live, and although he had chosen the Navy as a career and indeed bled blue and gold, he would not demand that his children follow suit. Moreover, he did not want them to grow up on a naval base for the simple reason that their experiences would be narrow. So he and Nancy drove the streets of Jacksonville looking for a house. It was difficult. In 1955, most junior officers earned $6,000 to $8,000 a year in base pay, with perhaps another $2,000 in housing allowances. In Jacksonville such a salary was barely enough to afford one of the numerous, miserable cinderblock affairs with a tin roof and a porch with storm shutters on a sandy quarter-acre lot. So they returned to Millport, where they spent Christmas. During the last week of 1954 they packed everything up and headed back to Jacksonville, this time with the children. The family moved into a motel and in off-duty hours Grover searched for more-permanent accomodations.

◢

In the 1950s an American male either enlisted in some branch of the military or was drafted into the Army. The 241 enlisted men in VW-4 had chosen the Navy for a variety of reasons—expectation of travel, a friend's recommendation, an adventure book read as a boy, or a disinclination to die in a foxhole in Korea. Jim Meyer enlisted in July 1952, went through boot camp in San Diego, and attended the Naval Air Technical Training Center in Norman, Oklahoma.

In early 1953 he began training in a six-week course in meteorology at Lakehurst, New Jersey. All instructors were enlisted personnel and aerologists, and there was no military regimentation. The barracks were like officers' quarters—two sailors in a room, each with a desk. The program itself was fairly intensive, with classes meeting all day, regular exams, and hands-on equipment training. For Meyer, who would be the first to say that he lacked a talent for higher mathematics, the most difficult part of the curriculum was coding and decoding weather data. Still, he made it through the program, and upon graduation he was made an "aerographer's mate." On hurricane missions his foremost job would be to determine wind direction and speed by looking at the sea.

He reported to Jax in January 1955. The night he arrived he was put in a motel. It felt good to be in Florida—he had not seen palm trees for a long time. A Navy van picked him up in the morning and took him to the front gate. There was a master of arms shack just inside the gate, and after checking in (he carried with him a large manila envelope with his naval and medical records), he was driven to the VW-4 hangar and shown the way to the barracks.

There were two barracks just south of the barn, and each housed thirty or forty men. They were long buildings with a front and rear entrance, no air conditioning in the summer, gas heat in the winter. Each building contained two rows of bunk beds along the outside walls, a metal locker nearby for each man, and a common head and shower that could accommodate a dozen at a time. At one end was a small office for the petty officer. In the center was a metal garbage can that did double duty as an alarm. The last man on night shift used a stick to bang reveille on the lid. In off-duty hours the men slept, wrote letters, had bull sessions, and listened to radios. They also spent a lot of off-duty time talking about their lives back home.

Most enlisted men had never been more than 50 miles from the place where they grew up, and the Navy offered quite an education. There were Irish Catholics from Cincinatti, Baptists from

Tuscaloosa, and following Eisenhower's 1948 order to integrate the armed services, there were black men in the squadron, a few serving on flight crews. Even for Jim Meyer it was an education. Once, he mentioned to an older sailor that in the showers he had noticed a tattoo of twin ships' propellers on both cheeks of a sailor's buttocks. He offered the observation only as an amusing note of local color, and was surprised to be told that that particular ornamentation was common. It was part of a rather ancient nautical superstition surviving into and transformed for the twentieth century. Roughly translated, it meant "to insure safe passage."

Most days enlisted men wore blue dungarees and a white hat. They went to mess, and at eight they reported to duty stations, where they spent most of their waking hours in the work of maintaining, repairing, and operating a fleet of aircraft.

In 1955 VW-4 was in transition, and its planes were a mixed lot. Most missions flew an aircraft that was a derivative of the commercial Lockheed Constellation. Crammed with six tons of electronic gear, it could stay aloft for eighteen hours. There were also several P2V Neptunes.[5] These were older patrol aircraft with two 3,500-horsepower Wright piston engines, designed for a crew of nine. In May, a few of the Neptunes were sent to St. Louis, where they had J-34 Westinghouse jet engines hung under either wing, outboard of the reciprocating engines. "Two turning, two burning," the crews called them. But the real prizes of the squadron, delivered earlier that year, were three Navy WC-121N Super Constellations. These were four-engine commercial aircraft reconfigured especially for weather reconnaissance. The planes were enormous. They could accommodate a crew of twenty-nine, working in three teams: flight, weather, and radar. The men called them "Super Connies," and their distinguishing feature, rising out of the

---

5. The P2V was a patrol aircraft—thus the *P*. It was the second land-based patrol aircraft in the Lockheed locker—thus the *2*. And it was designed by Lockheed's Vega division—thus the *V*.

fuselage just aft the flight deck, was a "hump." It held a search radar antenna that could sweep an area of 200,000 square miles. It was off limits to customs inspectors, and the prevailing joke was that the hump was where crews stashed their liquor.

An officer or enlisted man of Airborne Early Warning Squadron Four served in one of four departments. The men in the maintenance department pulled engines out of planes, greased them and rebuilt them, inspected airframes for stress, and tested and repaired radar and radio equipment. Operations people conducted ground and in-flight training and formulated mission procedures. These procedures were determined in part by hurricane science, and most of the science came through aerology, whose men were trained in the science of hurricanes and tropical climatology. Administration staff did paperwork, a great deal of it—watch lists, personnel records, and squadron directives. The department had an education office and a public information office, whose charges wrote and issued press releases, spoke to reporters, and especially during hurricane season, made presentations to local civics groups and high schools.

All this work was in the service of the flight crews. There were six such crews in VW-4, with nine men in each. Assignments to crews were provisional, and often a man would be bumped from a mission or "loaned" to another crew. Nonetheless, any given crew could be said to develop a certain character. Some, like Mackie's Crew Two, were especially congenial. In every photograph they are shown smiling, and it is clear that they enjoyed each other's company. Others, like Crew Six, seemed more serious.

Navy flight crews tended to be informal within the bounds of military customs and courtesy. Officers normally addressed one another by first name or nickname. A sailor would address an officer two ranks his senior as "mister." For their part, officers addressed enlisted personnel by their surnames. If such protocol seemed overly formal for young men working long hours in close quarters, it was a practice one grew used to, and crews built real camaraderie nonetheless.

The flight crews at Jax spent most days in training flights, some from Jacksonville down the coast to Miami, some out into the Atlantic to specified coordinates and back. Especially when a crew was breaking in a newer pilot, they spent whole days on the base and near it, doing landings and takeoffs called "touch and go's." Sometimes an enlisted man had more experience than an officer, and protocol was waived in the interests of that officer's education. On one routine flight off the coast a pilot decided to practice a hurricane penetration drill in clear and fair weather. Normally he would seek advice from the onboard aerologist, but the closest they had that day was Aerographer's Mate Meyer, so the pilot asked him for a heading that would put the plane into the wind at 500 feet off the water. Meyer gave him a heading, and a few minutes later thought to look at the waves. The pilot had taken another heading, a dangerous one. They were heading downwind. Had they been in a hurricane, they would already be dead. Meyer informed the pilot, who asked Meyer what to do. The enlisted man advised him to come about by 180 degrees. Once they were heading upwind, Meyer started giving 10-degree changes in heading, the changes they would make if they were actually penetrating a hurricane.

Flight crews were privileged to an activity the Navy called "long-range navigation flights," and the men themselves called "boon-doggles." Some of these were flights to naval air bases in the Caribbean. Others were across the Atlantic to bases in Britain, Denmark, Spain, Morocco, and the Azores. From points of view of the Navy, the flights made a lot of sense. They ensured that pilots and navigators kept up their skills. For pilots, it was likewise an agreeable arrangement. In addition to their regular salary, they received flight pay, which could be as much as $1,700 a year. And the enlisted men—who neither piloted nor navigated—saw the world.

And so the Hurricane Hunters lived with the accoutrements of war, both the necessary and the absurd. There was boredom and routine, and there were the small idiocies of bureaucracies and chains of command. But there were also the pleasures of new and unexpected perspectives. And sometimes, there was a sense of something large and dangerous just over the horizon.

➤

In 1955 the city of Jacksonville was a military boomtown—miles and miles of ranch houses, public schools, supermarkets, and miniature golf courses. Out all along U.S. Route 17, there were little one-story cinderblock bars and honky-tonks and motels with neon "Vacancy" signs, and every mile or so, a barbershop charging a dollar-fifty for a haircut. Neighborhoods of private residences were of the type common in communities near military installations in the American South: wide streets, rows of single-story houses, half-acre plots, patches of wiry grass that struggled to stay alive in the sandy, hard-packed ground, and a few scrub pines and palmettos, nothing reaching more than 8 or 10 feet in height.

Not all the civilians in Jacksonville appreciated the military presence; hand-lettered signs in some front yards read "SAILORS KEEP OFF THE GRASS." But the Navy had been in Jacksonville for sixteen years, and two houses out of ten were occupied by a naval officer and his family. One such residence lay a mile and a half to the northwest of Jax, on Timuquana Road. It was slightly grander than those around it. The one-story house was designed in what was called the "hacienda" style—a white stucco exterior with a red-tile roof. Inside was a large living room with a fireplace, three bedrooms, even maids' quarters. There was a side yard, and a school a few blocks away.

When Nancy saw the house, she was astonished. She thought her husband was joking. She could not understand how they would manage on his salary, but he assured her they would. In fact, their rent would be only a little more than they were used to paying.

Windham had found two rather unusually accommodating landlords. The owners and residents were two elderly sisters who intended to live out their remaining years in their second home, a beach house. He had persuaded them to leave half of their furniture and to let them move in sooner than the date cited in the lease. Nancy did not pretend to know what combination of innocent flirtation and flattery her husband had put to use. And by then, she knew better than to ask.

4

1955

In the first years of the twentieth century hurricanes that reached the United States seemed to direct themselves toward the Gulf Coast and southern Florida. That trend ended in 1953, when Hurricane Barbara skirted North Carolina's Outer Banks. The next year was far worse. In the last week of August, Hurricane Carol skirted North Carolina and moved northeast along the coast. When she reached southern New England, her winds were clocked at 100 miles an hour. Carol's eye made landfall on the eastern tip of Long Island, and although the worst winds remained at sea, gusts on Block Island reached 130 miles an hour. Before Carol dissipated, sixty people were dead.

Hurricane Edna appeared a few days later, and again New England was hit hard, with Cape Cod and the islands of Martha's Vineyard and Nantucket taking the worst of it. Edna churned northward along the coasts of Massachusetts and Maine, then into Nova Scotia. This time tens of thousands were able to flee inland, in large part because forecasters had given warning. Still, twenty were killed, and damage was estimated at $42 million. The season was far from over, and the worst was to come.

She would be called Hazel. Forecasters in San Juan and Miami observed an easterly wave east of the Lesser Antilles. On October 5, a Navy reconnaissance craft 50 miles east of Granada observed a "poorly defined eye" and winds of 95 miles an hour, and the S.S. *Atlantic Importer* passed through a squall, the wind coming from the south at hurricane velocity. Two days later another Navy reconnaissance plane encountered severe turbulence. One crewman was badly injured, and low-level missions were discontinued. On the tenth Hazel showed a turn to the northwest and then the north-northeast. Meteorologists clocked her winds at 100 miles per hour. Four villages on Haiti were destroyed. Larger cities were damaged by winds and high tides, and estimates for the number dead ranged from 400 to 1,000. By October 11 the storm had passed into the Atlantic, and on the twelfth she was between Cape Hatteras and Bermuda. Over the next few days her winds grew stronger—at one point reaching 150 miles per hour—and six people were killed when a sailboat capsized near Inagua.

A hurricane's size is measured in three ways: the diameter of the hurricane winds, the diameter of the gale winds, and the outer boundary of the area of low pressure. In an average hurricane, the diameter of hurricane force winds is 100 miles, and the diameter of its gale winds from 350 to 400 miles. There have been some rather extraordinary specimens. The hurricane winds of the "Great Atlantic Hurricane" of September 1944 had measured over 200 miles across, and its gales measured 600 miles across. Pacific typhoons, because they have more room to develop, have been known to have diameters large enough to cover the western half of the United States. As the size of Atlantic hurricanes go, Hazel was better than respectable. On October 14 her hurricane winds had a diameter greater than 120 miles and gales of more than 300 miles.

Residents along the North Carolina coast near Wilmington were mildly concerned with news of Hazel, but most forecasts had her hitting the coast farther north. Hazel defied expectations. There were scattered cumulus and stratocumulus clouds in the morning, and intermittent rain squalls by late afternoon. Hurricane warnings were ordered for Wilmington. By the evening of the fourteenth, the storm swell was breaking on the beach every twenty seconds and the tide was higher than anyone had ever seen it. A meteorologist was on the beach to check on sea conditions. He was sobered enough by what he saw that he persuaded a local radio station to issue an emergency broadcast on the spot. Officials began to realize the situation was serious, and they alerted state and village police, civil defense, and the Red Cross. The hurricane reached the coast in midmorning on October 15. Winds tore at buildings, and the storm surge rose. The shrimp boat *Nina Fay* was able to ride it out near Holden Beach Bridge. She was the only boat to remain afloat, and her captain said the wind was probably 150 miles an hour. From Myrtle Beach to Cedar Island, North Carolina—every fishing pier was demolished. The business section of Garden City was made rubble. At Wrightsville Beach the wind reached 125 miles an hour, and the storm surge submerged the whole island.

It soon became apparent that Hazel was unusual. Most hurricanes lose strength when they cross a shoreline, but this one seemed to be playing by a different set of rules. As she moved inland through Maryland, Pennsylvania, and western New York State, she actually became stronger. The reason was a major "convulsion" in the circulation pattern. Late on the twelfth, while Hazel was still off the coast of North Carolina, an area of low pressure began to form in the western Gulf of Alaska, and a trough of very cold air over western Canada began to push eastward. By the sixteenth Hazel had accelerated, traveling through the mid-Atlantic states at speeds of 60 miles an hour. Washington, D.C., was hit with winds of 78 miles an hour, the highest on record. Philadelphia reported peak gusts of 94 miles per hour, and the New York Weather Bureau Office recorded 113 miles per hour, another record. Control towers at airports were abandoned.

On the seventeenth, Hazel, redesignated an "extratropical cyclone," passed over Lake Ontario. Toronto had already been drenched by thunderstorms preceding the cold front, and the combined effect of convergence and lift over the steep frontal surface made for a record-breaking rainfall around the city. The watershed was already saturated, and in the western suburban area of the city, flood waters rose so quickly that cars were washed from roads and bridges. The Humber and Credit Rivers were inundated with seven inches of rain in a single day. Eighty people drowned and thousands were made homeless.

Gradually, the rains diminished. By October 18 the remnants of the storm had moved out over the Atlantic. Two days later Hazel was still producing strong winds and rains on the coasts of Scandinavia, a thousand miles away.

Hurricane Hazel was one of the most severe combined tropical and extratropical storms ever to hit the northeastern United States and southeastern Canada. By the time her wrath was spent, she had killed between 600 and 1,200 people. One lesson of Hazel was that predictions must take into account larger dynamics of the atmosphere called "broad-scale flow patterns." Carol and Hazel in 1954 and the New England Hurricane of 1938 all accelerated rapidly, in part because a low-pressure trough adjacent to the storm suddenly "deepened" and pulled the storm toward it. But there was a second, more disturbing lesson. Even in retrospect, no one could completely explain Hazel's movements. She was the storm that showed meteorologists how little they knew.

The year 1954 was seen as a freak, and most expected that 1955 would return to what had been the norm. There were, however, dissenters. Certain meteorologists were suggesting that the norm itself was changing. In early February the German Hydrographic Institute reported that warm-water fish—tuna and sardines—were being caught in the North Sea. Dr. Gunther Bohnecke, the institute's chief, suspected that the fish had extended their range northward because the waters off Norway, like many parts of the Northern Hemisphere, were growing warmer. Many agreed there was evidence of a general oceanic warming trend.

Atmospheric warming was different from oceanographic warming, but no one doubted they were related. As early as 1895 the Swedish chemist Svante Arrhenius had calculated that Earth's average temperature would rise by 10° Celsius (50° Fahrenheit) if atmospheric carbon dioxide were merely doubled. In 1955 something like that seemed to be happening. Roger Revelle of the Scripps Oceanographic Institute had been studying the subject in some depth. He found that codfish had moved north, glaciers were in retreat, Mexican armadillos were invading the Gulf Coast, and permanent snow lines on mountainsides had moved higher. In August of 1955 ocean temperatures off the coast of Maine were warmer than normal by 7° Fahrenheit.

If the warming was real, its other effects would not be so benign as fish caught beyond their usual range. Hurricanes were generated by an upwelling of warm air and moisture, and hurricanes first appear in mid-June because that is when waters are sufficiently warmed. Meteorologists thought that it followed logically that warmer waters—or waters that became warmer earlier and remained warm for longer periods of time—would generate more hurricanes. Indeed, since 1930 there had been a slight increase in the number of hurricanes in any given year. A severe hurricane had struck New England in 1938, another in 1944, and by 1954 the trend seemed to have greatly accelerated. The new frequency may well have been a product of warming temperatures, but it soon became clear that the chain of cause and effect, if it existed at all, was complex. Meteorologist Gordon Dunn found that sea temperatures below normal seemed to correlate with fewer hurricanes, but temperatures above normal did not correlate with *more* hurricanes.

Jerome Namias was a U.S. Weather Bureau meteorologist particularly interested in the connections between atmospheric warming and hurricanes. He believed that a warmer atmosphere meant more moist tropical air moving northward and more hurricanes steering north of the 35-degree latitude. They had more time to retain the warm central core, the characteristic that made them powerful. In February of 1955 Namias told a New York meeting of the American Meteorological Society that in coming seasons, hurricanes would be more likely to steer toward the eastern seaboard. The reason, he believed, was a change in the "planetary air current"—the great river of high-altitude wind that sweeps around Earth in temperate latitudes. Namias believed that it had shifted in such a way that brought more air from the Atlantic Ocean and less from Canada. Something similar was going on in the northeastern Pacific. Japan was being hit with more typhoons. Namias was certain that the typhoons, the hurricanes, and the tuna in the North Sea were connected. He just wasn't sure how.

⤙

The U.S. Weather Bureau names hurricanes in advance, usually a month or so before the start of the season in mid-June. Since 1953 the practice had been to consult a few "name the baby" books and decide on a set of names for the coming season. No one expected a new list would be needed much before early summer. But the first storm of 1955 arrived in January. And the bureau's "namers," caught unprepared, simply recycled the first name from the previous year. As it happened, Alice of 1955 was not especially powerful (her winds never reached speeds higher than 80 miles per hour), but she was a harbinger of a season the bureau would call, with some understatement, "active." As with most years, spring and early summer were quiet. In late July, Hurricane Brenda appeared and dissipated quickly and harmlessly. Then, in August, the season seemed to take a turn.

The hurricane named Connie was born on the third day of the month, in the mid-Atlantic, 600 miles west of Cape Verde. She tracked westward across the Caribbean, staying north of the islands. She veered north between the Bahamas and Bermuda and moved toward the U.S. coastline. Meteorologists knew she was likely to be a bad one, and they began to watch her carefully. A new storm, Diane, was following Connie. At her most powerful, Connie was 1,500 miles wide, when Diane was 400. The edges of the two storms interpenetrated each other, and for the first days of her life, Diane was actually inside Connie, a storm within a storm. The proximity of the storms made them subject to a phenomenon called the *Fujiwara effect*. In the 1920s Japanese meteorologist Sakuhei Fujiwara studied the interaction between the phenomenon of whirling fluids called *vortices*. He observed that two vortices, near each other, tend to rotate counterclockwise around a point somewhere between them; moreover, the vortices are mutually attracted. Connie was pulling Diane, and Diane, to a lesser degree, was pulling Connie. Both were moving toward the U.S. coastline.

Connie hit first. Her easternmost edge made landfall near Moorehead City, North Carolina. She tore up the coast, wrecking a schooner in Chesapeake Bay and killing all fourteen people aboard. She made only a glancing blow against the coast itself, and because the tide was low, she spent much of her fury against seawalls and sand banks. For three hours Connie looped slowly about and her winds diminished to 80 miles an hour. As she moved inland she was slowly dying, but not without a fight. She brought torrents of rain to the mid-Atlantic states and put the New Jersey shore under a foot of ocean. Her winds tore down power lines. Grand Central Station in New York City lost electricity, and for half a day La Guardia Airport was under a foot of water. In Long Island she brought floods, and everywhere she brought death. In Pennsylvania four people were killed; in New Jersey, six; in New York, eleven. Connie wreaked havoc for seven days and nights, then moved inland toward western New York State, where, in a gust of rain and wind, she finally died.

Meanwhile, Diane was in the Atlantic about 1,000 miles east of Miami, moving northwest at 10 miles an hour, pushing gale winds ahead of her. Her winds lost force when she neared the North Carolina coast. When forecasters announced that she posed little threat, summer vacationers once again took to the highways and beaches. The forecasters were right about her winds, but rains were more difficult to predict, and soon the rains turned relentless. On the morning of August 17, Diane moved into central Virginia. Then she turned east by northeast, passing over eastern Pennsylvania, New Jersey, and southern New England.

Her rains fell on saturated ground, and the waters flowed and surged, until streams and tributaries reached record levels. Highways and bridges were closed, rail service between New York and Boston was shut down, smaller cities lost power, and still the rains continued. In Stroudsburg, Pennsylvania, the Brodhead Creek rose 30 feet in fifteen minutes, leaving fifty dead. In southern New England dams overflowed and burst. Debris charged downstream, collected at narrows and against bridge supports, and suddenly dislodged. Torrents of water turned streets into channels, tore through pavement, and lifted buildings from their foundations.

Some scenes of the devastation might have emerged from a gothic hell. In Seymour, Connecticut, and Woonsocket, Rhode Island, floodwaters ripped through cemeteries, tearing up the earth and sending coffins bobbing downstream. In Putnam, Connecticut, the flood destroyed a chemical plant, and hundreds of barrels of burning magnesium floated in streets turned into canals. All through that long night one barrel after another would rupture. Some simply exploded like bombs; others rolled, turned, and leaked slowly, sending geysers of white-hot metal shrieking 200 feet into the air. The front pages of newspapers the next day showed photographs of downtown areas taken from the air. It was as though a giant had dropped buildings in the middle of a wide and raging river.

President Eisenhower declared six eastern states disaster areas and ordered federal relief. The Army, Red Cross, and civilian defense units began one of the largest rescue and rehabilitation efforts in U.S. history. They brought food, medicine, and emergency water-purification systems. People were housed in tents, churches, and schools. Officials put the death toll at 250, but by week's end hundreds were still missing and at least 100,000 were homeless. As to property damage, Diane would become known as the first "billion-dollar hurricane," the worst in U.S. history.

In the first few days of September a reconnaissance mission found Hurricane Gladys. Born not in the mid-Atlantic but in the wide bay in the southern Gulf of Mexico, she moved northwest along the coast for a few hundred miles, then turned southward and moved ashore in central Mexico. She was cause for worry, but her winds never exceeded 90 miles per hour, and by September 8 she had made landfall and dissipated.

The next one would be different. Born near Antigua on September 9, Hurricane Hilda moved north and began to track dead west, a few miles north of Puerto Rico and the Dominican Republic. Hilda seemed drawn to land. In fact, she seemed to follow island chains. She skirted the southern coast of Cuba and moved through the Cayman Islands. Her 115-mile-an-hour winds tore into the Yucatán Peninsula near Cozumel. Most hurricanes lose speed over land, because energy supplied by upwelling water is cut off and because the variegated topography confuses and slows winds. But as Hilda continued west across the Yucatán, her winds lessened only slightly. She crossed the Gulf of Mexico and made landfall again in Mexico. In a matter of hours she tore into the coast, destroying much of the city of Tampico.

Soon the Caribbean seemed crowded with storms. On September 10 a reconnaissance flight tracking Hilda had discovered a new one, Ione. She was the ninth hurricane of the season, born in the mid-Atlantic, about 50 miles south of where Diane was first sighted. She began to move west by southwest and tracked toward Venezuela. But on September 12 she suddenly turned northward and began to parallel the tracks of Connie and Diane. Again the U.S. coastline was threatened. Memories of Connie and Diane were fresh, and the eastern seaboard braced itself. Red and black hurricane pennants were flying from Cape Hatteras to Cape Cod. Larger craft moved out to sea; small boats were hauled ashore; beach dwellers boarded windows, packed their cars, and headed inland.

Ione hit North Carolina as predicted: boardwalks and beach-front cottages were demolished. The winds were only moderate gales, but local weather bureaus said that as she moved north, her winds would increase and her rains would become torrential. They reserved particular concern for New York City. The city had never suffered a direct hit from a hurricane, but it was directly in Ione's path. Every feature of Manhattan and the boroughs—a dense population, a low-lying topography with streets and railways running just above the high water mark—was ready-made for a disaster of historic proportions. Civil defense units prepared emergency crews, the Coast Guard issued warnings to ships, and the Board of Planning and Operations awaited the worst.

Then, Ione did not move north. Instead, she lingered off the Carolina coast. Soon radar showed her eye fading, her spiral arms dissolving into rain clouds. The system itself moved out to sea.

Anyone might have expected that the reaction of the public would be gratitude to the U.S. Weather Bureau for its caution. Instead, people were angry for an error that caused them to cancel vacations and trips they should not have had to cancel. Many editorial writers accused the bureau of warnings they called "hysterical." Jokes of a bumbling and error-prone weather service were at least as old as the Civil War, but this was a peculiarly virulent reaction, especially given its timing. It was as though Hazel and Diane and Connie had been forgotten.

In fact, some local forecasters had said Ione would dissipate. Among them was Princeton astronomer John Q. Stewart. Stewart told the press that the Weather Bureau would be well advised to rely less on radar and more on the barometer. That he was an astronomer and not a meteorologist was a fine point lost on newspapers, many of whom seemed pleased to be able to cite an authority questioning the bureau's methods. As for the sentiment of the bureau itself, no one knew better that predictions were tentative, that human understanding of hurricanes was dangerously insufficient. The bureau's forecasters knew what a hurricane could do, they believed they had erred on the side of caution, and they had no talent for the niceties of public relations. Publicly, their defense was a weak plea for appreciation of the difficulty with which predictions are made, and a statement that Ione's sudden turn oceanward was caused by an unexpected and uncharacteristic southerly veering of the jet stream. The public seemed to say, "Well—why couldn't you have predicted *that*?"

If most Americans had little appreciation for the difficulties forecasters confronted in making predictions, at least the Weather Bureau was an organization they could name. By contrast, few had heard of the Navy and Air Force weather reconnaissance squadrons, despite the fact that the members of those squadrons had saved probably hundreds of lives and millions of dollars in property damage. The reason for this ignorance was difficult to explain. There were no secrets associated with the crews or their operations. By 1955 they had been the subject of a few newspaper stories, and especially during hurricane season it was not unusual for a few pages on the crews to appear as part of a Sunday supplement. Seven years earlier, in fact, the glamour of brave men, airplanes, and storms had attracted the attention of Hollywood. In 1949 Twentieth Century Fox had released to American cinemas an opus called *Slattery's Hurricane*. It starred Richard Widmark, Linda Darnell, and Veronica Lake. Much of it had been filmed at Naval Air Station Miami, and as the studio's publicity department went to great lengths to make known, it was made with the full cooperation of the U.S. Navy. One of the squadron's crews had flown a Lockheed Constellation to cities in which the film premiered, and for a few weeks the men were treated like movie stars. But the film opened to mixed reviews, and soon enough audiences forgot it.

There was another bit of publicity, though, in 1954. It was coordinated by Edward R. Murrow, the journalist who gained fame for his shortwave radio broadcasts from London during the blitz, and was probably the most accurate representation of weather reconnaissance. Murrow and a cameraman accompanied a crew from the Air Force's 53rd Weather Reconnaissance Squadron into Hurricane Edna. The resulting film was aired on CBS television as a segment in a show called *See It Now*.

And so although the public heard bits and pieces about the crews almost since their beginning, their interest was never peaked. The weather reconnaissance squadrons would never enjoy the general adulation accorded war heroes or test pilots, and in 1955 few Americans knew anything about the men who flew into the violent hearts of storms. In fact, anyone hearing about the crews for the first time was likely to respond, "You mean men actually fly into hurricanes? On purpose?"

Meanwhile, in the summer and early fall of 1955 the Navy Hurricane Hunters, for the most part oblivious to the public's indifference, went quietly about their work. For Hurricane Connie they had flown ten missions that included flights into the eye. These were called *penetration missions*. They had also flown eleven radar missions—flights that included circumnavigating the storm and mapping its structure with radar. For Hilda, they had flown six penetration and four night radar missions. For Ione, six penetrations, three night radar, and one day radar mission. It was a challenging season too, in that they were testing new equipment and new aircraft. A crew flew the first reconnaissance mission in a Super Connie. A few weeks later, Lieutenant Commander Raymond C. Newman and a sixteen-man crew in another Super Connie penetrated the eye of Ione. It was a record-breaking eighteen-hour mission, and they spent four hours inside the 30-mile-wide eye.

A typical season sees eight tropical storms, five of which develop into hurricanes. But by early September 1955 there had already been nine, and the season was far from over. By mid month it would become the worst hurricane season of the century.

If Grover Windham thought about the recent course of events in his life, he had reason to be pleased. He had the advantages of a military career, and he was advancing quickly. He had been promoted to patrol plane commander on the first of the month. He enjoyed being near his family, and was growing to appreciate the house on Timuquana Road. Among its features was a study. He used it to do paperwork and to prepare for the tests necessary to gain promotion to commander, a rank he had a good chance of attaining before year's end. And as for the wife whom the last ten years had made him neglect, he did not know if he could make up for the lost time, but he could try. He and Nancy began a kind of second honeymoon. Saturday mornings Nan and Buz were under orders not to disturb their parents, and cereal and milk were left on a shelf in the refrigerator.

It was clear to anyone who saw the Windhams that they were very much in love. It was also clear that they were two strong-willed people. Naturally enough, they had disagreements. Grover thought that Nan and Buz should have a dog. It would teach them responsibility, he said. But Nancy had long had a mild fear of dogs and simply did not want one in the house. He would bring the subject up now and again, but on the canine issue she was a wall: the Windham household would have no dog. They had disagreements on more serious matters, too—for one, his career. Despite his reassurances, she had never quite warmed up to the idea of his spending so much time in Navy aircraft. In fact, she did not like the idea of her children's father in military aviation of any kind. Already that year there had been several accidents at Jax, and those crews had only been on routine training flights. They had not been trying to fly into a hurricane.

These disagreements always played out quickly and always the same way. They went into the bedroom and closed the door. There they would have a "discussion." He would make his case. She would tell him in articulate and direct terms that he was mistaken. He would counter, and she would return. And sooner or later one or the other would say something funny, and they would both laugh. Before long they would forget what they were arguing about.

Many of the choices they had made, the direction they had taken, were for the children. The neighborhood in which they lived, for instance. The public grammar school was two blocks away, and Grover liked the fact that he and Nancy could stand on the front porch and watch their children walk the whole way there. He had definite ideas about their education. When Nan turned nine, she was required to watch the evening news and read the front page of the newspaper every day. During dinner the family held discussions on current events.

Still, Windham felt some of the guilt of a father who had lost too much time. He had been on tours of duty for stretches of sixteen months and eighteen months. So much happens in a child's life. He had been determined to do better in this regard too, and he did. He began teaching his son to play the guitar. He arranged "lunch dates" with his daughter. For three or four days of the week he would be home at noon, and Nancy would prepare lunch for her husband and her daughter, then excuse herself.

During one such meal—it was a Friday—Nan was upset. In her third-grade class she had failed a spelling quiz. Worse, she had failed it because she had followed her father's advice. He had helped her study for the test on words like *book*—that is, words with consecutive *o*'s. The problem was that whenever he had spelled a word out loud, he had said "double *o*" and she had heard "*w. o.*" So she had failed the test. When she told her father, he laughed. There was a lot of laughter in the Windham household, and this laughter in particular may have been produced from a recollection of a moment in childhood, a gentle laughter born of delight. But to Nan it was merely the laugh of condescension. She was hurt, and when he was ready to leave, she would not give him a hug and a kiss good-bye.

His thoughts, perhaps, were elsewhere. A hurricane called Janet had raked across Barbados, and at the moment she was tracking west across the Caribbean. He had been given a mission with two passengers, both civilians—a reporter and a photographer from the *Toronto Daily Star*. They had been waiting a year for the flight, and a number of circumstances conspired to make it his. He was eager to demonstrate the skills of his crew and eager to share the feeling of being aloft in violent and spectacular weather. He and Crew Five would fly two missions on Janet. There would be a reconnaissance flight late Saturday night and Sunday morning. Then they would spend Sunday night at Guantánamo Bay and fly a penetration mission on Monday morning.

5

Miami

In 1955 the Hurricane Forecast Center Headquarters were located on the top floor of a sixteen-story building in downtown Miami. It was a rabbits' warren of cluttered offices crammed with drafting tables, teletype machines, and phones. In every office, walls were covered with synoptic charts, and a clock was set to Greenwich mean time, the time zone the military—and so the reconnaissance crews—called Zulu. During hurricane season the center installed a special teletype circuit that connected all Weather Bureau offices on the Gulf and South Atlantic Coasts, from Brownsville, Texas, to Charleston, South Carolina. Every station on those circuits received any observation or forecast placed on the line by any other station. Reports came in from passenger aircraft, from Coast Guard stations, from lighthouses, from oil rigs, and from national defense installations. There were special observers in Mexico, the West Indies, the Bahamas, and Cuba. Reports from ships came every six hours. When there was a hurri-

cane, reports came from the Air Force and Navy weather reconnaissance crews.

In September of 1955 the Hurricane Forecast Center had a
staff of twelve, and at any given time at least six of them were in the
offices, drawing and redrawing charts, typing bulletins, and studying data from radiosondes, pilot balloons, and ship reports. They
worked in eight- or ten-hour stretches, subsisting on coffee and
sandwiches. As soon as a tropical disturbance or hurricane was discovered, they prepared and issued warnings and advisories, and as
long as it remained a hurricane or a threat south of 50 degrees
north latitude and west of 35 degrees west longitude, they continued to issue advisories. They made announcements every six
hours, more often when there was some rapid or unexpected
development. From June on, the teletypes in the offices clicked
almost continuously.

The chief forecaster and *chargé d'affaires* at Miami, new since
June, was a thin, fifty-year-old Vermonter named Gordon Dunn.
He was one of four or five people in 1955 who knew more about
hurricanes than anyone alive. Dunn was the most recent representative of forecasters in a hundred-year history of institutionalized
weather forecasting.

In the first decades of the nineteenth century memories of any
given storm were local, and few appreciated that a single storm
might affect places separated by hundreds of miles. But by the
1840s James Espy and Elias Loomis had charted years of weather
data and had proved that storms move west to east across the
American continent. It was an important discovery, but it was next
to useless until there was means to convey the news faster than the
storm could travel. The telegraph was the obvious answer. In 1842
Samuel Morse set up a trial wire between Baltimore and
Washington, D.C. Seven years later five hundred stations across the
United States began to telegraph weather reports to Washington,
D.C. From these, the Smithsonian Institution produced daily

weather maps. The system worked tolerably well, until the Civil War interrupted and ultimately ended it. When peace came, there were a few small-scale attempts to revive the practice, the most successful one being devised by a private organization calling itself the Cincinnati Observatory.

Under the directorship of an astronomer named Cleveland Abbe, the observatory published daily weather maps and predictions that it modestly (and realistically) called "probabilities." The observatory's probabilities were often wildly inaccurate, but regular forecasting was so obviously useful that in 1870 President Ulysses S. Grant authorized a weather service within the Army, and on a regular basis, twenty-two stations of the Army Signal Corps made synchronous weather observations and telegraphed them to Washington.

In Europe, it would take a catastrophe to develop a permanent meteorological observation network. In 1854, during the Crimean War, a joint British-French naval fleet was operating in the Black Sea, near Balaklava, where the Light Brigade had made its disastrous charge a month earlier. On November 14, when a storm approached, much of the fleet made for the safety of open waters. But thirteen supply ships were caught near the rocky coast, and winds and heavy seas battered them. Those ships had been carrying provisions that would have sustained the armies through the winter. Because the supplies were lost, some eight thousand troops perished.

In an earlier era, such an event would have been deemed a disaster, attributed to fate or divine will and soon forgotten. But this was a time when nature herself seemed to bend to the will of men. The storm that had destroyed part of the fleet had been observed days earlier, several hundreds of miles west, over the Mediterranean; the French government ordered Urbain-Jean-Joseph Leverrier, director of the Paris Observatory, to examine the correlation. Leverrier gathered observations from around Europe; with these he drew a set of charts displaying the position of the storm at timed intervals. The result was something no one had ever seen: a map of the *course* of a body of wind and rain. Leverrier's conclusion was sobering. A network of weather observation stations could have given at least a day's warning.

The French government by then had an established telegraph department, and Leverrier, a scientist with enormous powers of persuasion, convinced his government to lend its services. On February 17, 1855, Napoleon III signed the order establishing the system, and within two years central Europe had a network of eighteen stations reporting to a central office that then issued a daily weather bulletin. Meanwhile, the British Parliament responded to the same disaster by ordering Captain Robert Fitzroy, Charles Darwin's captain on the *Beagle* and a longtime advocate of combining science with traditional forecasting techniques, to establish a meteorological office. He did, and on September 3, 1860, the office began issuing daily reports.

Soon there was more progress on the other side of the Atlantic. By 1878 the Army Signal Corps had 284 stations issuing complete reports twice in every twenty-four-hour period. An hour after a forecast was made, it was telegraphed to railroad stations and newspapers, and maps were printed and displayed in public places.

As to hurricanes in particular, in 1873 the signal corps began reports from Havana, Cuba, and Kingston, Jamaica. In the same year it issued "cautionary signals" and hurricane warnings for the Atlantic Coast from Cape May to New London. In 1880 the U.S. Weather Bureau was created, and the next year six stations in the Caribbean began issuing regular reports.

On April 25, 1898, the United States declared war against Spain, and American warships departed for the Caribbean with seventeen thousand officers and enlisted men. William Moore, chief of the Weather Bureau, knew that weather had determined outcomes of whole wars, and he showed President McKinley a map of the islands and hurricane tracks. It was the clearest possible demonstration that hurricanes were a real danger, capable of destroying the entire fleet. McKinley took Moore's point and admitted, "I am more afraid of a West Indian hurricane than I am of the entire Spanish Navy." He authorized procedural changes. Within the year, observers were on duty at islands throughout the Caribbean, and a fast cruiser was stationed at Key West to carry news to the fleet.

By the close of the nineteenth century there had been great progress in predicting paths of hurricanes. Yet there were also grim reminders that forecasting prowess was imperfect. In September 1900, a hurricane struck Galveston, Texas, killing over six thousand people. Although the Weather Bureau had forecast the storm four days earlier, it had not predicted the storm surge.

In the first decades of the twentieth century there were attempts to measure the upper atmosphere with balloons, kites, and aircraft, and European nations devised a real-time observing system. World War II brought further advances. The Allied Forces, who needed forecasting to plan long-range bombing, established a permanent network of stations. When the war ended, there was fairly complete coverage of the atmosphere above both North America and Europe. But there were serious deficiencies. For most intents and purposes, in an area of a million square miles—the mid-Atlantic, a broad expanse of open water between the African coast and the Lesser Antilles—there was simply no way to measure upper-level winds. It so happened that this was precisely where most hurricanes were spawned.

And so Gordon Dunn knew he was only at the most recent iteration of a long line of attempts to organize weather forecasting. The Hurricane Forecast Center, the particular weather office of which Dunn was now in charge, had come into being through the determined efforts of a scholarly looking gentleman with an affectation for bow ties. His name was Grady Norton. For twenty years Norton had broadcast his warnings and advisories over a dozen radio stations on the Atlantic and Gulf Coasts. During some storms he made broadcasts continuously and went days without rest. His voice became familiar and reassuring, and his listeners began to call him "Mr. Hurricane." Norton's forecasts were astonishingly accurate: during his tenure the average death count from a given hurricane dropped from five hundred to five, and in 1949 he received the Department of Commerce Silver Medal for Meritorious Service. But by 1954 he was in ill health, his work habits having overtaxed an already weak constitution. Norton's physician advised him to turn over responsibility to his assistants. He refused. On the night of October 9 of that year, as Hurricane Hazel was gaining strength near Haiti, Grady Norton died. His career had spanned twenty-two hurricane seasons.

Dunn had worked with Norton for years, and they had grown to know each other well—they had also grown more alike. Of course, now that Dunn held the office of chief forecaster, the newspapers emphasized differences. If Norton had been talkative, Dunn was quiet. If Norton was folksy, then Dunn was serious and staid. Gordon Dunn, the newspapers seemed to say, left behind him the sterile whiff of the laboratory. But this was at best a partial truth. Dunn's appreciation of the weather, like Norton's, was as much aesthetic as scientific. He often spoke of the "majesty of nature" and said that meteorologists, even though they were making forecasts for places thousands of miles distant, should work in a room with windows. In fact, there were several windows in the Hurricane Forecast Center Headquarters. Dunn's own office had a southward-facing balcony from which he liked to watch the clouds over the Everglades.

Dunn and his staff plotted reports on large outline maps called *synoptic charts*. *Synoptic* actually means "displaying a wide view," but in meteorology the word had come to mean "simultaneous," and a synoptic chart was a kind of snapshot, a display of phenomena that occurred simultaneously. At several points on any synoptic chart were dense clusters of hieroglyphics surrounding dark circles. These circles were data points; they showed the place of origin of a given report. Wind direction was indicated by a "pennant," whose staff emerged from that data point in the direction of the wind. "Feathers," lines drawn perpendicular to the pennant's staff, showed wind speed. A short feather meant 5 knots, a long one 10 knots, a long and a short 15 knots, and so on. Arranged in a small space around each data point were numbers that indicated visibility in kilometers, temperature, and atmospheric pressure, and symbols for cloud types, present weather, and weather since the last report. A given chart might have dozens of such points. All told, it was an incredibly economical system of scientific shorthand, evolved by meteorologists in less than a hundred years.

As the reports were received, assistants to the forecaster did the plotting. When they were finished, the forecasters began the actual analysis. They began by drawing curved lines between the data points. These were isobars, lines of equal air pressure. As they drew the isobars, the meteorologists adjusted the pressure values to sea level. They knew that certain data would confirm other data. Wind readings, for instance, were likely to bear a specific relation to pressure readings. They expected to see winds blowing nearly parallel to isobars, but crossing them slightly at a small angle, toward areas of lower pressure. They also expected, in the Northern Hemisphere, to find lower pressure to the left of the wind and isobars near each other in areas of strong wind. A good forecaster could see larger patterns take shape long before he had completed the chart. When he began to see isobars curving around an area of low pressure, for instance, he knew that he was probably charting a tropical depression.

⇀

In the first decade of the twentieth century, meteorologists began to use pilot balloons to make upper-air observations. A balloon was filled with enough hydrogen or helium to allow it to rise at a predetermined rate. As it rose, the aerologist tracked its azimuth and elevation with a theodolite, an instrument that worked much like a surveyor's transit. If the aerologist knew the balloon's rate of ascent, he could calculate wind direction and velocity, and if he attached a small light to the balloon, he could track it at night. It was possible to measure wind directions and velocities as high as 30,000 feet. But the technique had limitations.

To gain data on a hurricane, a balloon had to be launched within that hurricane or near it. This was a difficult proposition at best. It was true that a few balloons had been launched from weather stations that happened to lie directly in the paths of hurricanes. In 1912, for instance, the eye of a particularly obliging typhoon moved across a fully equipped weather observatory in Formosa, and the station was able to study the clear air of the eye. But no meteorologist could expect to witness such an event. The alternative—delivering an instrument to the proximity of a storm—was extraordinarily difficult. It was also dangerous. No ship's captain was likely to put his vessel in a hurricane's path so that a scientist could measure winds. Nonetheless, by the first decade of the twentieth century, meteorologists had managed to make balloon soundings within 100 miles of storm centers.

The findings were valuable—and utterly unexpected. As late as 1900 many meteorologists believed that hurricanes were relatively "shallow" atmospheric phenomena, their clouds and winds extending upward no farther than a mile. Some believed that people climbing mountains might actually look down on the storms. But balloons had tracked those upper levels to 40,000 feet, far above the tallest mountains. There were other discoveries. Some balloons, launched for the specific purpose of measuring cyclonic (counterclockwise) circulation at the upper levels, found small "anticyclonic" eddies at the same altitudes, 200 to 250 miles from the center.

Beginning about 1933, meteorologists began to affix meteoro-graphs to the balloons. These instruments recorded temperature, humidity, and pressure. The balloon rose to an altitude where it burst, and the meteorograph itself fell to the earth under a small parachute. An attached note offered a reward to anyone for returning it. Of course, by then the storm had long passed, and the data were useful only as a record of natural history. But by the late 1930s, engineers had developed radio transmitters that could send high-frequency signals to an observer. So meteorographs were equipped with transmitters, and the hybrid instrument was called a *radiosonde.* For gaining data on hurricanes, the radiosonde was a great improvement over the pilot balloon. Because the meteorolo-gist did not need to see it, the radiosonde could be launched into clouds. It rose through the hurricane or steering current until its balloon burst, usually somewhere between 60,000 and 100,000 feet, well above the storm's upper levels. If it was equipped with a radar antenna, the radiosonde could be tracked and a meteorolo-gist could obtain wind data. Ultimately though, the radiosonde's usefulness was limited because like the pilot balloon, it could not be steered or otherwise directed.

In the 1940s some suggested another possibilities for tracking. A storm produces electrical phenomena called *atmospherics* that can be detected by radio. It soon became clear that atmospherics could indicate the general shape of the storm's electrical fields. But after a few attempts to track storms with radios, meteorologists realized that the pattern of electrical fields was likely to be differ-ent from the pattern that mattered—the pattern of clouds or winds—and the technique was abandoned.

In the 1950s several meteorologists suggested that a hurricane might be tracked if a balloon and a radio transmitter could be made to remain in the eye. The idea was that an air reconnaissance crew might fly into the eye of a hurricane and release a balloon partly filled with helium and covered with a loose-fitting nylon envelope. As the balloon rose, lower pressures would allow it to expand until it filled and stiffened the envelope and could expand no more. At this point its density would exactly match that of the air around it, and the balloon would remain at that altitude. It might then be tracked from outside the storm with radar or radio. The hope was that the obliging balloon would drift in the gentle breezes in the eye, and when it neared the edge of the powerful currents in the wall, it would be pushed back toward the center.

The beliefs that the currents operated in this fashion, and that air in the eye was relatively stable, were born of a crude logic. Many reconnaissance crews had observed birds in the eye. It seemed obvious that the birds, having survived days in a hurricane, should be exhausted; they would be too weak to fly against strong winds. If powerful winds were pulling the birds into the eyewall, there would be no birds in the eye. Yet the birds *were* in the eye; therefore, there were no such winds.

Of course, the problem was how to deploy a balloon inside a hurricane. A balloon ejected from an aircraft in even a partially inflated state would be torn apart in the slipstream. Researchers used a wind tunnel to test a structure in a bomb bay that would deflect the slipstream around the balloon, but the results were inconclusive.

Air Force Captain Leo S. Bielinski came up with another approach for tracking hurricanes. He had been flying reconnaissance on Typhoon Doris in 1950 when he was thrown about violently, and his forearm struck a bulkhead with such force that he shattered a favorite wristwatch. He said that the loss of that particular piece of flight hardware inspired him to devise a way to track hurricanes that might pose fewer dangers than flying reconnaissance. No one was quite sure whether he was joking about his motivation, but in subsequent years he spent a great deal of time and a substantial amount of his own funds designing something he called a "Typhoon Homer." It was an uninflated balloon, a cartridge of pressurized helium, a radio transmitter, and a float, tied together in a small package. The whole apparatus was attached to a parachute, and Bielinski's idea was that it would be ejected from the aircraft much like a dropsonde. It would descend under the parachute to the water surface, where the float would rest on the water. A few moments later the balloon would inflate and carry the radio (still attached by a line to the float) to a predetermined altitude, where it would begin to transmit data. Bielinski estimated that the device would operate for a week, a day or so short of the lifetime of the average hurricane. There were several attempts to deploy it, but every time some part of the apparatus failed.

By 1955, the science of seismology offered yet another way to track hurricanes. Meteorologists had long understood that parts of the atmosphere could not be isolated from other parts; now seismologists were suggesting that the atmosphere could not be separated from the planet it enveloped. It is easy to think of the whole of Earth's atmosphere as insubstantial, as weightless as light. It is true that a given volume of air weighs less than almost anything else in our experience, but it is also true that there is a great deal of air. It extends upward to an altitude of perhaps 60 miles before it thins into what is generally regarded as the edge of space, the altitude at which 99 percent of the atmosphere is below, the altitude at which the control surfaces on aircraft have no effect. Most of humanity inhabits the atmosphere's depths, where it pushes down on every square foot with 2,000 pounds, and on every square mile with a pressure of 25 million tons.

There are countering forces equally powerful. Pressures from deep within the earth push upward, and so over some parts of the earth's crust, air and earth are locked in a titanic stalemate.

Ordinarily these forces are so well matched that neither moves, and the fact of the stalemate is itself imperceptible. But sometimes, as when a wrestler adjusts a foot or slips, the balance of forces shifts. And in the case of the atmosphere and tectonic plates, the shift has enormous consequences.

In the 1920s a meteorologist named C. F. Brooks determined that a drop in barometric pressure of 2 inches removes a load of 2 million tons of atmosphere from each square mile of surface. The resulting rise in water level, as much as 10 feet, would add 9 million tons to each square mile. And the net difference would be an addition of 7 million tons. He believed that the weight—or more precisely, the sudden change in weight—could trigger an earthquake. Indeed, an earthquake had accompanied the storm that struck Barbados in 1780. In the 1940s seismologists discovered another way a hurricane might generate movements in the earth. They realized that the tremendous surface waves of hurricanes move so much water that they can actually cause vibrations in the ocean floor. Such vibrations had been detected in the Caribbean's basins, some parts of which were 16,000 feet deep.

In late 1943, the aerological section of the Navy, at the recommendation of the Joint Meteorological Committee, activated a "Hurricane Microseismic Research Project." The idea was to track a seagoing hurricane continuously from onshore, triangulating its changing position with three seismographs. Geologists understood something of the ocean floor—they knew that the American Plate lay beneath most of North America, and its southern edge was sliding westward past the Caribbean Plate. They knew the fault traced a line that passed north of Puerto Rico and Hispaniola and curved south of Cuba and through Guatamala in Central America. But they knew very little of the actual composition and structure of the floor, the features that most influenced wave propogation. For this reason, tracking by seismograph was difficult. Nonetheless, the first such station was put into operation in 1944 at Guantánamo Bay, and its results, verified by reconnaissance flights, were promising. The network was expanded to cover the entire Caribbean. In September 1955 parts of the project were still operating.

In the year 1955 a new technology was brought to bear on the problem. The first hurricane-tracking radar station was established at Cape Hatteras, North Carolina. The station detected Hurricane Connie and gave the U.S. Weather Bureau its first pictures of a hurricane by radio facsimile; the technology had its own limitations. Ground radar had a range of 150 to 200 miles, a limit prescribed by the earth's shape, simple geometry, and physics; the earth is curved, but radio waves travel in straight lines.

But even radar was not the last word. There was much talk of the Air Age giving way to the Space Age, and most expected that meteorology would be a part of it. Five years earlier the Army Signal Corps had launched rockets to an altitude of 300,000 feet from the White Sands Missile Range in New Mexico, and already there had been discussion of orbital reconnaissance. In 1951 a group working for the RAND Corporation had produced a report entitled "Inquiry into the Feasibility of Weather Reconnaissance from a Satellite Vehicle." In 1955 though, such ideas were the stuff of science fiction. Most tracking was accomplished by reports from islands. When a hurricane was more than a hundred miles or so from any land weather station, the only way to track it was to send men into it.

If tracking a hurricane was problematic and prone to error, it was not nearly as difficult as prediction. In 1955, forecasting a hurricane's path was part science and part art. There were several forecasting techniques, used separately and in concert.

The technique called *analogue* involved doing the most with the least. It relied on the fact that hurricanes appearing in a certain area and at a certain time of the season are likely to follow similar tracks. If a given hurricane had been measured near St. Thomas with 100-mile-per-hour winds and a pressure of 28 inches, and had taken a course north by northwest, then it seemed reasonable to assume that a second hurricane at St. Thomas, showing the same winds and pressure, might take the same course. Finding an analogue for any given storm was a fairly straightforward procedure, and thanks to a meteorologist named Charles L. Mitchell, there were thousands of records from which to draw. In the 1920s Mitchell had studied ships' logs and daily weather maps of the Weather Bureau and replotted storm tracks of all the storms between 1887 and 1922.

A given storm, of course, was likely to have more than one analogue. In fact, anyone tracking hurricanes over more than a few years would discover whole sets of analogues and begin to discern certain patterns. One pattern had to do with the point of recurvature, the place where the storm might alter its initial track from northwesterly to northeasterly. As the hurricane season advanced, the storms recurved at points farther and farther westward. The trend was long recognized by peoples in the Caribbean and by the local dioceses of the Roman Catholic Church. In the nineteenth century ecclesiastic authority ordained that priests in Puerto Rico should recite the prayer *Ad repellendat tempestates* ("to repel storms") during mass in August and September but not in October. Priests in Cuba were to recite the prayer in mass in September and October but never in August.

An associate of Gordon Dunn's named Jose A. Colon had enjoyed considerable success using the analogue technique to forecast recurvature, but the technique had limitations. Colon had the least confidence in predictions for areas between 20 degrees and 30 degrees north latitude, roughly from the southernmost shore of Cuba to northern Florida, where the easterlies and westerlies confused systems of pressure and winds. Unfortunately, these were also the latitudes from which hurricanes began to approach the U.S. coastline, and precisely the area for which forecasting was needed most.

A forecast method called *simple extrapolation* was used for every-day predictions. If weather today was partly cloudy with a high in the fifties, unless a new variable appeared, it was likely that tomorrow would be the same. Extrapolation was particularly useful in predicting the movements of hurricanes, because a hurricane track within any twenty-four-hour period seldom diverged by more than 10 percent from the track of the previous twenty-four hours. But again, the technique was better suited to some areas than others. It was accurate 80 percent of the time in the easterly trade-wind belt, especially south of 20 degrees north latitude, the latitude of the southernmost shore of Cuba. But like the analogue method, extrapolation was likely to be confounded at the latitudes between Cuba and Florida. Farther north, it was even less reliable. Storms could be pulled by great lows over the North American continent and could be made to accelerate suddenly and with little warning in any of several directions. North of 25 degrees north latitude, extrapolation was useless.

Meteorologists realized that the movement of any hurricane is largely determined by the direction and the speed of the air current in which it is embedded. They called it the *steering current*. It was a great river of air likely to be several hundred miles wide (a diameter considerably larger than the hurricane it contained) and extending upward to altitudes of 30,000 feet. But meteorologists had difficulty determining its exact dimensions. Because it was difficult to know where the storm ended and the current began, it was difficult to decide where to launch a radiosonde. Even when they managed to obtain a reading, they could not be sure what it meant, as no one could be certain of the degree to which any measurement was representative of the larger current.

One group suggested the easiest measurement might be taken at the altitude considered *above* the hurricane, in that place where cyclonic circulation is virtually nonexistent. In a weak storm that altitude might be as low as 20,000 feet and in a mature storm, as high as 50,000 feet. In 1952, a meteorologist named Elizabeth Jordan used a working definition of the steering current as the mean flow from the surface to 30,000 feet and extending over a band 8 degrees latitude in width and centered on the storm. She discovered that on average, hurricanes traveled with this current. Jordan and others suspected that if one could predict the path of that flow, one could predict the path of the hurricane. However, two years earlier a researcher named L. Sherman had published evidence that the steering current could account for only about half of the observed changes in direction for any given hurricane. By 1955, meteorologists were still divided over the issue, but mounting evidence sided with Sherman. It seemed that the hurricane was something more than a cork bobbing downstream. The storm affected the steering current in which it lived, and so to some degree determined its own direction. If a storm's course were determined only by forces outside it, one might expect it to be drawn into a trough of low pressure ahead of it. But in fact, a hurricane produces an outflow of great masses of air that may build a ridge "downstream." The air would fill a low-pressure trough lying ahead and to the right of the hurricane, and the hurricane would continue on its course, having been pulled in the direction of that trough only temporarily, if at all.

In October of 1950 the Navy Bureau of Aeronautics began a project to research and develop new forecasting methods, including techniques to predict hurricane tracks. Again, meteorologists confronted a paucity of data, and the methods they proposed were rather ingenious means to squeeze blood from a stone. Meteorologists Herbert Riehl and William Haggard decided that a horizontal cross section of winds at about 18,500 feet was a fair representation of the mean wind flow down to the surface. They did not bother trying to determine winds at the top of a hurricane. Neither did they bother trying to measure winds directly. Instead, they estimated winds from a pressure chart: the more closely packed the isobars, the higher the winds in that area.

A tropical climatologist named Robert H. Simpson proposed another way to predict a storm's path. He knew the core of a hurricane was warmer than its surroundings and that the outflow from the eye produced a belt of warm air ahead of the storm. He called it a "warm tongue." Usually it appeared slightly to the right of and ahead of the storm, and parallel to the storm's track. Most significantly for forecasters, it could precede the storm by as much as twenty-four hours. Although the warm tongue was difficult to locate with thermometers, one of its visible effects—shields of altostratus and cirrostratus clouds—was likely to move ahead of the storm. Simpson suspected that a sudden and rapid reorientation in these clouds could foretell a change in the storm's course.

At the height of Janet's life cycle, the atmosphere in her vicinity weighed about 1 million tons less than normal. And the earth's tremendous upward pressures, usually held at bay, were released. Early on the morning of the fifth day of Janet's life a seismograph in Mobile, Alabama, recorded the distinctive signature of earthquake tremors. A seismologist reported that a quake recorded in two separate shocks seemed to have occurred on the ocean floor just north of Honduras. It was "very severe," with an intensity of 8.8 on the Richter scale. Had the quakes been on land, destruction would have been considerable.

By 11 P.M. on Thursday, September 22, Janet had left the Windward Islands behind. She was in the Caribbean Sea, 500 miles southeast of Puerto Rico and 100 miles south-southwest of Martinique, churning west at 12 miles an hour. The storm was 200 miles wide, winds were at 115 miles per hour near the center, and gales extended outward 140 miles in the northern semicircle and 60 miles in the southern semicircle. Puerto Rico remained on the alert. Walter Davis, a forecaster at the Miami Weather Bureau, told the press, "It has a well-defined eye and probably will show a westerly trend for a while."

Janet continued west, growing in size. By midday on September 23 she was 225 miles wide. Davis thought it was possible that the gale-force winds of her southern edges would skirt the small archipelago called the Netherlands Antilles—the islands of Bonaire, Curacao, and Aruba. He issued a report that predicted "continued movement . . . towards the west or west northeast at about the same rate during the night with some increase in intensity." At 9:00 P.M. on Friday the Paraguaná Peninsula and the Netherlands Antilles were ordered to hoist northwest storm warnings. Two hours later a Navy reconnaissance aircraft was in Janet's eye. The navigators reported the eye's position to be about 360 miles almost due south of San Juan, and estimated the storm's forward speed at 14 miles an hour. Measured by gale winds, Janet was 240 miles across.

Davis was only partially right. On Saturday, September 24, the Netherlands Antilles caught a great deal of rain, but the center of the storm passed 100 miles to their north. Winds near her edges were relatively calm at 30 miles an hour, and even the winds nearer her center were clocked at a mere 75 to 85 miles an hour. Suddenly Janet had lost so much strength she could barely be called a hurricane. She brushed close to the islands off Venezuela and then weakened further. To Davis, the behavior was a surprise. There would be others.

By early Saturday, Janet's winds had diminished further, but in the afternoon a reconnaissance flight found she had regained strength, with 100-mile-an-hour gusts near the eye. Davis said, "She is following a serpentine path, her eye is pulsating in size, and her intensity varies." He noted that her behavior was "eccentric."

There had been some concern that Janet would track toward populated areas—Cuba, Jamaica, the U.S. mainland. Now it seemed that she would follow a more or less straight path through the

Caribbean between the tenth and fifteenth parallel, staying well south of most islands. She was headed toward Central America and would probably strike Belize or Nicaragua. But at her present speed of 12 miles an hour she would not make landfall for at least two days. By late Sunday evening Janet was holding steady on the same westward course 240 miles south of Jamaica, and her speed had increased to 16 miles an hour. At present, Dunn and the Miami forecasters saw no reason to expect her to turn north, but they alerted Jamaica nevertheless. It paid to be cautious, particularly with a storm this powerful.

Especially during hurricane season, forecasters in Miami received calls from newspapers. A reporter pressed Dunn to explain Janet's erratic behavior, specifically her recent slowing. Dunn knew that in early stages, a storm may have short-period fluctuations in intensity, a change in wind speeds of 40 miles an hour in as little as half a day. He also knew that land may impede a hurricane, but it was difficult to see how the topography of Barbados—a small teardrop-shaped island only 20 miles wide, its highest point a mere 900 feet—could have such profound effects. So much was unknown. And when the reporter asked Dunn why Janet had slowed, he did not complain that he was a civil service employee expected to make forecasts that would be factored into decisions involving hundreds of thousands of people and dollars. He did not speak of continuity, or upper-level steering currents, or points of recurvature. He did not speak of the analogue method. Instead, he merely said, "We don't know what happened." Then for a moment he allowed his empiricism to falter, and quipped, "Maybe she just decided to rest a while."

6

Briefing

5:00 A.M. EST / 0900 Zulu

On the night of September 24, Crew Five began a night reconnaissance of Janet. Like most night missions, it was a radar circumnavigation. To all but the pilot, copilot, and radar operator, such missions were likely to be fairly boring. Still, the flight was demanding and lasted for eleven hours—most of Saturday night and the predawn hours of Sunday morning. When it was over, Crew Five landed at McCalla Field at Guantánamo Bay ("Gitmo," in Navy vernacular), the point of departure for Monday's mission. The overnight stop would save them time and fuel.

By the standards of naval air stations, Gitmo was quiet. It was a sleepy sort of place, and for long stretches of the day the only movement was the little green iguanas scrambling over the rocks. Especially during hurricane season, nights were humid and hot, and the facilities on the base—enlisted men's barracks and officers' quarters alike—were fairly primitive. There was no air conditioning, and no screens on windows. Insects were everywhere; most bunks came with netting. For Crew Five, sleep could not have come easily.

Yet at 5:00 A.M. on Monday, rested or not, they began another workday. It was still quiet, too early even for the iguanas. The door of the officers' quarters opened, and five men emerged, barely visible in the half-light. They walked toward the Air Operations Building, where they were met by two men in civilian dress. The group went inside and found the weather office. Windham opened the door and stood aside, allowing the newsmen to enter the room first. He flipped a light switch. There was a table and chairs, and a desk with a teletype machine. The officers dragged the chairs around and sat, and Windham pulled a message off the teletype and scanned it quickly:

FM OL/8 HQ HURRICANE FORECAST CENTER MIAMI FLORIDA TO RRCP NWS GUANTANAMO UNCLASSIFIED SENDS 26 SEPTEMBER RECON PLAN OF THE DAY FOR 26 SEPTEMBER FOLLOWS 1. NWS . . . FLT ONE . . . P2V DEPART GUANTANAMO APPROX 16/0630 Z. TO 14.80 N 76.30 W RECON AT 1000 FT OR BELOW AT PILOTS DISCRETION. STORM EXPECTED TO BE VICINITY OF 14.80 N 76.30 W AT 26/1200 Z. DESTINATION AT PILOTS DISCRETION.

As orders went, this was fairly typical. All instructions from Fleet Hurricane Warning Center in Miami included specifics as to time of takeoff, route of flight, and destination airport. But the men in Miami knew that hurricanes could change direction quickly, and appreciated that the crew itself might have better information. They recognized too, that while they worked in dry, air-conditioned, and well-lit offices, the crew would be actually entering the storm. For these reasons they granted each crew a considerable degree of autonomy, and orders they sent always included phrases like "at pilot's discretion" or "deviate at will."

If a flight were taking off from Miami, the crew's officers would be given instructions by the center's personnel. But at Gitmo on the morning of September 26, Windham and his men—Copilot Herlong, Navigators Morgan and Greaney, and Aerologist Buck— were mostly on their own.

On one wall was a synoptic chart of the central Caribbean. It showed lines of isobars and the weaving path of Janet over the last forty-eight hours. Buck studied it for a few minutes. Then he and the navigators figured their route in terms of time and fuel. It would be a standard penetration mission and include two entries into the eye. The first would be made at about 700 feet. They would circle inside the eye, and Buck would take readings. Then they would depart the eye, clear the heaviest weather, and circumnavigate the storm while the aviation electronics man performed radar surveillance. Six hours later they would climb to 19,000 feet and make a second penetration into the eye. From that altitude they would deploy an instrument called a *dropsonde,* and copy its transmissions as it descended to the water surface. At about 2:00 P.M. they would depart the eye and then leave the vicinity of the storm. They expected to be back at McCalla Field by 4:30.

An urn of coffee had been set up on a table near the wall, and it was both welcome and necessary. They sipped the coffee and they talked a little about other flights.

Before Crew Five's radar circumnavigation, there had been several reconnaissance flights of Janet, and everyone in that room knew that something strange had happened to the second one. Captain Ken Mackie and Crew Two had been tracking Hurricane Ione when their radar observer saw Janet. They began a preliminary reconnaissance. They expected Janet to be mild—a "baby" was Mackie's word. But on approach they were surprised. Mackie's aerologist and copilot had both tracked Hazel in 1954, and both said that already Janet's turbulence was worse than Hazel's had been at that stage.

Crew Two penetrated Janet as she was skirting Barbados, and

they were inside the eye at low altitude, 400 or 500 hundred feet, near enough to the water surface to have a good view. The greater the wind in a hurricane eye, the more water is churned into white-caps, and it was obvious that winds in Janet's eye were fierce. In debriefings, Mackie said the water looked like buttermilk. He also said that the turbulence at 400 feet had been so severe he could not understand why his plane had not been shaken apart. The nav-igator, Lieutenant Jess Prestyly, was the only member of the crew who seemed aware that they were dangerously near Barbados, but he did not call for a course change—he stayed at his post and qui-etly and dutifully called out coordinates. Either no one understood the implications or no one heard the coordinates, and Prestyly stared at his charts while his breathing rate increased and his skin turned clammy. Finally, as the island grew nearer, he hyperventi-lated and blacked out. The crew administered oxygen, and con-vinced that his condition was not serious, finished their reconnaissance of the eye, and then made a fast trip to San Juan. Prestyly recovered quickly.

Postflight inspection revealed that the flight had been even rougher than the crew had realized. Four hundred feet was gener-ally thought to be a safe altitude, but maintenance crews found salt water caked on the bottom of the aircraft's wings.

To a reader of signs, the experience of Lieutenant Prestyly and Crew Two suggested there was something unsettling about this par-ticular hurricane. Indeed, the head of the San Juan Weather Bureau had said this could become the worst of the year.

By September 25, against all expectations Janet had become a monster—a hurricane with winds of 135 miles per hour, tracking almost due west. Fortunately, that path would take her well south of the major islands of Puerto Rico and Hispanola. At the time of Crew Five's preflight briefing, Janet was in open ocean about 300 miles southwest of Jamaica and regaining strength. Gale-force winds extended from the center to 125 to 150 miles, and her most severe winds near the eye were being clocked at 110 miles an hour. She was pursuing a rather serpentine course, following roughly the same path as Hazel had. Most thought she would reach the central Caribbean sometime late Saturday, but her precise course was uncertain. There were light winds that might cause her to turn northwest.

The officers of Crew Five did not pretend to know what was out there over the ocean. But they had each flown enough missions to know that it probably had very little to do with what they were looking at. In all likelihood it had transformed itself by now. Everything signified by points on chart was a guess, and by the time anyone saw the guess, it was likely to have already passed.

➤

They filed their flight plan with the Operations Office, and Windham briefed the enlisted crew. There were four. The highest-ranking, the crew chief, was Aviation Mechanic First Class J. P. Windham Jr. (no kin to the commander). With him were Aviation Electronics Man First Class Joseph F. Combs, Aviation Electronics Technician Second Class Julius J. Mann, and Airman Kenneth L. Clegg.

By now the sun was well above the horizon. Already it was hot, and the hangars and administration buildings were casting long shadows. The base was still mostly quiet, although the day's operations were beginning, and there were sounds of engines in the distance. McCalla Field was the home of utility squadron VU-10, which assisted surface units by providing target towing and aerial spotting of gunfire. Units of the Atlantic Fleet were there too, using Gitmo for battle training and operational readiness tests. But it was still early, and most activity on the field was associated with Crew Five's mission. A man in the ground crew was decoupling a tractor that had towed a P2V Navy Neptune from the hangar. A fuel truck was pulling away from the plane.

Eleven men walked across the tarmac toward the plane: five officers in white duty uniforms, with parachute harnesses dangling; four enlisted men in standard Navy-issue wrinkled coveralls and duty caps; and two civilians dressed in dark slacks and white shirts—the newsmen, reporter Alfred O. Tate and photographer Douglas Cronk. At Cronk's request, there was an unusual bit of ceremony. The nine Navy men arranged themselves in the traditional formation of crew photographs: the five officers in the first row, crouching on one knee, the four enlisted men standing directly behind.

Mann and Clegg were both twenty-two years old; Grover Windham was the "old man" of the group at thirty-four. JP Windham was thirty-two, and the rest were between twenty-four and twenty-six years old. Six of them—Windham, Greaney, Buck, Morgan, JP Windham, and Clegg—were married. All told, they represented a fair cross section of American class and geography. Buck was from a small city a few miles from Boston, Morgan was from a Detroit suburb, JP was from a little crossroads town in east Texas. It would be Windham's tenth flight into a hurricane and Herlong's fourteenth. It would be Airman Clegg's first.

The men of Crew Five were as different from each other as members of any military group were likely to be in the mid-1950s, and yet it is easy to imagine them talking. Excepting Herlong, the officers had families and homes in Jacksonville. They likely spoke of the work, another flight, a shift in crew assignments, or a friend in another squadron who had gained a promotion. The enlisted men talked about what they did on Saturday nights in their hometowns, about liberty, and what they would do and where they would live when their time was up. The two unmarried enlisted men—Combs and Mann—perhaps talked about women or the absence of women. As it happened, the first game of the World Series was scheduled for Wednesday. It would be the sixth "Subway Series," with the Yankees a strong 13-10 favorite against the Brooklyn

Dodgers. The Yankees' Mickey Mantle had injured his right leg, and there was doubt as to whether he would start. And so they also talked of teams and odds and Mantle's injury. In short, the men of Crew Five talked about what all men talk about. Sometimes too, they talked about the weather.

The P2V had two lower hatches, one just behind the nose gear, the other farther back, about 8 feet behind the trailing edges of the wings. Herlong entered through the forward hatch, climbed onto the flight deck, moved forward into the cockpit, and settled into the right seat. Then, one after another, Morgan, Greaney, Mann, and Buck pulled themselves through the hatch and took their stations in midsection. The rest—Combs, Clegg, and the two newsmen—entered through the rear hatch.

Inside the aircraft, the men began checking equipment. Meanwhile, on the tarmac outside, Commander Windham and Crew Chief Windham did a walkaround, looking for hydraulic fuel leaks and oil leaks, making sure control surfaces were moving freely. The procedure was *pro forma*—the ground crew had already inspected the plane.

To all but the most discriminating eye, the six P2Vs from Jax were identical. Yet the crews themselves could tell them apart. In fact, crews assigned guard duty did not regard such work as a hardship because it was easy to develop affection as well as a rather proprietary attitude for a given plane. Even if the markings were removed, most men could identify their aircraft by any number of peculiarities—a scratch on a wing section, an engine sound.

The plane assigned to Windham's crew was known as "Five," and its radio code name was "Snowcloud Five." On September 26, 1955, the man who knew the plane most intimately was JP Windham. It was his duty to perform preflight and postflight inspections, giving particular attention to the engine for general condition and for fuel leaks. He supervised the removal and replacement of starters, generators, flight control surfaces, propellers, pressure transmitters, and oil filters. When a mission was completed, he would write up reports of engine performance, malfunctions, and total fuel consumption. Crew Chief Windham knew the sounds of the two 3,500-horsepower Wright engines better than anyone. He could detect a barely detectable change in pitch, a nearly subsonic shudder beneath the steady rumble.

He knew that the plane had flown several missions without incident, most recently their night reconnaissance of Janet. It had received standard checks for every thirty hours of flying time, its last check having been made two days earlier, on September 24. Total time logged for the airframe itself was 1,164 hours. After the last flight the port engine had logged 1,297 hours, 420 since its last overhaul. Total time for the starboard engine was 934 hours, 524 since its last overhaul. It had been his recommendation that the plane be certified for this flight. This morning he had determined that all was well.

Then Crew Chief Windham entered through the forward hatch and assumed his station at mid deck. Finally, Commander Windham entered through the aft hatch and began the internal inspection, moving forward through the plane.

All aircraft are designed from the outside in, and on the Neptune it showed. From outside the P2V looked spacious. In fact though, the deck cut through the plane's centerline: the lower half was taken up by the bomb bay, the radar dome, and wheel wells. The upper starboard half was crammed with electronic equipment. Only the upper port half was open space available for crew. Although the aircraft was 90 feet long from nose to tail stinger, only about 60 of the 90 feet was habitable space. Inside, especially mid deck, with bulkheads and radio equipment and oxygen hoses and wiring, it looked not so much like the interior of an aircraft as the interior of a submarine. Moving through the fuselage was difficult and not encouraged.

In the aft section of the aircraft were two large square ports that could be used as escape hatches. Seats were mounted in the deck near both. These were the rear observer stations—vantages that offered views of the engines as well as the ocean. Clegg was in one seat, Alf Tate the other. Commander Windham stepped forward across the hatch and the dropsonde racks and dropsonde chamber. From here the plane grew still more cramped. The deck was raised to accommodate the bomb bay beneath, and Windham could not stand fully upright. To his right was Combs, already checking frequencies. He sat facing aft in a dark monk's cell of a station, equipped with a surface for writing, and a small swivel lamp.

Mounted against the bulkhead to Windham's left was a four-gallon tank of drinking water and the "galley"—a two-burner electric stove sitting on a small refrigerator about the size of a kitchen drawer. Both were unusual features on military aircraft, but necessary in a plane intended for long flights.

The radio station and galley were built into an area just aft of a curving sheet of aluminum that was both the wing root and the skin of a fuel tank. The wing root actually bisected the fuselage. To move farther forward, Windham had to climb over it. (Although the P2V was a long-range plane, its designers made no accommodations for sleeping, but it was easy for a crewman to curl up on this surface, put his back against a bulkhead, pull his cap over his eyes, and catch some shut-eye. Men would take advantage of this on boondoggles or night radar missions.) A canister was mounted on a seam where the wing root met the port hull. Inside it, in a canvas sack about the size of a sleeping bag, were two life rafts.

Keeping his head low, Windham slid about 6 feet over the curving aluminum surface, with 3 feet space of overhead. He stepped down on a hydraulic tank and dropped again onto the deck, facing forward. Still he could not stand fully upright.

Against the starboard bulkhead was a row of duty stations. Mounted on a track in the deck were four aluminum-frame seats, all facing starboard: engineer's station, two navigators' stations, and the radar operator's station. And now Crew Chief Windham, Navigators Greaney and Morgan, and Radar Operator Mann were there, already busy. Some overhead light came from the astrodome, but these men, especially Mann, preferred it dark, to read radar better. Perhaps saying something, perhaps putting a hand on a man's shoulder, Windham squeezed past.

He made his way forward into the cockpit. Herlong, in the right seat, was checking fuel gauges and electrical systems. Lieutenant George W. Herlong was twenty-five years old. He was darkly handsome, and could have been mistaken for Windham's younger brother. He had enlisted in the Navy three years earlier, in August 1952, and had been ordered to Officers Candidate School in Newport, Rhode Island, six months after that. On June 29, 1954, he completed flight training and was designated a naval aviator. He had not had the benefit of Annapolis polish, but anyone who knew him said he had the "officer and a gentleman" manner.

As patrol plane second pilot, Herlong was to help others perform their jobs. He assisted the crew in planning missions by obtaining pertinent weather forecasts, intelligence reports, and maps. He assisted the pilot in operating controls and equipment on the ground and in flight. He assisted the navigator in charting the mission route and calculating the route information and fuel requirements. Of course, he was to take emergency procedure actions as required by the flight manual or the pilot. Generally, the patrol plane commander controlled the aircraft during takeoff and landing, but the second pilot might be in control for long periods at any given time. If the weather became rough, and there was every expectation that it would, Windham and Herlong would operate the controls together.

Windham slid into the left seat and made himself comfortable. To his immediate right were the engine throttles and a hand microphone. The seats were close enough that Windham could touch Herlong's shoulder without fully extending his arm.

The cockpit felt like the front seat of a Volkswagen, with the doors and roof replaced with large curving Plexiglas windows. A plane with that much glass can get hot while sitting on the runway, and for this reason the overhead windows could be swung outward and locked in place. It was nearly 6:00 A.M. The sun was only barely above the horizon, and already Herlong had opened the windows.

Windham checked fuel and fuel selectors, electrical switches, gear and flap positions, warning lights, cowl flaps, and brakes. He pushed throttles forward and the engines responded with a roar, coughing blue smoke. He and Herlong began the run-up. Windham pushed the control yoke around and checked flight controls for freedom and direction of movement. He checked flap, trim, throttle, and rpm settings. He checked the ignition system and pushed throttles forward and pulled them back. The engines responded again, and he adjusted propeller pitch.

Windham and Herlong closed and locked the overhead windows. Then Windham called for checks over the interphone and gave a "thumbs up" to the ground crew. Taking care to stay clear of the propellers, they pulled away the wheel chocks.

1

Geographia Naturalis

In the early seventeenth century a German geographer named Bernhardus Varenius published a work called *Geographia Naturalis* in which he described hurricanes as whirlwinds. Many had lived through winds arising from opposite compass directions, and for centuries the idea that hurricanes were circular storms was part of folk wisdom. But documentation was poor, and proof of a scientific kind was lacking. As late as the mid-1700s, knowledge of violent weather was rudimentary. There was no agreed upon distinction among tornadoes, nor'easters, thunderstorms, and hurricanes. Daniel Defoe wondered whether a storm was "the motion of the air . . . whether it is a Dilation, a previous Contraction, and then violent Extension as in Gunpowder, whether the motion is direct, circular, or oblique."

Those who thought much about storms assumed they were stationary. The first suspicions that they actually traveled great distances arose in the middle of the eighteenth century, from an

American better known for other pursuits. On the night of October 21, 1743, Benjamin Franklin had been in Philadelphia preparing to view an eclipse of the moon. But a storm obscured the skies, and his preparations were for naught. A few days later, though, his frustration turned to puzzlement. He read that the eclipse had been observed from Boston, some 250 miles to the northeast, but that the city experienced severe weather a day later. It seemed to Franklin that this was in all probability the same storm, and that it had moved northeast along the Atlantic Coast. What struck Franklin as particularly curious was that the storm's winds—at least as he had experienced them—had blown from the northeast, the very compass point toward which he hypothesized the storm was moving. He suggested that there was a pattern of winds *within* a storm that were not necessarily the same as its over-all direction of movement. But he admitted he could not discern the nature of that pattern.

In the nineteenth century Heinrich Wilhelm Brandes, professor of mathematics at Breslau and of physics at Leipzig, collected meteorological observations and constructed weather maps that showed winds and pressures over central Europe. He concluded that a storm was "a barometrical depression, produced by some unknown cause, which advances from west to east; the air blows generally from all sides and constantly towards the centre of the depression." Brandes made a special study of the Christmas Eve Storm of 1821. He was astounded at the low pressure and wondered "whether a mass of air in the neighborhood of the Atlantic coast entirely disappeared, or whether the jaws of the ocean opened to absorb the air, or showers produced by electricity lessened its volume."

A better understanding of the nature of storms would result from the work of another American, a man named William Redfield. Redfield was trained as a leatherworker, but by his early thirties he had moved through several professions; eventually he would become superintendent of the Hudson River Barge Line. Like many Americans in the nineteenth century, Redfield's avocations had little in common with his profession. He was fascinated by natural phenomena of all varieties; he was in the habit of taking long walks through the countryside.

In autumn of 1821 a terrific hurricane had swept through Long Island and southern New England, and a month later its effects were still evident. Redfield was beginning one of his rambles near Middletown, Connecticut, when he noticed trees that had fallen in a single direction to the northwest. He deduced, reasonably enough, that the destructive winds had arisen from the southeast and thought no more of it. But as he reached northwestern Connecticut, some 60 or 70 miles from Middletown, he was surprised to see trees fallen to the southeast, as though winds there had blown from the northwest. It occurred to him that he was seeing the effects of a single enormous storm, perhaps hundreds of miles across. He hypothesized that the shape of the storm was circular. He called it a "whirlwind."

Redfield began to study newspaper accounts of the storm and to exchange letters with harbormasters along the Atlantic seaboard. Soon he had enough information to trace the storm's path from the Caribbean. In 1831 the *American Journal of Science* published his findings and his theory of what he called "cyclonic whirlwinds." The paper posited that all large storms along the Atlantic Coast are systems of winds that rotate counterclockwise around a calm area. Redfield greatly overestimated the size (suggesting that they measure 1,000 miles across) and their speed (asserting that their forward motion averages 30 miles an hour), but in most other particulars he was essentially correct. He claimed that the storms could travel a distance equal to the length of a continent. He also claimed that they were likely to follow a parabolic course, northwesterly until reaching the Atlantic Coast of the United States, then moving north along that coast, and at a point between 25 and 35 degrees north latitude (the 800 or so miles between Miami and Cape Hatteras), turning to the northeast.

Redfield's paper further posited that the global wind pattern was produced entirely by gravitational forces on a rotating earth. All the commonly measured particulars of the atmosphere—barometric pressure, temperature, and moisture—had wind currents as their first cause. Although Redfield admitted that the sun heated air and that temperature differentials put air into motion, he believed that the contribution of this heating was relatively insignificant: should it cease, he claimed, the earth's winds would continue to whirl. He believed that hurricanes in particular were produced by an interaction between moving air and the topography of the Caribbean islands. As stones in a streamed deflect water flowing against them, those islands deflected the westerly trade winds of the North Atlantic into swirling masses of air, some of which were likely to grow into hurricanes.

In ensuing years Redfield continued to gather evidence for the theory, making his most persuasive case in a paper entitled "Observations on the Storm of December 15, 1839," which he read in 1841 before a meeting of the American Philosophical Society. Redfield had numerous supporters, and in time he also had an intellectual rival and opponent. His name was James Pollard Espy. In 1831, when he was forty-six (Redfield was then forty-two), Espy had made professional associations that would endure through a long career. In 1834 the Franklin Institute and the American Philosophical Society established the Joint Committee on Meteorology and made Espy its chairman. Espy was nothing if not ambitious. He hoped to explain what he considered the complete inventory of meteorological phenomena—"rain, hail, snow, waterspouts, landspouts [the term *tornado* had yet to enter the lexicon], winds and barometric fluctuations."

Espy's theory of hurricane formation was based in long-established physical laws on the behavior of gases as it had been understood for nearly two hundred years. His accomplishment had been to apply this behavior to a specific situation. He posited that when the air near the surface of the earth was heated, it formed rising columns of air: "As these columns rise, their upper parts will come under less pressure, and the air will therefore expand; as it expands it will grow colder, about one degree and a quarter for every hundred yards of its ascent. . . . The ascending columns will carry up with them the aqueous vapor which they contain, and if they rise high enough, the cold . . . will condense some of this vapor into cloud." Espy's theory differed from Redfield's in every conceivable way. Redfield's winds whirled around a central point, whereas Espy's winds converged inward to a central area from where they were pulled upward. Redfield's winds were formed by the earth's rotation and gravity; Espy's winds were driven by heat from the sun.

In 1834, Redfield and Espy began what neither could know would become a protracted and bitter public dispute over the nature of storms. Much of the debate was conducted through papers in scientific journals and presentations before scientific societies, and some of the controversy worked itself into larger and more public venues. Redfield suggested that Espy assimilated conventional ideas uncritically, sharing a "grand error into which the whole school of meteorologists have fallen." For his part, Espy examined Redfield's 1821 observations and calculated that a whirlwind of the type Redfield described was impossible. It violated the laws of physics. The whirling air, Espy said, would not remain in a tightly circumscribed space, but rather would spiral outward away from its center. No sooner would Redfield's storm come into existence than it would be torn apart by its own centrifugal motion. Espy further argued that Redfield's suggestion that the West Indies caused air to form whirls did not explain how such phenomena could persist for days; neither did it explain the rainfall or low atmospheric pressure that accompanied such storms. Redfield answered these objections vaguely, but he raised the debate's ambient temperature a bit, by suggesting that Espy misquoted him, confused facts well established by observations, and—most damning of all—stole his ideas.

In the meantime, Lieutenant Colonel William Reid of the Royal Engineers was dispatched to Barbados to inspect the damage of a hurricane that swept across the island in 1831. Reid had read of Redfield's "whirlwind" theory, and he thought it explained the effects he was observing. Soon the two men formed an intellectual alliance, growing more and more convinced that hurricanes were whirlwinds.

There was a persistent idea, promulgated by the Royal Academy among others, that until meteorology gave birth to overarching theories of the nature of weather and climate, it could not be regarded as a true science. It would remain, at best, the realm of untrained amateurs, mere collectors of data. When scientists of professional societies accused Redfield and Reid of avoiding theory, they responded rather ingeniously. Reid composed a 400-page treatise entitled *An Attempt to Develop a Law of Storms by Means of Facts, Arranged According to Place and Time; And Hence to Point Out a Cause for the Variable Winds, With a View to Practical Use in Navigation.* The title's emphasis on method—*"by Means of Facts"*—turned the accusation on its head, suggesting that it was precisely Espy's *overreliance* on theory that had blinded him to obvious truths.

Meanwhile, Espy set about to re-examine Redfield's first case— the storm of 1821. He demonstrated that the data in Redfield's 1831 paper could as easily support his own theory of inwelling and rising air. For his part, Redfield suggested that Espy's winds blew inward only when Espy deliberately misrepresented the sequence of events, remarking, "I did not anticipate so complete an evasion of all the distinguishing points at issue, and so barren an effort at confusing and mystifying. . . ."

By 1837 Espy had begun to make public lectures as part of the lyceum movement, that grand American experiment in public education. He was a popular and engaging speaker, and in part because he began to offer schemes for causing rain by setting fire to tracts of forest, he was often introduced as the "Storm King." The rainmaking proposal was ridiculed by some scientists, but many were impressed by Espy himself, one anonymous writer to a newspaper letter column calling him into the company of "Galileo, Harvey and Franklin." Indeed, many respected American scientists, among them Joseph Henry, the first secretary of the Smithsonian Institution, were convinced that Espy's "convective" theory of storms was basically sound.

There was a third participant in what some were beginning to call the "great storm debate." He was Robert Hare, a professor of chemistry at the University of Pennsylvania. It was Hare's contention that the sky and the earth could be thought of as two adjoining "oceans" of opposite electrical charge. Clouds were electrified by the "celestial ocean" and caused an accumulation of opposite charge on the ground beneath. This charge diminished atmospheric pressure and pulled air inward and then upward in a dynamic much like that proposed by Espy.

Hare's entry into the fray only served to heighten tensions. In February of 1843 Espy wrote to a sympathizer, "Is it not remarkable that Mr. Redfield in his controversy with Prof. Hare, persists in the assertion that storms travel towards the N.E. when you show that your great storm commenced in Quebec about the same time it did at C. Hatteras? And sneers at me on the same subject? Speak out on this point to the world . . . how can men permit themselves to be so blinded?"

In 1848 at the inaugural meeting of the American Association for the Advancement of Science, Hare argued against the very *possibility* of Redfield's circular whirlwinds, claiming that a mass of whirling air could not possibly be sustained because it lacked both a "restraining vessel" and a "constant stirrer." Espy had worked with the Army Medical Department and the Navy, and his "Second Report on Meteorology" was issued as a government publication. Redfield worried that Espy's association with the government gave him an unfair advantage and in 1849 he asked the secretary of the Navy to recognize him officially as a theorist of whirlwinds. He also proposed that the Navy use Reid's new work, *Progress of the Development of the Law of Storms,* as a navigational aid and an Annapolis textbook. Meanwhile, Hare began to criticize Espy too, and made an appeal to nationalistic sentiments by noting that the French Academy of Sciences had supported Espy and calling for Americans to free themselves of continental "intellectual tyranny." He had stopped short of calling Espy unpatriotic and treasonous, but only barely.

The debate over the nature of hurricanes waged for twenty-three years and became so heated and bitter that the author of the *U.S. Patent Office Annual Report of 1858* noted wryly that the situation made it seem "as if the violent commotions of the atmosphere induced a sympathetic effect on the minds of those who attempted to study them." After 1852 Redfield lost momentum. He published summaries and gathered data from the Pacific. He died in 1857 at the age of sixty-eight. Espy would survive him by three years, and during that time he re-examined many of the records on which Reid derived his theories. Espy confided to a European colleague, "I am now seventy three years old, and it would give me much pleasure to see, before I die, my labors begin to be useful to mankind." Hare's endgame was the strangest of the three. He abandoned science altogether, to devote his energies to spiritualism.

In the late nineteenth century others made significant contributions to the science of hurricanes. They were an unusual group, and some experiments were as ingenious as they were strange. Elias Loomis, an astronomer and meteorologist at Western Reserve

College, noticed that many accounts of the aftermath of violent winds described fowl "picked clean of feathers." In 1842 he realized that this phenomenon offered a way to estimate the speed of hurricane winds. Loomis lacked the means to generate a wind of hurricane force on a fowl (wind tunnels would not appear for several decades); he could, however, propel a foul through still air at considerable speed. The materials for his experiment were a six-pound cannon, five ounces of powder, and a freshly killed chicken. In a paper published the same year he reported, "The body was town into small fragments, only a part of which could be found." He calculated the velocity to be 500 feet per second, or 341 miles per hour, and he concluded that "with a less velocity, it is probable most of the feathers might be pulled out without mutilating the body."

Among the best and most immediately applicable work was that of a Jesuit priest in Cuba, Father Benito Viñes. He was meteorological director of Havana'a Royal College of Belén. From 1870 to 1892, Viñes studied the storms and made significant discoveries. He found that summer hurricanes tend to track directly westward; autumn hurricanes were likelier to track westward until they reached Cuba, then veer northward along the U.S. coast. He observed that hurricanes were often preceded by the high thin cloud known as cirrostratus plumiformes.

At the more theoretical end of the field was a Nashville schoolteacher named William Ferrel. Ferrel was innocent of Gaspard Coriolis's discovery of a force that appears when a body moves within an accelerated system, but in 1858 he suggested that a similar process made possible the formation of hurricanes. "If a body is moving in any direction," Ferrel said, "a force, arising from the earth's rotation . . . always deflects it to the right in the Northern Hemisphere, and to the left in the southern." Cleveland Abbe thought it a seminal piece of scholarship, and perhaps the most important single work in the history of meteorology. It was, he said, the *principia meteorologica.*[6]

The great storm debate may have seemed mere academic infighting, yet it concerned a subject about which specific knowledge (or the lack thereof) could mean sudden and violent death. Indeed, hurricanes were striking the Caribbean with frightening regularity, and every storm confirmed the conviction of all participants that their proper understanding was of paramount importance for scientists and (more immediately) for navigators and coastal dwellers. The Barbados hurricane whose aftermath Reid witnessed had occurred in 1831, the year in which Redfield's first paper was published. It had killed 1,477 people and laid waste to most of the island. The knowledge that such devastation occurred periodically did little to mitigate the shock of those seeing it for the first time. An account from a Bridgetown newspaper read, "To whichever point of the compass the eye was directed, a grand but distressing ruin presented itself. The whole face of the country was laid waste; no sign of vegetation was apparent, except here and there small patches of a sickly green. The surface of the ground appeared as if fire had run through the land, scorching and burning up the production of the earth. The few remaining trees, stripped of the bows and foliage, wore a cold and wintry aspect; and numerous seats in the environs of Bridgetown, formerly concealed amid thick groves, were now exposed and in ruins. . . ."

In 1834 a hurricane hit the island of Dominica, and in 1837 at least eight hurricanes swept through the West Indies. In the nineteenth century there were many descriptions of hurricanes from inhabitants of coasts or islands, but the most interesting—and perhaps the most dramatic—were from seagoing vessels. In December

---

6. In time, climatological studies of the tropics would show that hurricanes cannot begin within 5 degrees latitude of the equator, where the Coriolis effect is simply too weak to induce a circulation. They become more likely as latitudes increase from 5 to 15 degrees. Without the Coriolis effect, winds would blow almost directly inward from high to low pressure, and there would be no development of the cyclonic circulation.

1852 the ship *Equestrian* was bound from Calcutta to the West Indies. Captain Robonson described an encounter with a "severe hurricane":

> *On the morning of the 24th the weather was very dirty, the wind strong at N.E. and sea so high, we were compelled to run nearly right before it. The glass was still stationary. During the forenoon the eastern sky cleared away, the sun came out, and I obtained for the first time for several days good sights for longitude and latitude. . . . As the sky kept open to S.E. and East the greater part of the afternoon, I had great hopes we were fast getting out of harm's way, and I assure you this considerably lightened a heart not wholly at ease with the care of 350 souls. These hopes were doomed to be short lived, for about 4h. P.M. the barometer was observed falling, but being about the time of its lowest tide range, the warning conveyed by it was not so apparent. At 5h. P.M., it still continued to fall, showing no time was to be lost in making our final preparations.*

Robonson's crew made ready. They close reefed and re-secured the furled sails, got extra sheets on the foresail, and gathered all the axes in one place, should they be needed to cut free fallen masts and spars.

> *This work was barely completed ere it came astern thick and heavy, the rain in torrents beating down and against the masts with amazing force, and the gusts of wind howling fearfully as they swept through the rigging; it became perfectly dark considerably before its usual time. At 8h. P.M. the glass 29.40; the ship groaning fearfully as she flew before the tempest. At 9h., by the light thrown upwards by the foam, we could see the maintopsail giving way: with much difficulty it was got in, but the storm was still increasing in violence. At 10h. the foresail blew into ribands and was gone in a few seconds; the foretopsail soon after followed, but*

so densely thick was it that we were not aware of the exact moment of its departure. We had a hope in the storm main trysail, but, although stretched against the main rigging, it was blown into tatters in a short time and we were left in the total power of the maddened elements, which were roaring and howling fearfully over the ship as she rounded to.

The crew spent the night manning the pumps. Robonson wrote that daylight "ushered in a most dreary Christmas day." The wind was veering to south with increased violence, and the barometer was still dropping.

At 10h. A.M. the mizen topmast, unable to bear its force longer, came down bringing all the yards, gaff, and part of top with it, and to be brief at 1h. 30m. P.M. the head of the mainmast was wrung off close to the rigging, and down came the mainmast with a fearful crash, as it smashed across the bulwark. At this time the storm was at its height, and seemed appeased with the ravage it had done to us; for by the time the wreck was cut away a visible change was taking place, the wind abating, the western sky clearing, and dirt and gloom settling to the S.E. the wind veering to the S.W., we were now evidently on the storm's N.W. border.

After carefully considering the storm, the shifts of wind, the ship's course and drift, and other attendant circumstances, it was evident to me that this cyclone had for the first two or three days been moving to the S.W., and suddenly on the afternoon of the 24th diverged to the S.E; this is a circumstance deserving attention, for had we hove to we should most certainly, although unconsciously, have laid ourselves in its path. As it was the few hours run we had, until bereft of sail, barely carried us clear of the vortex, which, considering the violence we experienced, must have been fearful to contemplate.

Some meteorologists were wasting no time waiting for the approval of academies and conferences. Experiences like that of the *Equestrian* were inspiring them to translate observation into instructions for determining the course of a hurricane and directing a ship away from it. The author of several works in this vein was an Englishman named Henry Piddington. In the 1830s Piddington was president of the Marine Courts of Inquiry at Calcutta, and part of his assignment had been to examine accounts of hurricanes.

Piddington was particularly interested in ships' observations of severe storms in the Bay of Bengal and the Arabian Sea. Of the cases he studied, perhaps the strangest was that of the brig *Charles Heddles*. In 1845 the ship was used to transport cattle between Mauritius and Madagascar. On February 22, a day after departing Mauritius, Captain Finck and his crew found themselves in the vicinity of a fierce storm. Finck decided that they would try to outrun it, or at least run before it. The storm increased, and its winds veered around all compass points, and soon the ship was laboring in heavy seas. The crew expected that it would cease, but to their increasing dismay, it did not. They had passed through disbelief to resignation and back to disbelief when, three days later, they were still in the storm. They were exhausted, their sails and rigging had long been ripped away, and the ship was taking on water. They were very nearly desperate. Finally, on February 27 the sky cleared, and Finck was able to make a sun sighting and establish bearings. To his astonishment, he discovered they were a few miles off the coast of Mauritius. They had taken a week to be blown in a circle. Later reports of the storm's movement were compared to Finck's reckoning, and showed that the ship had been carried many times around the storm center, moving with the storm. A chart of its course would have looked like a watch spring drawn out, a series of loops arcing north to the west of Mauritius.

Piddington proposed a theory of hurricane structure that

agreed, in essence, with Redfield and Reid's ideas, although he found winds to be inclined slightly inward, or "incurved." He named the storms "cyclones" from the Greek word meaning "coiled like a snake," and the term quickly came into widespread use to mean not only hurricanes but temperate-zone storms as well. He showed that successive observations of wind could indicate the direction of the center of the storm, and readings of the barometer could indicate its distance. Piddington devised a kind of visual aid he called a "horn card." It was made by heating and flattening a plaque of horn or hoof and splitting it to produce a fine and rather fragile "leaf." The leaf was coated with tallow and placed under extreme pressure in a heated vise until it became transparent. The result was a rectangular plate that was dried, cut and molded, and etched with a diagram of hurricane winds. The horn card was waterproof and partly transparent. It could be placed over a page of compass directions and turned at will. A mariner could determine his position within the storm and see how best to navigate out of it.

Piddington thought the methods of Redfield and Reid—examining fallen trees and studying historical accounts—hopelessly indirect. It was as though they were trying to learn an animal's behavior by looking at its fossil when an abundance of perfectly healthy specimens was living in their midst. He knew that a more direct approach was difficult, if not impossible. Still, he believed that there was a clear need for actual investigations and that someday men would dare to undertake them. And in 1845 he offered a prophecy: *"The day will yet come when ships will be sent out to investigate the nature and course of storms and hurricanes, as they are now sent out to reach the poles or to survey pestilential coasts, or on any other scientific service."*

8

Wheels Up

6:33 A.M. EST / 1133 Zulu

The P2V rose into the dawn sky. In the cockpit Windham retracted the landing gear and then the wing flaps. Herlong switched UHF frequencies on the radio and notified the crew that they were leveling off at 1,500 feet for a calibration run. Windham scanned the row of dials before him—airspeed indicator, altimeter, attitude indicator, and heading indicator. Herlong checked tachometers, oil pressure gauges, manifold pressure gauges, and fuel gauges. They read through the climb checklist. Windham richened the mixtures and boosted the rpm. He pulled back on the yoke and pushed the throttles forward. The plane climbed, and he brought it to a cruise altitude of 8,000 feet. The crew made another check of all systems, and when Windham was satisfied that the plane was ready, he took a heading west by southwest.

Although Crew Chief Windham had a seat in mid deck, for much of the flight he stood behind Commander Windham and

Herlong, or leaned in the cramped space behind the cockpit. Mostly, he acted as another pair of eyes. He observed engine instruments, system indicators, tachometers, and torquemeters. He monitored circuit breakers, fuel flow, temperature and pressure indicators, electrical voltage and loads, and altitude indicators. He observed warning lights and fire detection indicators. He might recommend adjusting engine controls to maintain the required power during the climb and cruise part of the flight, and at any given moment he was prepared to recommend corrective action.

The P2V Navy Neptune was not the newest aircraft at Jax in September 1955. Both the jet-assisted version of the P2V and the Super Connies were more advanced and faster. Neither was it the largest. Put the P2V on a football field, and all but a few feet would fit between one end zone and the thirty-yard line. And while the Super Connie could carry a crew of twenty-nine in comfort, the P2V was designed for only nine. But the P2V was reliable and trusted, and by 1955 it was the workhorse and mainstay of Navy weather reconnaissance.

The Neptune had an interesting pedigree. In 1941, Lockheed Aircraft's Vega division had begun the design of a twin-engine bomber called "Model 26." It would use the new Wright R-3350 Cyclone Engine, and even with only two engines, it would be able to carry a larger bomb load for greater distances than could workhorses like the four-engine B-17. But in 1941 the Army Air Force considered Model 26 a relatively low priority, and soon enough those Wright R-3350 Cyclones were diverted to a larger and top-secret project—the long-range bomber that would become the Boeing B-29 Superfortress. Still, development of Model 26 proceeded, and in April 1944 the Navy ordered fifteen of the aircraft. They would be too late to see the war. The first one was flown on May 17, 1945, a little more than a week after the Germans surrendered.

The P2V had a rather remarkable 200-mile-per-hour difference between top speed and patrol speed and a tremendously long range, made evident when a plane christened *The Turtle* made a nonstop demonstration flight from Perth, Australia, to Columbus, Ohio. The distance was 11,236 miles, a record for piston-powered aircraft that would stand unchallenged for forty years.

The plane had several unusual features. One was its enormous vertical tail—its area was 18 percent of the total wing area on the plane. The tail was meant to increase directional stability, allowing a pilot to spend less time struggling with the fishtailing motion called *yaw.* Indeed, the Neptune seemed to perform with the agility of smaller aircraft. A Lockheed test pilot named Stan Beltz flew an early version. He performed a slow roll on one engine, flew it at 385 miles an hour, pulled out of a dive at nearly 3*gs*, performed a few power stalls, and made some violent yaws. He also performed several deadstick landings—that is, landings with both engines feathered.

It was not uncommon for a plane to spend five years in development, and especially during wartime it was not uncommon for needs to shift and for research and development to discover new applications of materials and designs. The result was inevitably a mongrel, and in the case of the P2V it was precisely these mixed bloodlines that ensured it a long service life and a wide range of missions. The Neptune would be in continuous production for twenty years. It seemed there was little it could not do. During the Korean War, Neptunes were used in combat for ground attack, mine laying, and day and night bombing. In the first years of the 1950s some had their landing gear replaced with skis so they could fly missions in the Arctic and Antarctic. Others were fitted with rockets and launched from aircraft carriers. The Navy used the planes for "open water reconnaissance," which meant hunting Soviet submarines. A few were used during the Cold War on missions that are still classified top secret.

There were variants of the Neptune, each differentiated from its predecessor with a dash and a numeral—P2V-2, P2V-3, and so on. The Dash Three replaced armament with electronics, most of it fit into a radar dome in the belly. The Dash Four had a turbo-compound engine, and it had auxiliary fuel tanks built into aerodynamic pods on the tips of its wings.

The Dash Five altered the silhouette of the plane rather dramatically, with a conical aerodynamic cowling on the tail section. The cowling looked like a tail stinger. It was about 12 feet long and had been designed as the housing for the Magnetic Anomaly Detector (MAD), a device used to detect submarines by the magnetic material in their hulls. The MAD was so sensitive that the housing had to be made of fiberglass, and even its tail lights had to be nonmagnetic. Because even the small amounts of magnetic material in the engines could impede its operation, the MAD had to be as far from the engines as possible. Some versions of the MAD had been towed on a cable behind the plane.

The Dash Five featured another design change. The forward section of the starboard pod was made of clear Plexiglas and held a 75-million-candlepower searchlight for tracking submarines. It was incredibly powerful. In January of 1954 a Neptune pilot from Naval Air Station Iwakuni, Japan, climbed to 8,000 feet and turned on the searchlight, acting as a beacon for a group of fighters who were returning to base disoriented and low on fuel. The fighter group saw the beacon from 50 miles away.

Lockheed received many orders for the Dash Five, and more than four hundred were built. It subcontracted half the production to other manufacturers—Chance Vought, Tempco Aircraft, Kaiser-Fraser Aircraft Division. The version called P2V-5J made numerous accommodations for weather reconnaissance. The guns were replaced with instruments, a radar dome was installed beneath its belly, and the MAD system inside the tail housing was replaced with more weather-sensing equipment.

The Navy's first hurricane surveillance flights had been made in seaplanes—PBM Mariners. The first full-time reconnaissance squadron, VPB-114, used four-engine PB4Y Privateers, and the Navy aviators considered the exchange of pontoons for two extra engines a fair trade. But by the mid-1950s the Privateers were getting old, and the Navy was phasing them out and replacing them with the twin-engine P2V. Weather reconnaissance crews, grown accustomed to the Privateers, had reservations about entering a hurricane with only two engines. But on the afternoon of September 15, 1953, a crew in a P2V Neptune reconnoitered Hurricane Edna, approximately 240 miles north of Puerto Rico. In debriefings, the pilot and copilot reported a successful flight. They had encountered 100-mile-an-hour winds in the eyewall, and inside the 23-mile-wide eye they had effected a circular climb. The Neptune itself came through its paces well, suffering only some peeled paint on the leading edges of its wings.

Asked about their feelings on the Neptune, most crews in 1955 called it cramped and prone to hydraulic problems. Some pilots said the wings were stiff, and in turbulence this made for an especially bumpy ride. Other pilots said it handled well—there were servomechanisms for the control surfaces. And several admitted that like the B-17 of legend, to which it bore a passing resemblance, the P2V could take an incredible amount of punishment. The "Old Sailor," as it came to be called, always got you home.

The first P2V Neptunes delivered to Jacksonville had arrived a few years earlier. Windham's was a relative latecomer. Officially known as Aircraft P2V-5J, Bureau Number 131442, it had been accepted from Lockheed on March 1, 1954. It had been flown first by Patrol Squadron Eighteen, who operated it through March 1955. In January of that year the plane's nose gear had collapsed during a landing rollout, damaging both propellers and the radar dome. The harm was judged to be minor. Fixes were made, and the plane was accepted by Airborne Early Warning Squadron Four on

March 31, 1955, and moved to Jax. It flew a few training missions in late spring, and in July it was flown to Naval Air Station Norfolk for a "J" configuration, a major overhaul to install weather-sensing equipment. In early 1955 the Navy had directed that all land-based patrol aircraft be painted in an overall seaplane gray, replacing the sea blue worn by Navy aircraft for more than a decade. The plane was given a new coat of paint and assigned to Crew Five. It arrived at Jax on September 1, in time for what forecasters generally regard as the climax of the hurricane season.

Lieutenant William A. Buck Jr. had strong features and a square jaw that made him look like a good mechanic. He was only twenty-five, but because he was prone to serious expressions, most who saw him for the first time guessed him to be thirty.

As the aerologist, Buck was the mission's mind and its memory. He made the preflight inspection of meteorological instrumentation, including the altimeters, total temperature system, sea-surface temperature instrumentation, dew-point hygrometer system, and meteorological altimeter system. He coordinated his work with the Hurricane Forecast Center, and he was responsible for completing the mission to its satisfaction. Buck also coordinated mission requirements with Windham and the navigators to include the route, weather observation position, dropsonde-release points, special observation requirements, and altitude or altitudes to be flown. With Combs, he ensured that the mission's weather data would be received by the staff in Miami.

Buck was a graduate of the aerological engineering course given at the Navy postgraduate school in Monterey, California. The Navy defined aerology as "the study of the atmosphere and upper air weather patterns surrounding and supporting airborne structures." It was a field with a brief but interesting history. In 1918 Dr. Alexander G. McAdie of Harvard's Blue Hill Observatory

taught one of the Navy's first courses in the subject. He said that
aerology differed from meteorology most significantly in its point
of view. While meteorology was atmospheric science from the perspective of the "automobilist," aerology was atmospheric science
from the point of view of the aviator. By the late 1940s Navy aerologists were required to pass a series of ground school courses that
would allow them to qualify for a flight status akin to that of navigators. In 1946 the Navy began to assign aerological officers to
weather reconnaissance squadrons. The Navy established the rating called "Aerographer's Mate." Thereafter, the officers were
called *aerologists*.

In the spring and summer of 1955, William Buck and
Aerographer's Mate Jim Meyer developed a friendship, in part
because of shared interest, and in part because they worked
together in the Aerology Office and flew together on numerous
missions, sharing the crowded space in the observer's station. It
was not a unique situation, but it was certainly rare. For the most
part officers and enlisted men had no great desire to mix. They led
rather different lives. Most officers lived in Jacksonville; all enlisted
men lived in the barracks. But Lieutenant Buck could be unusually
personable. The men of VW-4 used to play football out behind the
barracks, and Buck acted as coach to Meyer's quarterback. Not
only did he invite Meyer to his home for dinner with him and his
wife Barbara, but when he did so, he asked the sailor to name his
favorite dish. A few nights later, when Meyer arrived at the modest
ranch house a few miles from base, he was greeted with the warm
fragrance of marinara sauce.

A few days before Crew Five's night reconnaissance of Janet,
Buck had seen Meyer in the Aerology Office, and told him that he
was being bumped to make room for two Canadian newsmen.
Meyer always looked forward to missions, and he was disappointed.
But he took the news with a philosophical shrug, telling himself
there would surely be more flights—the season had several weeks

to go. This time, he would work in the Aerology Office, taking the plane's coordinates from the Hurricane Forecast Center and plotting its course southward from Cuba. Meanwhile, aboard the aircraft, Buck would do double-duty as aerologist and aerographer.

Now Buck moved forward through the plane's mid deck, with the photographer Doug Cronk behind him. They stopped near the crew chief's station. Had Buck and Cronk continued farther forward, they would have entered the cockpit. But instead the lieutenant knelt and opened a hatch in the deck. He put his hands on the frame and lowered himself into a well until his feet touched a lower deck. Cronk followed him down, crouched, then reached up and closed the hatch above. Buck crawled forward into a narrow tunnel like a large ventilation duct and began to pull himself through it. Cronk was behind him, and they crawled and pulled themselves for several feet. To the right was the forward escape hatch and the nose wheel well, with the retracted wheel inside. Straight ahead, the tunnel opened into a larger space.

This was the forward observer's station. In earlier versions of the P2V, it had been the position of the forward gunner, or the man trying to sight the reflection of the sun off a periscope. When the plane was reconfigured for weather reconnaissance, it became the station of the aerographer. It was a relatively spacious area—6 feet across, its forward half a Plexiglas bubble. The seat, a lightweight frame of aluminum tubing and a footrest, was mounted roughly in the center. To the right, within easy reach, were a radar altimeter, a barometer, and a wet- and dry-bulb thermometer.

The position offered a panoramic view, capable of inducing vertigo if one were not used to it. But Buck was used to it. He could sit there, put his feet on the frame, and watch the ocean slide by beneath. Pilots had been known to term his kind "weather guessers" or "balloon blowers." If you asked him, Buck might admit that he did not understand the crew's casual disinterest in the weather. As far as he was concerned, there was no place on Earth— or above it—better than the observation station of a P2V. It was a solitary vantage. To sit there was like becoming a boy again, climbing a tree.

They were traveling at nearly 200 miles an hour. But at this altitude, with no landmarks and the horizon stretching in all directions, they felt motionless, suspended. Nearly a hundred years earlier, Herman Melville described the same sensations as experienced from the masthead of a whale ship: "Lulled into such an opium-like listlessness of vacant, unconscious reverie is this absent-minded youth by the blending cadence of waves with thoughts, that at last he loses his identity; takes the mystic ocean at his feet for the visible image of that deep, blue, bottomless soul, pervading mankind and nature; and every strange, half-seen, gliding, beautiful thing that eludes him; every dimly discovered, uprising fin of some discernible form, seems to him the embodiment of those elusive thoughts that only people the soul by continually flitting through it."

True, there were differences—in the P2V there would be no gentle rolling of the ship, no breezes felt on the cheek. And it was not quiet; there was the unceasing sound of engines. But because the engine sounds were steady, it was possible to allow one's attention to slip. It was possible to think. A man in the observer's station was separated, apart—and there was at least the illusion that he was alone.

Of course, this time he was not alone. The man holding a camera and kneeling on the deck to Buck's left—in the only remaining available area—had a youthful appearance that belied wide experience. Already Doug Cronk had seen more of the world than most would ever see. During World War II he had served as a signalman on frigates and destroyers, and he had been with Canadian troops in Korea. On assignment aboard a Royal Canadian Navy minesweeper, he took over the signal watch, and by all accounts worked as expertly as he had while running a convoy escort during the war. Cronk's ongoing assignment for the *Toronto Daily Star* was photography, but he was hardly passive during interviews. In fact, he was likely to ask as many questions as the reporter he accompanied. He had an insatiable curiosity about the world and the people in it. Ill-suited to introspection, Cronk described his predilections simply and straightforwardly: "I like to see things." At the moment, there was plenty to see.

Gitmo and the island of Cuba were well behind them now, and outside was an immense bright emptiness. To the port was the rising sun, and in the water directly beneath a million tiny crenellated reflections, returning to blue on either side. The sky was a lighter blue. There were a few streaks of high clouds. To starboard, the sea was a deep aqua, turning lighter green in shallows. Stretching to the horizon to starboard the mottling of colors gradually faded, the details gradually growing indistinct until they dissolved into a band of mist on the western horizon. As the plane headed southwest, the sky lightened in the east, and the waters below turned from gray to pale blue and emerald. The water directly beneath was like green glass.

They flew south by southwest across the stretch of water called the Jamaica Channel. It was a little more than 200 miles to the island of the same name—they would fly across its western part— over St. Ann's Bay and soon Kingston and finally Spanish Town, which should be visible on their starboard side. Finally, out over the southern coast and into the open waters of the Caribbean.

A hurricane may be first detected by its swells. Waves generated by a hurricane travel between 30 and 50 miles an hour. When they move beyond the area of the storm, they lose strength, or as oceanographers say, "decay." But they do not disappear. Rather, they transform themselves into the smooth undulating form called *swells*. In the Atlantic Ocean and Caribbean Sea, swells may move several hundred miles ahead of the hurricane center, and in some instances as much as 2,000 miles. Smaller swells propagate in all directions, and a chart of swells from a hurricane looks like ripples from a rock dropped in a pond. Swells moving across shallow water reflect, diffract, and refract—and they may bend to fit a gradually shoaling bottom. From altitudes above a few hundred feet, swells are all but invisible, unless they strike a shallow bottom.

Sometimes Buck and Cronk could see lines of white breakers where the swells had struck a coral reef just below the surface. Those regularly spaced curving white lines were the first indications of the storm, but the information they carried was already old. Buck knew that at the moment Janet's eye was passing over a point about 250 miles equidistant from Jamaica to the north, Nicaragua's Costa de Mosquitos to the west, and the northern coast of Colombia to the south. The breakers were the remnants of an earlier Janet; the direction from which they came was where she had been a day ago. Soon though, there would be fresher signs. In an hour they would see clouds. Then they would begin to feel her winds.

⟜

To a weather reconnaissance crew, coffee was as necessary as fuel, and they would drink it all the way out. The men in the cockpit would drink it coming back. Although coffee detail was usually given to the crewmember with the lightest duties, it was regarded as an important assignment. One unlucky radar operator had mistakenly filled thermoses with hot water. Well into the mission his error was discovered, and the navigator told him that Jonah had been thrown overboard for less. Today the responsibility for brewing and serving belonged to Airman Kenneth L. Clegg, the twenty-two-year-old man from Cranston, Rhode Island. Clegg was aboard as a photographer. The Navy recognized the public relations possibilities to be gained from the presence of Tate and

Cronk, and photographs of the Canadian newsmen with the crew would demonstrate an interest in their work that went beyond the gates at Jax.

Tradition was that the man assigned coffee detail broke out the coffee as soon as the flight was reasonably level. Clegg, near the "galley," put a thermos on the wing root for whoever was on the other side—probably Mann or Greaney—to carry to the cockpit. As Buck would not have left his station, Clegg, carrying a thermos, pulled himself through the tunnel to make a special delivery.

In the duty stations in mid deck there were a few yawns. The coffee was poured from a thermos, and someone asked one of the navigators the distance to Jamaica. There was some talk over the interphone, and a man removed his headset and shouted a question or a joke to someone nearby.

For most of the crew, that first coffee involved the last bit of communication that was nonprofessional. From here until they were in the eye, they were separated from each other by bulkheads, by the sound of engines. They were also separated by assigned tasks and their own spheres of attention. Windham and Herlong would be scanning the instrument panel almost as a habit, speaking a little without keying the interphone mike. Crew Chief Windham would be crouching behind, watching the engine indicator. Below and forward, Buck and the photographer were most probably shouting a few questions and answers back and forth, the aerologist explaining the dry-bulb thermometer or perhaps recounting another mission. Cronk would be listening, asking questions, watching the seas beneath. In mid deck Greaney and Morgan would be checking equipment, plotting the course with a compass and chart, and glancing at the rotating hand of Mann's radar every now and then for the first sign of the storm. Aft the wing root sat Combs, in his own backward-facing monk's cell, listening passively for calls from Miami or Gitmo or Jax. Finally in the rear, reporter Alf Tate was scribbling notes, and across from him was Airman

Clegg, given a job that required the least to do and the most time to think. Clegg was nervous about his first close encounter with a hurricane, and back in the barracks he had asked Jim Meyer a lot of questions. Meyer told him the worst part was the eyewall. The eye itself, he said, was "something to see." For the moment, Clegg could only look out the port and wait for the bumps to begin.

Civilian aircraft crews carried on long, layered conversations on the interphone, sliding easily between two subjects with entirely different vocabularies without so much as a beat and never confusing the threads. But in a Navy aircrew there is little talk over the radio because the commander wants to keep channels clear. So the crew were probably mostly quiet, scanning instruments, sipping their coffee, even a little bored.

9

"A Radically Inexact Science"

By the late nineteenth century the telegraph had made communication among weather stations efficient, and whole nations had begun cooperating and sharing data. Meteorologists had actually begun to track storms. Much as the forecast method called analogue could be used to predict tracks of hurricanes, so it could be used to make more general forecasts. Essentially, meteorologists would search records to find a day when data were similar to the present, examine records of the following day, and use those records to create a forecast of the weather tomorrow. If a certain combination of humidity and westerly winds led to rain in the past, so the same humidity and westerly winds probably would lead to rain in the future.

Over time the records accumulated, and meteorologists were able to derive rules. A rule might state, for instance, that sustained wind from a certain direction at a certain time of year was likely to be followed by a certain amount of rainfall. But as there were more and more examples and patterns to compare, the analogue system grew increasingly unwieldy. By the 1930s rules numbered in the hundreds, most had qualifications and exceptions, and many rules contradicted other rules. Early in his career, meteorologist Jerome Namias had tried to memorize them and failed. He said, "I soon had to give up since my mind didn't have enough storage." Meteorologists were not the only ones inconvenienced. The people they made the forecasts *for* knew that all too often the predictions were vague and as often as not, simply wrong.

So by the first years of the twentieth century there was observation and comparison, but a real theory of larger atmospheric dynamics was nowhere in sight, and its absence remained the chief reason why many continued to think meteorology unworthy of being termed a proper science. There was one man, however, who believed that all that was needed was the careful application of the proper tools. And those tools, he believed, were very much at hand.

His name was Vilhelm Bjerknes. He had the sharp, angular features of a nineteenth-century schoolmaster, and in 1903 he was a forty-one-year-old professor of physics at the University of Stockholm. To be a physicist early in the twentieth century was to ascribe to a doctrine called *determinism.* Its central assumption was that if one could know all of the forces operating in the cosmos and the respective positions of all the parts of the cosmos, one would necessarily also know the future and the past of—quite literally—everything.[7] Bjerknes did not think he knew all the parts and all the forces even of a small part of the atmosphere. But he did think that he could learn the relevant forces and that he could

---

7. The clearest formulation of "universal determinism" was from Pierre-Simon de Laplace in his *Essai philosophique sur les probabilités* (1814). He asserted that from a complete specification of the state of the universe at a given instant (the positions and velocities of all bodies), a superhuman intelligence knowing all the laws of nature could infer and know all past and future states of the universe.

determine the important parts. He could know, in other words, *enough.*

In 1904 Bjerknes suggested that one might make a prediction first by measuring the present atmospheric conditions of a given area in detail. One would then examine "known boundary conditions," that is, weather just outside the edges of that area. Finally, one would perform a kind of thought experiment, applying to both sets of atmospheric conditions the laws of thermodynamics and hydrodynamics. Bjerknes was aware that he was talking about a formidable effort, some on a relatively theoretical plane (thermodynamics and hydrodynamics had heretofore been separate fields) and some that was practical and mundane. Bjerknes wanted an ambitious program, and to accomplish it he needed scientists, trained observers to perform kite and balloon soundings, telegraphs to communicate among stations, administrators to coordinate work, and a clerical staff to keep records. Bjerknes knew that every prediction would require so many readings and calculations that by the time a forecast was made, the day for which it was made was likely to have passed. It hardly mattered. Applications and predictions could come later. At least for the time being, he was concerned only with establishing a model and creating a set of overarching theories of atmospheric motions that could be questioned, tested, and refined.

Bjerknes sought financing wherever he could, and worked tirelessly through several changes in circumstances. In 1913, the German government coaxed him away from Sweden, naming him director of an institute of geophysics at the university in Leipzig. Late in the summer of 1914, because Bjerknes and his group were under the employ of the German government, they were tasked to make forecasts for the military planners. The Swede did not enjoy such work, not so much for pacifist sensibilities, but because he regarded day-to-day meteorology as "a radically inexact science." To his great relief, in 1917 he was invited to Norway to the new

Bergen Geophysical Institute, and he returned to the work of creating a theory on the workings of the atmosphere.

In the first years of the twentieth century, most meteorologists regarded the barometer as the major instrument of weather forecasting. Its great advantage was that it disregarded localized winds and temperatures in lieu of a larger picture, and it had long demonstrated that an onset of low atmospheric pressure heralded a storm. A forecaster collected reports of barometric pressure from as many stations as possible, marked those locations on a chart, and between points of equal pressures drew the isobars, thus dividing areas of high and low pressure. He thereby outlined a "field" of low pressure whose boundaries corresponded with those of the storm.

Such charting was possible, of course, only in areas where barometric readings could be made. Norway was handicapped by the absence of any stations in the North Sea to its west. There was no sure way to measure atmospheric pressure in the very region from which most of Norway's weather originated. In Bergen, Bjerknes and several assistants turned the situation to their advantage. They devised a method of taking readings at a distance, by watching clouds. They called it *indirect aerology*. It was a method at least as old as Aristotle, but it was also a method that would give birth to a new science. By 1919 Bjerknes was ready to draw some rather revolutionary conclusions about the nature of weather. It was his contention that the atmosphere was composed of great masses of air. Weather changes, he said, not because of differences in pressure but rather because these masses of air move. One might identify a given mass of air not only by barometric pressure but also by associated temperature, humidity, and clouds. And between these masses one could identify discrete boundaries—or, as he called them, *fronts*. As to cyclones in particular, he believed that every cyclone began when a mass of warm air pushed itself into a larger mass of colder air. On its eastern edge the warm air flowed up and over the colder denser air. When the warm air cooled, its water vapor condensed into clouds, and on the western edge of the warm air mass, the colder air pushed beneath with enough force to cause sudden precipitation.

Bjerknes had half jokingly called his assistants "apostles," an allusion to their possession of a new and important sort of doctrine and his hope that they would disseminate it. By the 1930s most meteorologists outside Scandinavia had come to admit that fronts existed, but few thought they could be of much importance in understanding hurricanes. The idea that a storm was a whirlwind, as posited by William Redfield, was by this time deeply rooted, and meteorologists found it difficult to reconcile with Bjerknes's idea of a wavelike distortion.

➤

Even as Bjerknes was developing his "indirect" means to understand the atmosphere, pilots were exploring it more directly. In 1919 the Navy, as a kind of demonstration of the capabilities of aircraft, staged the first mass trans-Atlantic flight. On May 16 three Curtiss NC flying boats departed Trepassey Bay, Newfoundland. Forty-nine destroyers positioned at 50-mile intervals across the North Atlantic, were expected to aid in rescue, to offer navigational beacons, and to provide weather forecasting. Ten of them had meteorological equipment aboard. Despite the resources supporting the operation, it was difficult. Two of the three aircraft were hampered by bad weather and thick fog and were forced to give up halfway. Only one aircraft completed the entire flight to Plymouth, England.

Nonetheless, it was quite a feat at the time. It was also an auspicious beginning to the long and accomplished career of the Navy forecaster for the operation. He was a young ensign named Francis Reichelderfer. From 1922 to 1928, Reichelderfer served as aerological officer in the Bureau of Aeronautics. In 1931 the Navy sent him to Norway to study frontal weather analysis under Bjerknes.

He returned the following year and wrote a report that was so highly regarded that the Navy was persuaded to adopt Bjerknes's methods. In the years that followed, Reichelderfer instituted courses in meteorology in the United States Naval Academy and several universities. In 1938 President Roosevelt appointed him chief of the Weather Bureau, and he wasted no time in gathering within it former students of the Norwegian school. By the 1940s, in large part through Reichelderfer's efforts, most meteorologists regarded Bjerknes and his associates as brilliant, and their discovery of frontal systems among the most important contributions to what was becoming a science of weather.

Meanwhile, in the preceding half century there had been little progress in understanding the particular meteorological phenomenon called the hurricane. As to the work of Redfield, Espy, and the others, like the blind men trying to understand the elephant, none were entirely wrong and all were partly right. By the 1930s understanding of the process called *cyclogenesis* had progressed somewhat, having combined Redfield's whirlwinds, Espy's ideas of convection, William Ferrel's application of the discoveries of Coriolis, and Father Viñes's detailed observations.

But much was unknown. In the 1930s no one was entirely sure how a hurricane formed, although there were several ideas. In the mid nineteenth century Heinrich Wilhelm Dove had proposed a "countercurrent" theory. He knew that regions in which hurricanes are formed are bound on the north and south by trade winds moving in opposite directions, and he suggested that the air currents at their interface could be twisted, beginning a spiral motion that could grow into a cyclone. For some fifty years Dove's hypothesis was modified by various authors, and by the 1930s several meteorologists had combined the countercurrent idea with Bjerknes's frontal hypothesis. They applied the Norwegian "air mass" ideas to tropical weather, looked for fronts in the lower latitudes, and saw (or thought they saw) phenomena very like them.

The precise dynamics of a hurricane presented another mystery. Meteorologists knew that in a "stable" cyclone—that is, a cyclone that is neither strengthening nor weakening—exactly as much air is flowing into the storm as is leaving it. The whole system operated much like a chimney. As low pressure pulling air up a chimney will make a fire at its base burn faster, so air leaving a hurricane will speed its circulation and intensify the overall storm. In the 1930s meteorologists knew the inflow along the ocean surface was tremendous. Obviously it moved upward into the storm, but they did not know exactly where. Some thought the upwelling might occur at the edges. Others suspected areas inside. Much of the evidence they had suggested it did *not* happen at the center.

In 1935 a meteorologist named Bernhard Haurwitz had studied records of the Manila typhoon of 1882 and concluded that "the air in the center is very much drier, indicating that in the eye of the storm we have a downward current which brings warm and dry air to the ground. This air in the center probably comes from the surrounding regions of the cyclone, and has lost part of its moisture content by precipitation during previous ascent." Most students of tropical climatology knew that any theory of downward-moving air in the eye presented problems. Ivan Ray Tannehill, in a respected 1938 work on hurricanes, wrote, "If true, it is a paradox for we must assume that the tropical cyclone as a whole involves ascending currents on a grand scale to account for the torrential rainfall and to provide an outlet for the vast quantity of air that is carried inward at the surface." The air being pulled in had to be going somewhere. On this particular question, it seemed meteorologists were no better off than Heinrich Brandes, a hundred years before, wondering whether it was absorbed by "the jaws of the ocean."

Meanwhile, other long-held beliefs were being overturned. Herbert Riehl was the meteorologist who would later attempt to track a hurricane's path by measuring winds at 18,000 feet. In 1942 he was a German expatriate and a professor at the University of

Chicago. He had already done good work in tropical climatology, and in 1943 he was invited to join the faculty at the Institute of Tropical Meteorology at the University of Puerto Rico, Río Piedras. On the evening of Riehl's arrival, he and some of the new staff walked along the beach. It was a warm tropical night, and they admired the trade cumuli to the west, its edges dramatically back-lit by moonlight. They knew the clouds were approaching, but were unconcerned. Riehl and the others had been schooled in the "ice crystal" theory of rain, which held that raindrops formed around ice crystals and could not form without them. They knew the clouds in question were at an altitude where the temperature was well above freezing. But soon they heard raindrops pelting the sand. The landscape before them grew dim, then disappeared entirely. It was raining. The shower increased and in moments grew to a downpour. The scientists ran for cover, and a few minutes later they were standing under a roof, shivering and drenched to the skin. They had received their first lesson in tropical meteorology, namely, that rain is possible in above-freezing temperatures. It was clear that much that they knew was wrong. In the tropics, they would have to begin again.

10

A Ride on Railroad Tracks

A little after 7:00 A.M., reporter Alfred O. Tate made his way forward through the fuselage. During the outward-bound leg his nominal position was in the rear, with Clegg. But as long as the ride was smooth, he took the opportunity to move about the plane. He talked a bit with Combs, then slid over the wing root into the midsection, and watched Greaney and Morgan over their shoulders. Now and then he asked a question. He moved forward again. Crew Chief Windham stepped aside and returned to his station. There was a little room behind the pilots' seats, and for a while Tate crouched there, half in the cockpit, half in mid deck. He listened, shouted a few more questions, and bracing himself against the bulkhead, scribbled some notes.

Alf Tate did not look the part of a globe-trotting journalist cum adventurer. At forty-four, he was balding, and anyone seeing him on the street might have taken him for an accountant. But he had worked for the *Toronto Daily Star* for nearly half his life, and in that time he had managed to get himself in and out of more than a few close scrapes. During the war he had been a photographic officer in the Royal Canadian Navy, spending eighteen months on convoy patrol in the North Atlantic. In the summer of 1944 the *Star* gave him a roving assignment to "cover the invasion." It was exactly the sort of thing he loved—a leash just long enough to let him go anywhere he thought there might be an interesting story. Or, as his colleagues at the paper would say, to get him into trouble. Like many war correspondents, Tate seemed to possess an unshakable belief in his own immortality. He had been among the first ashore at Normandy, and troops on advanced assault later said they had been amazed to see him, camera and equipment bag in tow, edging forward under fire.

In 1955 Tate and Cronk were a kind of team. Kindred spirits, they had been chronicling dangerous pursuits for years. Tate in particular had long been fascinated with hurricanes and the men who flew into them. He used to say that someday he wanted to telephone a story from inside the eye. He and Cronk had been trying for a year to fly with a weather reconnaissance mission, and they had been ready to visit Hurricane Hazel. For a number of reasons—including the particularly unpredictable behavior of Hazel herself—their assignment was postponed.

In September of 1955 they had another chance, as Janet began to move west across the Caribbean. While the storm was near Barbados, the newsmen prepared to take a passenger flight from Toronto. Another photographer from the *Star* named Eric Cole had accompanied them to the airport for the express purpose of taking their photos. Evidently they were becoming a news story themselves. The three arrived at the airport to find that the flight was delayed two hours, and Tate and Cronk chafed about that a bit. For a while they considered driving south to Cleveland to make their connection, but they wound up deciding to wait. They were in high spirits, and joked about the fact that Cole's camera did not work. Cronk had to lend him his own so Cole could take the photos. Tate was a bit chagrined that the *Star* would bother to send along a photographer to document the beginning of another routine assignment, and they all laughed a little about their own sudden newsworthiness. They said the pictures would be used only if they failed to return.

There was good reason for Tate's presence on the mission. The experience of flying through a hurricane was known to a handful of men, and for the most part, those few were not loquacious. On occasion, a few details of the experience were shared with laypersons. Especially in Miami and the communities along the Florida coast, the Hurricane Hunters enjoyed some small notoriety. A patrol plane commander named Bud Shipman had flown PB4Y-2s in three hurricane seasons from 1950 to 1952, and he recounted a few of the more-challenging missions before civic groups. After one of Shipman's recitations, a questioner asked what he did in the moments in the eyewall, the most turbulent part of the storm where downdrafts threaten to push the plane into the sea. Shipman just grinned a little and muttered something about getting your best hope and hanging on. His crew chief happened to be part of the guests and added, "You also talk to the airplane." The questioner nodded as though he understood, and left them alone. Shipman looked at his crew chief and said, "What was that about, Breckenridge?" And the enlisted man replied, "Well, when we were in Betsy, and in the worst of it, you kept saying 'Up, you son of a bitch—up!'"

A one-sentence answer like Shipman's was about as close as any of the crews came to breathless narrative. They might call a given flight "rough" or joke that it had been "a bit bumpy out there," but that was all. Certainly part of the reason was sheer exhaustion. Missions lasted ten or twelve hours and required heightened awareness on the part of the pilot and copilot for periods of twenty and thirty minutes at a time. Most returning crews were too tired to do anything but fill out a few forms and fall into their bunks. Nonetheless, the almost complete absence of detailed descriptions was curious. Ivan Ray Tannehill was particularly bewildered by the situation. He had poured over thousands of mission reports and found only a handful of narratives of the flights and descriptions of the storms. All he could surmise was that the men were simply in awe. "The vastness of the thing," he said, "seemed to leave them speechless."

Whatever the reason for crews' disinclination to description, journalists were more than willing to pick up the slack. Indeed, newsmen had been hitching rides into hurricanes almost from the start. As early as 1944, a reporter from the *Miami Star* named Milt Sosin had accompanied a crew into the Great Atlantic Hurricane, and by 1955 dozens of reporters had taken the ride. Most of their stories had style best described as "boys' adventure." Still, a reader had to credit their humility. One wrote,

> *Suddenly the plane keeled over on one side, the left wing tip dipped down vertically, and for a moment I thought the end had come. I gulped for breath as the plane dropped. The sea rushed up towards us; huge waves reared up and mocked us, clawing up at the wing tip . . . as if trying to swallow us in one. A greater burst from the engines, a hovering sensation for a second and then, with the whole plane shuddering under the strain, our nose once again tilted upward. I felt weak and with difficulty breathed again.*
>
> *I was growing sick in the bomb aimer's bay, stretched over a pile of parachutes and hanging on to the navigator's chair for dear life. Some baggage, roped down beforehand, now lay strewn across the gangway. Parachutes, life jackets, water cans and camera cases were thrown about into heaps. The photographer, trying in vain to take pictures out of the window, was knocked down and sent flying across the fuselage. His arms were bruised from repeated efforts. My stomach was everywhere but where it should have been.*

Everything went black. The plane was thrown from side to side and the floor under my feet dropped. We emerged from a big cloud into an eerie and uncanny pink half-light. The photographer clambered from the floor and tried to look out. He thought the reddish light was an engine on fire.

The Air Force and Navy were ambivalent on the matter of journalists as guests. It was another balance of risk against risk, the chance of favorable publicity versus the possibility of loss of life. Edward Murrow's broadcast in 1954 had been arranged by Air Force Major William C. Anderson. At least by the standards of weather reconnaissance missions, the flight had been smooth. Hurricane Edna made for what was called a "storybook setup," and in his broadcast Murrow described her 20-mile-wide eye as "magnificent." Major Anderson told the press that the flight's success demonstrated the superb abilities of crews. Privately though, he had been more than a little anxious. When the newsmen and crew returned safely, he enjoyed the first good night's sleep he had had in two weeks.

On the morning of September 26, Alf Tate was crouching awkwardly in a space between the cockpit and the midsection, and over the backs of two men he watched the sea outside reflecting the glare of a sun now well above the horizon. He could not know that one of the few men who had flown into hurricanes and also talked readily about the experience was, at that moment, piloting the aircraft.

Grover Windham enjoyed the hangar talk almost as much as the flying. He told stories of missions at parties. He also told them to his children—or at least he told a certain version. It was as though he wanted Nan and Buz to experience everything. If he could not bring them along on missions, he would do the next best thing.

He would take Nan, sit her on his knees facing forward, and say he was going to show her what it was like to fly into a hurricane. He would slowly begin rocking back and forth. Then he would say, "It's like being in a car riding on railroad tracks." He would describe the clouds and the way the sea looked below them. He would tell her what it was like to see the storm as a gray wall on the horizon, and tell her what it was like to enter the clouds. He would lift his heel and roll the ball of his foot a few times, bouncing her on his knee. He would describe the clouds moving past the plane, and his knee would bounce her faster and faster, "until you're going a hundred miles an hour." By now the knee would be bumping her up and down so fast she would nearly fall off his lap and then *whump!*—he would stop: "You're in the eye." And then he would pull her closer until his head was touching hers. His voice would turn quiet, nearly a whisper in her ear.

"It's calm. There's no wind. The sun is so bright you can barely see. You look down at the ocean, and it's like glass. But when you look up, you see the storm, still there all around you. The winds, the rain, and waves crashing around the edge of the eye. It's beautiful. But you know you have to get back home, and to do that you have to get back on those railroad tracks . . ."

And then his knee would start again. . . .

11

The Pioneers

Soon after the Galveston Hurricane of 1900, there was some hope that wireless messages from ships at sea could offer warning in enough time. The first ocean weather report came from the steamship *New York*, on December 3, 1905, and the first wireless report of a hurricane was received four years later, from the SS *Cartago*, off the coast of the Yucatán. In ensuing years, such reports became common. The practice was interrupted briefly by World War I but resumed after 1919, when the Weather Bureau adopted a standard policy of gathering reports from oceangoing vessels and transmitting warnings to any in the vicinity of a hurricane or its predicted path. Ship captains were grateful for the practice, but others became victims of its success. Those same ship captains, hearing the warnings and having no wish to put their vessels at risk, steamed out of the storm's path. Consequently, fewer and fewer reports came from ships near the hurricane, and in a day or two there were not enough reports for the Weather Bureau to locate it. The storm became, in a term that many living on the Gulf or Atlantic Coasts found unsettling, "lost." In the 1920s and 1930s, several hurricanes were lost in the Gulf of Mexico, and by the time they were found again it was too late to evacuate.

Some citizens voiced proposals for a coastal storm patrol. The Weather Bureau responded that such a plan was ill-advised and unworkable. For a vessel to get near enough for its crew to see a storm would put it in danger. A vessel heading south into the Caribbean to meet a westward-heading storm would be in the storm's path. Moreover, no vessel could be expected to outrun a hurricane: the distance a ship could make in a good day in rough water would not provide an acceptable margin of safety. Even putting such fears aside, it was difficult to imagine circumstances under which even a single reconnaissance would be implemented. If the bureau had enough ship reports to know where to send a cutter, they had no need to send it, and if they had no ship reports, they would not know *where* to send it.

For a while the matter was forgotten. But the hurricane season of 1933 saw twenty-one tropical storms in the Caribbean, breaking all records. There were new proposals for hurricane reconnaissance. In August 1937 President Roosevelt arranged a conference on the subject and turned its supervision over to his son James, instructing him to say that the administration believed that sending Coast Guard vessels into hurricanes would be dangerous and was unlikely to yield useful results. But the Coast Guard had an energetic new commandant, Admiral Russell Randolph Waesche. He had not been informed of the president's decision, but he was the first to speak. To the astonishment of many present, he endorsed the idea in full. He promised to send cutters into the Gulf upon request from the Weather Bureau. And so began one of the strangest, if shortest, eras in hurricane reconnaissance. As per the agreement, Coast Guard cutters would leave port at the behest of the Weather Bureau, but in open water the commander's first responsibility was the safety of his vessel, and no commander would deliberately put that vessel in harm's way. The Weather Bureau, having no desire to be responsible for the deaths of Coast Guard crews, seldom called. After two years of mutual and polite disregard on the parts of both participants, the scheme was quietly forgotten.

At that White House conference, a few had voiced thoughts of tracking hurricanes with aircraft. The idea was that planes would circumnavigate the storm, take three or more bearings, and estimate the location of its center. Six years later when the United States entered World War II, the bureau considered contracting commercial flyers to reconnoiter storms. When the request was presented to the Bureau of the Budget, the examiners asked the Weather Bureau to consider using the Army and Navy. The pilots themselves regarded these schemes—even reconnoitering storms from a distance—with little enthusiasm. They need not have worried. By 1942 there was some talk, but by then there were greater military needs and too few pilots to waste.

In neither of these discussions did anyone seriously suggest sending an aircraft *into* a hurricane. The simple reason was that no one knew what was inside. In some respects the understanding of hurricanes had advanced little since the days of William Redfield and James Espy, and such ignorance would have immediate repercussions for anyone entertaining ideas of controlled flight through a storm. On this count there was a specific fear. Although meteorologists knew the air in the eye was quiet at sea level, upper levels remained *aeris incognita*. Those levels could be where the air was pulled outward from the eye. A few suspected that winds in the eye at altitudes of more than a few thousand feet might be violent enough to throw an aircraft outward into the furious chaos of the eyewall.

In many fields of science and engineering, theoreticians con-
ceive and plan the first entry into a new realm. This was the case
with the Air Force's efforts to break the sound barrier. Although
the pilots of the "right stuff" legend certainly were brave, the part
of the myth that paints them as the high-noon sort of hero, the
lone challenger of the high frontier, is less than accurate. Chuck
Yeager, Scott Crossfield, and all the other pilots testing the new
aircraft at Edwards Air Force Base in the late 1940s and 1950s had
ample training and preparation. In fact, on the fateful morning in
1947 when Yeager entered the history books, he was armed with
the considerable knowledge of the Army's aeronautical engineers,
the theories of physicist Theodore von Karmann, and the experience of hundreds of previous flights flown by him and others. He
also had the Bell X-1, an aircraft designed and built for the specific purpose of flying faster than sound. Few knew that three
years earlier another pilot undertook a similarly courageous flight
into the unknown, and he did it with no official sanction, no engineers, no theories other than his own, and no aircraft designed
for that purpose.

In the summer of 1943, British pilots were being trained as
instructors in instrument flying at Bryan Field in Texas. The lead
instructor was a forty-year-old Army Air Force colonel from
Savannah. His name was Joseph B. Duckworth. In civilian life
Duckworth had been a pilot for Eastern Airlines. During the war he
had become a vocal advocate of instrument flying, working to initiate and organize the school at Bryan Field. The planes used in training were North American AT-6s. They were single-engine, two-place
trainers that the British called "Harvards," a sly reference to their
educational function. But the name was not entirely complimentary.
Some of the British, especially those who had already flown in combat, thought their training merited better planes, perhaps P-51s or
P-38s, and it was their contention that the AT-6s were flimsy.
Duckworth was a bit tired of the talk, but most days he just took it.

After the Japanese attack on Pearl Harbor, the American merchant marine stopped radioing weather messages, and on weather maps, oceans were left blank. Finding and tracking hurricanes became increasingly difficult. With every approaching storm, policy makers wrestled with the same dilemma: the risk of enemies knowing the position of Allied fleets, weighed against the risk of a civilian population ignorant of an approaching storm. In 1943 German U-boat activity was expected in the Gulf of Mexico, and all ships' radio broadcasts, including weather and storm broadcasts, were silenced. For the data used to issue storm warnings, Weather Bureau forecasters had relied on reports from ships at sea and land-based weather offices. It was by these means that on the morning of July 27, Bryan Field was alerted that a hurricane was coming ashore at Galveston. There was concern for the planes, and there were rumors that headquarters would order that they be flown farther north. For the British officers, such rumors validated their low opinion of the aircraft. They made a few remarks over breakfast that morning, and finally Duckworth had enough. He proposed a bet. He would fly an AT-6 into the hurricane and back. The flight would demonstrate the AT-6's airworthiness once and for all; it would incidentally confirm the value of instrument flying, also a subject of some derision. At first the Brits thought he was joking. But it soon became clear that he was stone serious, and the bet was on. The loser could expect to buy drinks in the officers' club.

Duckworth would need a navigator, and the only one on base that morning was also sitting at the table. Lieutenant Ralph O'Hair was by nature a bit more conservative than the man who offered the invitation, and doubted the wisdom of an "experimental instrument flight" conceived in the time it took for their coffee to cool. But he also had long admired Duckworth's skill as a pilot. So when Duckworth looked at him and said he could use some company, O'Hair agreed to supply it.

Probably neither the Brits nor Duckworth himself understood

the risk he was about to take. It was true that because of radio blackouts, the British by 1943 had much experience flying routine weather missions. They flew courses over the Atlantic, the North Sea, and Europe, and they flew in storms. But they had little appreciation for the severity of weather in the Western Hemisphere, and it is likely that those at the table suspected *hurricane* was merely an American word for "severe thunderstorm." As for Duckworth himself, he had flown in storms, and he may well have been one of the best instrument pilots alive. His thinking was that as long as he stayed at a reasonably high altitude and gave himself enough room to recover from a stall, he would be fine. He had only two concerns. One was that static from the rain would be so heavy that they could not use the navigation radio. The other was the single Pratt & Whitney R-1340-47 radial engine. If rain cooled the cylinder heads enough, a strong possibility in the tremendous downpour inside a hurricane, the engine would fail.

On the afternoon of July 27, 1943, Duckworth and O'Hair departed the Army Air Force base in Bryan, Texas, on a course south by southeast.

The hurricane was small and intense, tracking inland a short distance from Galveston. By afternoon her winds were clocked at 80 to 100 miles an hour on Galveston Bay and in Chambers County to the east. The AT-6 entered the storm's clouds at an altitude between 4,000 and 9,000 feet. Almost immediately it was buffeted about so violently that O'Hair would later say it was like "being tossed about like a stick in a dog's mouth." The sheets of rain drumming against the aircraft's skin were louder than the engine, and Duckworth realized the AT-6 was not necessarily the best plane for the job. Its sliding mullioned canopy was notoriously leaky, and water was streaming into various parts of the cockpit.

It had been Duckworth's plan merely to fly somewhere into the storm and turn around. He had no specific intention of reconnoitering the eye. But suddenly the clouds grew lighter, and they broke into clear air and sunshine. They could see the Texas countryside 5,000 feet below. It was rangeland, open country somewhere between Galveston and Houston. When they looked upward, they saw the clouds at the upper rim illuminated by sun, and a clear sky directly above. The eyewall of darker clouds surrounded them, O'Hair would later say, like a "shower curtain." The wall was in the shape of a leaning cone about 10 miles across, and the lower section seemed to be dragging from contact with the ground. For several minutes they circled inside the eye, and made their exit the same direction they had entered. Soon they were back at Bryan Field.

The base weather officer, Lieutenant William Jones-Burdick, was there to greet them, slightly miffed that he had not been invited. O'Hair had had enough. He said it was his first and last flight into a hurricane. But Duckworth was still game, and a few hours later he took the AT-6 back for more, with Jones-Burdick in the other seat. As they neared the storm, they experienced moderate to light turbulence, some static on communication and navigation radios, and light rain. They spent about fifteen minutes inside the eye. Then, for the second time that day, pilot and passenger returned safely to Bryan Field.

That night at the officers' club, the British bought the drinks.

Duckworth had proved the airworthiness—or *stormworthiness*—of the AT-6. There had been no damage to his plane, and he and the two men had survived two flights unhurt. A few weeks later there was a story in a local paper, and Duckworth received a call from Brigadier General Luke Smith, who told him that he was being considered for the Distinguished Flying Cross.

It was not long before word of the flights reached Washington, where they came to the attention of Weather Bureau Chief Reichelderfer. He asked Duckworth and Jones-Burdick for a report, and in due course the pilot and weather officer supplied one. Parts of it sounded a little like the enforced writing of schoolboys apologizing for a prank: "It is to be regretted that the flight was not planned to satisfy a larger objective than our personal curiosity. We hope that another opportunity may soon present itself for a more careful study." Nowhere did the report mention the wager with British pilots and the matter of the AT-6. It did, however, include detailed notes, a brief narrative, and findings. Of those findings, Reichelderfer judged two of particular significance. First, even at 5,000 feet the air was far warmer than the air in the surrounding clouds. Second, at that altitude there was a remarkable absence of updrafts or turbulence. The calm air at the center, until then experienced only at sea level or ground level, extended upward to at least a mile and a half. This was very good news. It seemed that fears of violent winds at upper levels in the center were unwarranted, and airborne reconnaissance of the eye itself was possible.

It happened that a few other instructors at Bryan, learning of Duckworth's flight, took a B-25 into the same hurricane a day later. And in the next weeks and months, others followed, inspired by the challenge of flying in weather and of putting skills and reflexes to a new kind of test. Such missions were possible because it was wartime, and protocol was relatively lax. There was no shortage of men ready to take advantage of the situation, and suddenly it seemed that officers at air bases all over the Midwest and Southeast United States were pulling whatever strings could be pulled and somehow or other wrangling permission to undertake what they called "investigative weather missions."

It would not be long before a pilot effected a flight into a hurricane over open ocean.

On August 20, 1943, Captain G. H. MacDougall and an Army Air Force crew flew into an Atlantic hurricane near Antigua. It was only the second fully developed storm of 1943. It had begun in mid-Atlantic and was tracking on a north-northwest course toward Bermuda. They entered at 10,000 feet, an altitude that required oxygen, and they flew through thin clouds that refracted sunlight to create what MacDougall described as a "bluish twilight." They judged the position of the eye first from compass readings, and then went on instruments, flying "uphill" in a direction that caused the needle on the pressure altimeter to drop steadily. Soon they entered a clearer area they assumed was the eye, came off oxygen, and descended to an altitude of 1,000 feet. They looked below.

Until that moment, everyone who had ever seen the ocean surface from within a hurricane's eye saw it from that surface. As impressive as those views were, they were blocked every few seconds by high seas. No one had ever had a broad perspective, free of obstruction. MacDougall and his crew were seeing the waters from above, at the height of an eight-story building, so the view of the surface was flattened and foreshortened, and to the untrained eye there would have been little sense of relief or vertical scale. But these were men who were acquainted with the look of water from altitude and who could read shadows of seas and spray. They knew that they were looking at something spectacular. MacDougall said, "For those of us who had spent enough time in the Caribbean to be familiar with the magnitude of the waves usually encountered, it was hard to believe what we saw below. The seas were tremendous and the crests were being blown off in long swirls that must easily have exceeded seventy miles per hour."

A month later Second Lieutenant Paul Ekern, stationed at the Army Air Force weather station at Tinker Field near Oklahoma City, made plans to fly into another hurricane. He was not a pilot. In fact, he was only a second lieutenant in the Army Air Force. But he had an insatiable curiosity and a knack for persuading the powers that be to see his point of view. Ekern had a friend on base, Sergeant Jack Huennekens, and together they made what a subsequent report would call "arrangements" to reconnoiter a storm that was churning in the Gulf of Mexico. They were quite open about their intentions but met some resistance from higher levels of command.

The storm itself seemed patient. It looped off the Texas coast for three days. In that time Ekern's flight plan was approved, and he found a pilot, an Army Air Force officer named John Griffin. He also secured an aircraft, a B-17 Flying Fortress. Meanwhile, word of their plan had spread to other bases. A Navy aerologist showed up at Tinker Field, asking for Ekern's whereabouts. He was Gerald Finger from the Naval Training Station in Norman, Oklahoma. He had with him an "aerometeorograph," a device that could measure pressure, humidity, and temperature. When he told Ekern he wanted to be aboard, the lieutenant realized he had devised the first intraservice hurricane reconnaissance.

So on the September 18 the four departed for south Texas and then the Gulf, where they first saw the storm. They entered at 30,000 feet, above most of the clouds, and flew toward the eye. The hurricane was weakening. But as Finger's record suggests, it was nonetheless impressive:

1712	*Started meteorograph record for a check. Altitude 30,000 feet. Altimeter set at 30.10″. Occasional turbulence. A single cumulonimbus cloud to the East reaching to flight level. Blue sea visible through breaks in the clouds.*
1715	*Clear to the sea below. A rainbow visible in rainshowers from the huge cumulonimbus whose cloud top must rise to 40,000 or 45,000 ft with the base thirty miles in diameter.*
1720	*Clear below, with broken to overcast on all sides. Seem to be in the eye. One tremendous cunb to the East of the clear space must easily rise to 15,000 feet above flight level.*
1725	*Heavy rainshowers in cumulonimbus. Eastern sides of the clouds are darker.*
1726	*Vivid lightning . . . cloud to cloud.*

They circled inside for three hours, while Finger collected data on temperature, humidity, and pressure. They descended to 12,000 feet, when fuel began to run low. Then they began the return.

Many in the Army Air Force and Navy thought the flights of MacDougall and Ekern were just a few foolhardy souls having some fun. They were intriguing experiments, perhaps of some consequence for scientific purposes, but of no real strategic use. But to meteorologists, the results of each of these flights were encouraging. The pilots found fewer gusts and less turbulence than they had expected, and a few went so far as to say that conditions on the peripheries of thunderstorms were worse. As to negotiating through the outer layers, it seemed almost easy—a simple matter, as Duckworth had believed, of maintaining altitude. When the 1943 season ended, the Army reported both flights to the Weather Bureau, whose recommendations were forwarded to the Joint Chiefs of Staff. The chiefs, in turn, referred the matter to their meteorological committee. The members of the committee had long recognized the need to forewarn the public. Now they recognized too, for the first time, that it was possible to call aerial reconnaissance into play.

All indications were that deployment would not be especially difficult. There were experienced crews; to protect convoys and ferry goods and people, Army Air Force pilots had flown thousands of missions across the Atlantic in rough weather. There were reliable planes. And now, there was the political will. On February 15, 1944, the meteorological committee approved a plan for the coming year, and by June pilots and aircraft were prepared to initiate weather reconnaissance missions.

The Navy, the Army, and the Weather Bureau coordinated to become Miami Joint Weather Central. They did not task a particular group with aerial reconnaissance; rather, they used a number of squadrons in the Caribbean and the Gulf of Mexico. The alliance of the Hurricane Forecast Center and the Navy was made with the delicacy usually relegated to relations between sovereign nations, and that delicacy was reflected in its language. For one, the Hurricane Forecast Center did not "order" an investigative flight— it "requested" one. But no request would ever be refused.

On September 8, 1944, there were signs of a disturbance northeast of Puerto Rico. Its central pressure was below 27 inches, and it covered a wide area. Again the meteorologists were seeing their ideas undermined. In 1944 the U.S. Weather Bureau classified a hurricane's life into four stages: *formative, immaturity, maturity,* and *decay.* The stage of immaturity occurred when circulation reached maximum intensity and when the hurricane itself was most symmetrical and most compact. The stage of maturity occurred when the hurricane had spread out over a wide area and had begun to weaken. At the time, these categories were widely accepted: they had been adopted by the new Institute of Tropical Meteorology in Puerto Rico and described in a leading textbook. But this particular storm defied the classifications. When it entered its third stage, when it should have been spreading and weakening, it was spreading and *gaining strength.*

Ships were avoiding the vicinity of the storm, and there were no regular weather reports. Grady Norton, then chief of the Hurricane Forecast Center, had a bad feeling about it, and on the morning of September 10 he used a secure line to call the Navy and the Army Air Force and request reconnaissance. In a matter of hours a Navy plane approached the storm, which was tracking northeast off the Carolinas. The crew met extreme turbulence, torrential rain, and winds in excess of 140 miles an hour. A few hours later, an Army Air Force pilot and copilot entered the storm. They had difficulty controlling their aircraft, and both later reported that at several moments they thought it was about to be ripped apart. They managed to make it back to base and found 150 rivets sheared from one wing alone.

The Army Air Force had an expression that conveyed the bru-
tal natural selection that seemed inevitable in aviator or pilot training: "There are bold pilots and there are old pilots, but there are
no bold, old pilots." At higher levels there was some feeling that
junior officers—by definition, relatively inexperienced pilots—
should be disallowed from hurricane reconnaissance. Colonel
Floyd B. Wood was a veteran flyer in the Air Force. He suspected
that the conditions encountered by Duckworth, MacDougall, and
Ekern were unusual, and he feared that their good fortune might
foster a sense of security that could prove dangerous. Besides, word
of mouth was merely that these men flew into hurricanes. No one
bothered to say that Ekern's hurricane had been weakening, and
flying conditions were probably no different from those in heavy
rainclouds and wind. Wood wanted to see for himself what a severe
storm might be like, and the system moving up the coast toward
Washington offered an opportunity. He invited the participation of
two others, First Lieutenant Frank Record of the Air Force Forecast
Branch, and Major Harry Wexler, the research executive of the
Weather Division. All three were in positions of some authority,
and without much difficulty they secured a Douglas A-20. Wood
took the pilot's seat, and Record and Wexler stationed themselves
in the rear gunner's compartment. As they settled into their stations, Wexler called Wood over the interphone and said he hoped
the pilot intended to make it a round-trip. Wood responded that
he would do his best. At 2 P.M., they were airborne and headed east.

The storm was near the mouth of Chesapeake Bay, and again
airmen experienced a wholly new perspective. It was a view no one
had seen and few had imagined. Wood said he watched the waters
below as "a freighter plowing through the Bay was being swept
from bow to stern by huge waves which at times appeared to engulf
the whole vessel at once." He said he kept thinking that if they had
to ditch, no life raft or life jacket would have kept them alive. What
surprised him most was that he had to compensate for a strong and

steady downcurrent. Meteorologists associated precipitation with rising air, but they were flying through heavy rain and the air was most definitely *descending*. He was fighting to maintain altitude.

The light grew dimmer, the rain heavier, and the ride bumpy. Meanwhile, Wexler was taking notes. He said, "Suddenly with an upward lurch the airplane broke into a cloud where there was considerably more light and no rain. Here the sun was dimly visible through the cloud. The air was very turbulent." Wexler too was about to find a phenomenon he had not expected, specifically, an ascending current in the eye. He said, "The pilot informed us over the interphone that on entering the cloud the plane was lifted suddenly from 3000 feet to 5000 feet, and that he had to nose the plane down to keep from being carried higher."

The three men believed they were near the center but could not find it. At an altitude of 5,000 feet Wood changed course for Norfolk. Then they encountered the hurricane's layers they had met on entry, but in reverse—heavy rainfall and a dark band of descending air. They emerged from the storm at a point 30 miles east-northeast of Norfolk, and a few hours after they had departed they were back on the ground. But they were not sure exactly where they had been. They had to guess from drift, compass headings, and estimated ground speed. Nonetheless, the three took a sheet of chart paper and roughed out the familiar isobaric lines. The result looked a lot like all the weather charts that had preceded it. But in fact, it was the first of its kind. The twelve or so data points derived from compass headings did not represent readings from separate sources, but measurements from a single source that had moved, tracing a curving path across the isobaric lines through a hurricane toward the eye and out again.

The torrential rainfall and the vast quantity of inward-rushing air at the surface would seem to require ascending air in many parts of the hurricane, including the eye. Yet accepted theory was that there was ascending motion throughout the hurricane, and descending air in the eye. It was what Ivan Ray Tannehill had acknowledged as a paradox. And now meteorologists seemed to have the answer. All evidence from Wood's flight showed that they had it exactly reversed. In fact, the air in the eye *ascended*. The proposition was so difficult to believe, so flatly counterintuitive, that Wexler took pains to say that the three aboard were in agreement. In a paper published some months later, he referred to them as "witnesses" and presented the paper's conclusion almost apologetically, as the explanation of the last resort: "The immense hurricane cloud system being maintained by ascending motion passing through a relatively narrow throat near the storm's center may not seem very reasonable, but the observations allow no other interpretation." In fact, it would resolve Tannehill's paradox by demonstrating that one of its underlying assumptions was simply in error.

But once again, the larger lesson was how little they knew. The published papers in meteorological journals of the 1930s and early 1940s cited records collected in the previous century. It gave one pause to realize that the theory of descending air in the eye had been based in part on measurements taken in 1882. It was some of the best data they had, and it was nearly seventy years old.

As for pilots flying through the storm, Colonel Wood had specific recommendations. Reconnaissance, he said, should begin at about 30,000 feet, above the worst of the winds. Once an aircraft had gained the eye, it could descend safely. But he stressed that the storm he and his fellow officers reconnoitered had reached temperate latitudes and was greatly weakened. It might not represent a true tropical cyclone. He cautioned, "Although one of the more important points indicated by our experience . . . is that hurricanes can very probably be successfully flown through after they have reached temperate latitudes, it should not be accepted as conclusive proof that all hurricanes may be flown through. Any pilot who . . . might desire to repeat the experience is advised that any hurricane should be approached gingerly and with a view toward making an immediate 180 degree change in his track."

Vessels riding the seas beneath had not fared as well. A destroyer, a minesweeper, and two Coast Guard cutters were lost. In time the storm into which Wood and the others had flown would be called the Great Atlantic Hurricane.

Meanwhile, the Army had contracted a Transcontinental & Western Air airline pilot named Robert Buck and a civilian crew of four to conduct a variety of missions requiring them to fly through heavy weather. They were provided a refitted B-17 as a test bed for new versions of radio and navigation equipment, and when they began most flights they had no idea where they would land. Buck and his crew were in the business of going where the air took them, which is exactly what they did—until their fuel ran low. Buck knew it was an unusual job. More than once he had tried to explain to nonaviators that he had actually learned to like flying in bad weather, as did his crew. He said his radio engineer in particular "always wishes, even when we're holding on for life itself, that the weather was just a little worse than it is."

On October 19, 1944, a month after Wood's flight, Buck's crew investigated a hurricane. They flew from their home base in Kansas City and met the storm near Alma, Georgia. They planned to fly through it for 200 miles. Assuming the hurricane did not make a radical change of course, they would probably land at Jacksonville. This would be more than a quick hit-and-run sort of mission. Their flight plan would allow pilot and crew to gather a series of data points for temperature, wind, and precipitation from the ground to about 30,000 feet. With that information they would have a vertical cross section of the storm. Buck was instructed to observe carefully and to take photographs.

They began their climb into the storm from 4,000 feet, where they were between a stratus deck and under an altocumulus deck. At 6,500 feet they entered the altocumuli, and at 7,000 feet they hit

Weather kites were used to bring recording instruments to high levels.
Courtesy National Oceanic and Atmospheric Administration.

Waves and storm tide from the New England Hurricane of 1938. Courtesy National Oceanic and Atmospheric Administration.

(Above) Snowcloud Five upon takeoff. Courtesy Dane Youell.

(Below) The eye of a hurricane, with a central cloud dome. Courtesy National Oceanic and Atmospheric Administration.

Nancy Windham. Courtesy: Nancy Windham DeFevers.

Grover Windham. Courtesy Nancy Windham DeFevers.

Hurricane eyewall. Courtesy National Oceanic and Atmospheric Administration.

updrafts that lifted them at a rate of what Buck estimated was 400 feet per minute. He described it as a peculiar type of turbulence. It was, he said, "Not rough air in the usual sense, but rather that choppy feeling, and although it wasn't violent you could feel it had teeth in it. . . . The bumps were vicious, and although they weren't bad you felt something big was on its way."

At 10,000 feet the turbulence ceased and the plane broke out of the first layer. The temperature was 7° Celsius (44.6° Fahrenheit). It was raining hard and visibility was poor. Buck said he could tell they were between layers because the fog part of the cloud was not "wisping" over the wings between the engines. They climbed higher. At 11,000 feet the rain became sleet, and at 12,700 feet the air was at the freezing point and they were flying through snow. They continued to climb, and soon they lost radio reception.

Buck and his crew were in a B-17 at 13,000 feet and in 100-mile-an-hour winds without navigational aids. They were in no immediate danger, but like mariners of the previous century, if they became disoriented, they could easily find themselves heading into the worst part of the storm. Buck tried to imagine the center of the storm so he could guess where to change the drift correction and how much to change it. The cockpit had a lot of distractions, and he was having difficulty visualizing the storm properly. But there was a metal control box at his elbow, and it occurred to him he might use it as a sketch pad. He reached into a pocket on his flightsuit and took out a crayon pencil and drew a circle on the box. He made some lines for winds and pressed the crayon against the metal to make a dot where he thought Jacksonville was and another where he thought they were. It was an ad hoc version of the "horn card" made for sailors a hundred years earlier. With it, he was able to understand their position inside the storm.

At 14,000 feet the rain turned to snow, great wet flakes. Buck noticed that it stuck on the windshield wipers and in little corners on the wing fairing and the ignition harness and the propeller governor control line. It was cause for some concern. If enough wet snow got into the carburetor scoops, it could play havoc with the engines.

At 19,400 feet the temperature had dropped three more degrees, and at 20,000 feet the radio beam came in again, and he found he was east of where he thought he was. He realized his 30-degree right drift correction was now a 30-degree *left* drift. Somehow, they had passed the center and slipped sideways into another quadrant, a westerly one. Then they left the storm. At 24,000 feet the clouds thinned and at 25,000 they broke out the side near the top. Buck turned east to be able to see it. The storm had the structure of a cold front—cumulus and cirrus clouds all mixed in together. It looked, he said, "rough and nasty." He wondered where he had gone through it—that is, how near the hurricane's center—and he could not tell. There was a deck of clouds far below him, and an oval-shaped depression that they knew must be the eye. But like Colonel Wood, Buck was not sure where he had been.

The photographs Buck took were published in the June 1945 issue of the *Journal of the American Meteorological Society.* The issue also included a photograph of the hurricane cloud taken from ground level and touched up to render a visual profile of Buck's flight. A line began below the cloud, curved upward, ran horizontally through the cloud, and descended. Beneath the photograph was a brief narrative, and Buck's recommendations to any pilots contemplating similar flights. He said that if navigation radios cannot operate due to static, there was a chance of an aircraft becoming lost. He said that so long as the pilot maintained an altitude of at least 8,000 feet, there was little danger of structural failure or loss of control.

The first men to fly into hurricanes were known to each other mostly by word of mouth. They did not think of themselves as a group, let alone an elite group, yet they were the first explorers of a place like none on Earth. It was a place where rain could fall sideways and even upwards, where temperatures could be colder than those at the Arctic Circle, where light and water assumed fantastic, unreal shapes. In more ways than even they understood, it was a new place.

The cooperation of the Hurricane Forecast Center and the Navy in 1943 was a clear indication that the first missions into hurricanes had been recognized as successful. Nonetheless, some doubted the usefulness of storm reconnaissance. But in December 1944, the same year of the flights of Wood and Buck, there occurred a disaster of such proportions that even the skeptics were persuaded that not only was it necessary for men to fly into hurricanes, but also it was necessary to develop an airborne navigation technology that might tell them exactly where, within those hurricanes, they had flown.

12

Halsey's Typhoon

Forward of the wing root, Crew Five's navigators sat facing an instrument panel mounted against a starboard bulkhead. Lieutenant Thomas Lawrence Greaney was twenty-six. Originally from Pittsburgh, he lived with his wife Margaret in Jacksonville in a modest home a few miles from the Windhams. To his right was Thomas R. Morgan, age twenty-four. A reservist, Morgan lived with his wife Joan in the community of Orange Park. The VW-4 operations department appreciated that the navigator's duties were too many for one man, and by 1955 most missions used two navigators.

Greaney and Morgan's workday had begun back at Gitmo well before takeoff. They had prepared a navigation flight plan that included route, headings, and altitudes; checkpoints; estimated time of arrival at the storm; and estimated fuel consumption. As part of preflight check they had inspected compasses, sextants, the radio and radar sets. Throughout the mission they were expected to supply Commander Windham information on position, heading, wind direction, and speed. They were also expected to report their own ground speed and estimated time of arrival. At any moment they might have to act as machinists and electricians, checking their equipment and fixing it when it broke. And like most of the crew, Greaney and Morgan were also record keepers and file clerks. They kept a log during the mission, and when it was over they would write maintenance reports.

Set into the hull almost directly above Morgan was a Plexiglas bubble held inside an aluminum ring measuring about 3 feet across. It was called an *astrodome*. The whole assembly, frame and dome, weighed perhaps 20 pounds. It could be unlocked, pulled inside the plane, and leaned against a bulkhead so that anyone could exit through the opening. The inside lower edge of the dome was painted with small tic marks representing 360 degrees, with 0 degrees being directly forward. On clear nights Morgan could look up through the astrodome and make sightings on stars. To learn his heading, all he had to do was identify a known star or constellation, use it to determine true compass directions, then use the scale to adjust for the difference. On the night radar mission that was Crew Five's previous flight, he had done exactly that.

Most navigators liked the astrodome. It could yield fairly accurate readings, and there was something reassuring about using the stars that navigators had used for centuries, the same stars Marco Polo and Columbus used. It was only during daytime flights that the astrodome became an annoyance. It let light into the flight deck and made the radar screen difficult to read. And when the aircraft was flying through rain, the frame was known to leak water.

If the crew were near land, the coastline would appear on Julius Mann's radar scope. It was the easiest means to see their position—like watching themselves as a point over a slowly scrolling map. The radar would give them a navigational fix that would be accurate within 5 miles. The problem was that as a navigational aid, radar was useful only when they were near enough a coastline or an island that it appeared on the scope.

The navigators had another electronic device at their disposal. It was called a *loran* (the word is a hybrid acronym for "long-range navigation"), and it calculated their position by measuring the time it took for two low-frequency radio signals broadcast from stations onshore to reach the receiver on the aircraft. The loran could provide a fix with an accuracy of 10 miles. But loran stations were rare in the Caribbean, and no aircraft could count on being within range of any two. Moreover, loran signal was just above the standard broadcast band, and *precipitation static*—that is, the static caused by rain—could tear up a signal. Crews lost radio contact so routinely to precipitation static that they joked about it. One radio operator told Miami, "We are still lost, but we are making excellent time." Finally, loran was a grand idea in concept, and helped on occasion, but it was a technology no navigator depended on.

For the most part, Greaney and Morgan relied on the tried-and-true navigation method called *dead reckoning.* They used the compass to learn their heading and the airspeed indicator to learn their speed. They also needed to know their drift—that is, the distance and direction in which the wind was pushing them off course. The easiest way to estimate the wind's effect on them was to observe its effect on the seas below. Set into the floor near Morgan's station was a low-power telescope called a *driftmeter.* It was mounted upright and stuck straight out of the deck. Morgan could rotate his chair 180 degrees, lean over and look into its eyepiece, and observe the direction of spindrift and whitecaps against a calibrated scale set in the glass. If Morgan used dead reckoning alone, he could estimate their position with an accuracy of 25 miles.

The navigation instruments used by Morgan and Greaney were compromises and half-solutions, a collection of imperfect technologies that were a response to an event that had occurred more than a decade earlier, several thousand miles away, in another ocean.

It was mid-December 1944, exactly a week before Christmas. Eighty-six vessels of U.S. Navy Task Force 38 were in the Philippine Sea, 300 miles east of Luzon. There were eight battleships, thirteen carriers, fifteen cruisers, and fifty destroyers, all operating under the command of Admiral William F. Halsey aboard the flagship *New Jersey*. The carriers had just completed three days of raids against Japanese airfields when oil tankers began refueling operations. Wind was coming from the northeast at 30 miles an hour, and seas were choppy. Crews managed to wrestle hoses aboard, but they were working on heaving decks, and the steady rising and falling kept pulling fuel lines from their housings. When conditions deteriorated from difficult to dangerous, Halsey ordered refueling to cease until they could find calmer waters.

Halsey's chief meteorologist on the *New Jersey* was Commander George F. Kosco. In 1944 an American weather officer in the Pacific had little to work with. The Navy had weather stations on only a few captured islands, and pilots who were flying or had flown through weather were reluctant to break radio silence to report it. Fleet Weather Central in Pearl Harbor issued regular radio reports to ships, but even its knowledge was spotty. Consequently, Kosco's predictions were based on what few reports he did have, and his own best judgment.

Kosco believed that the storm they were encountering was northeast of the fleet. There was a cold front over them, and Kosco was convinced that it would slow the storm, forcing it to curve farther away to the northeast. He advised Halsey accordingly, and the admiral, hoping to increase distance from the storm and buy them a margin of safety, ordered the fleet south, on a course that put the cold front between them and the storm. By afternoon, the ships' barometers were rising again, and they thought they were out of the worst of it. But they were wrong. Soon the ships' bows were plunging into seas, and walls of green water were washing over decks. The task force was headed directly toward the center of the typhoon, which they now realized had been following them from the southeast. The falling barometer and a shift in wind direction meant they were in it.

Crews were ordered to lash down all moveable gear and to lower elevators on all ships. Helmsmen adjusted headings to place the ships in the trough of the seas and reduced speed to minimum. Still, they were not prepared for what would come. Soon winds increased to 80, 90, then 100 miles an hour. Seas rose to 70 feet. Some twenty vessels were caught in the worst part of the storm, and Halsey had no choice but to release them from formation so they might ride it out better. The carrier USS *San Jacinto* was among them. It was rolling 40 degrees and more. To see the wave crests, the men on board had to look *up*. Every time it rolled, its deck upended like a table, and everything not secured slid sideways. Aircraft broke loose and crashed into superstructures. In the confined spaces below, matters were worse. The hanger deck held ten of the heavier planes in two rows of five, lashed down. When the ship rolled, the weight of the planes began pulling the lines. One plane broke loose and slid into the one near it. The ship rolled again, and both planes careened across the deck, crashing into spare engines, belly tanks, and loading tractors. The ship rolled yet again, and the planes and wreckage smashed into the eight other planes. Soon enough, a mass of several tons of metal was sliding across the deck, which had been made slippery with spilled oil and gasoline. The planes shifted and slid again with every roll. Every now and then a wing or some heavy equipment would hit and rupture an outside bulkhead, and soon rain and seas flooded the deck. Flames and smoke appeared in the hanger, and the automatic sprinkling system was turned on. There were racks of machine gun ammunition stored on deck too, and as they were struck by debris or flames, one by one they began to explode.

Aboard nearby vessels, the situation was as bad or worse. Ships were very nearly capsizing. Decks were awash; winds and seas swept away lifeboats and davits. Men tried to secure gear that had gone adrift, but winds made it impossible. Switchboards and electrical machinery shorted out, and there were fires from short circuits. There was no electrical power, no lights, no radar, no radio. Engine rooms were flooded waist deep. Ship-to-ship communication was impossible, and even communication within vessels was difficult. All ships were rapidly taking on water.

By the time it was over, three destroyers, USS *Hull*, USS *Spence*, and USS *Monaghan*, had capsized and gone down with almost all hands. A cruiser, five aircraft carriers, and three destroyers suffered extensive damage. On three carriers, some 146 planes were lost or damaged beyond repair by fires or impact from when they broke loose. Many planes had simply been swept overboard. Seven hundred and ninety men had been lost or killed, and another eighty injured.

Following a court of inquiry, Admiral Chester W. Nimitz, commander in chief of the U.S. Pacific Fleet, observed that it was "the greatest loss that we have taken in the Pacific without compensatory return since the First Battle of Savo" in January 1942. For Nimitz, it was about hubris. Technology had given a false sense of invulnerability. But no battleship could defeat a storm. His "Pacific Fleet Confidential Letter" called for a renewed awareness of sea conditions and warned against overreliance on technology. The conclusions claimed there had been insufficient attention to lessons more than a hundred years old. Indeed, Halsey's weather observers had neglected a dictum impressed upon mariners by Henry Piddington: face the wind, and the storm's center will be roughly 110 degrees to the starboard.

In June 1945, Halsey and Kosco were unfortunate enough to

be with the Third Fleet when it was caught in the center of another typhoon. The flight deck of the carrier *Hornet* caved in, and seventy-six aircraft were destroyed. If Nimitz decried lack of seamanship, Halsey questioned the near absence of reconnaissance data. He later said, "I wish to state unequivocally that both in December 1944, and the June 1945, typhoons the weather warning service did not provide the accurate and timely information necessary to enable me to take evasive action." In the aftermath, the Pacific Fleet established new weather stations in the Caroline Islands and, as they were secured, Manila, Iwo Jima, and Okinawa.

Although news of the war captured the headlines, in fact hurricanes and typhoons had wreaked havoc throughout the 1940s. Halsey's typhoon was only the most recent example. The hurricane that hit south Texas on July 27 of the previous year—the same hurricane Duckworth had flown through—had left nineteen dead. In October 1944 a storm had approached the port of Mazatlán, Mexico. Professor Pablo Schiaffino was chief of the meteorological observatory there, and he had expected communication from a colleague at a weather station on Mariá Madre island. It never came. A later report stated, "No contact was made . . . and it is now believed that the station was completely destroyed and Señor Carbayal in charge of the station was killed." Forecasters, it seemed, could not even save themselves.

It was for these reasons that in December 1944, forecasters, mission planners, pilots, weather officers, and aerologists attended a conference in Washington to evaluate the state of the new art of airborne hurricane reconnaissance. There was considerable optimism. As recently as 1942, many had doubted that reconnaissance by aircraft was even feasible. Now, a mere two years later, it already proved itself worth the cost and effort. But recommending and authorizing reconnaissance was one thing. Actually flying into a storm and reconnoitering it in such a way as to assist forecasters was quite another. Forecasters needed two sets of data. To predict a hurricane's development, they needed to know atmospheric pressure at its core. Changes in pressure indicated whether the hurricane was gaining or losing strength. To predict a hurricane's path, they needed to know the exact position of the eye over the course of a few days. If a forecaster could fix a series of positions for the eye, he could plot a precise track of the storm's past course, which in turn would allow him to extrapolate its future course. The position of the eye would also enable him to estimate the overall diameter of the hurricane's winds.

To the uninitiated, a hurricane radar image is roughly circular. In fact, though, the eye is likely to be slightly off-center. Measured in clouds or the outer pressure boundary, the shape of the whole storm is amorphous and constantly shifting, a great skirt pulling in one edge, extending the opposite. In 1944 it was difficult to know which parts would be gone in a few hours and which parts would likely endure for the rest of its short life. This asymmetry was even more apparent if the measure was not clouds but wind speed. The focal point of the winds, the actual circulation center of the hurricane, was called the *wind eye*, and at any given moment in the life of any hurricane it was likely to be at a different position than the cloud eye. A meteorologist who knew the exact position of the wind eye could also determine the probable diameter of the hurricane as measured by the winds that would hit, say, the Texas coast. He would also know the location of the leading right quadrant.

The leading right quadrant is the most dangerous part of any hurricane, for several reasons. The winds themselves are strongest in that quadrant because it is where the hurricane's rotary motion is added to its forward motion. It is as though a boxer were throwing a right hook and moving forward at the same time. Hurricane winds of 100 miles an hour might, in that quadrant, gain 12 miles an hour in absolute speed. And because wind increases its force on an object with the square of its velocity, that extra 12 miles an hour would represent an increase in force not of 12 percent, but of 24 percent. Winds there would be almost a fourth again more powerful than winds in other parts of the storm.

Those winds, in turn, create a second danger. Over open ocean the height of a wave is determined for the most part by three factors: wind speed, length of time the wind has been blowing over the water, and "fetch," the distance the wind has been blowing over a straight path. The leading right quadrant is the place where two of these factors may reach their greatest possible development. The waves there are pushed by the strongest winds and are pushed for the longest time in the direction in which the storm is moving. So the leading right quadrant is likely to be where the hurricane's waves are highest. In an average hurricane, waves build to 35 or 40 feet, and in larger storms they can reach heights of 45 or 50 feet. If a 60-mile-an-hour wind were to blow for three days over a 1,500-mile fetch, the highest tenth of the waves produced would reach 100 feet. Such conditions, while rare, are quite possible in a hurricane—especially in its leading right quadrant.

By far the greatest danger presented by the leading right quadrant is a phenomenon called the *storm surge*. Piddington, who called it a "storm tide," explained its origins in a general way. His idea was that a mass of water was pulled above sea level by lowered atmospheric pressure, and when the water was confined within a bay or river mouth, that effect was increased. By 1944 his theory had been much embellished but remained essentially unchanged. The lowered pressure in the vicinity of a hurricane draws the surface beneath it upward. The force is substantial: an area of ocean surface might be drawn as much as 2 feet higher than the surrounding water into a dome or "hill" that might measure 50 miles across. If the storm reaches coastal waters, the surge may be drawn into shallows, and the water may rise farther, as much as 20 feet. At the same time, the breaking waves are driven with so much force that they create a landward-flowing surface current that moves faster than water can return seaward along the bottom.

Some surges crashed onto shorelands as a whole, causing flash flooding of coasts and destruction on a massive scale. In the first half of the twentieth century, more than three fourths of the deaths in any given hurricane were the result of the storm surge.

The combined effect of storm surge and unusually high waves is likely to be devastation. In 1886, Indianola, Texas, was destroyed so completely by a storm surge that it was never rebuilt. William Reid had described part of the Bermuda storm of 1839: it "carried boats into fields above the usual high water mark, and removed several rocks, containing by measurement twenty cubic feet, some of them bearing evidence of having been broken off from the beds on which they rested, by the surge." Isaac M. Cline, the Weather Bureau chief during the Galveston Hurricane in 1900 experienced a surge of 4 feet in a few seconds. He reported, "I was standing at my front door, which was partly open, watching the water which was flowing with great rapidity from east to west. The water at this time was about eight inches deep in my residence and the sudden rise of four feet brought it above my waist before I could change my position." The New England Hurricane of 1938 hit Long Island with a surge of 40 feet, higher than the low skyline of beach houses. A witness to the storm wave first believed it was a "thick and high bank of fog rolling in fast from the ocean. . . . When it came closer we saw that it wasn't fog. It was water."

At the conference in December 1944, all were aware of the necessity of identifying the probable size and position of the leading right quadrant. Among the possibilities discussed was a procedure for airborne reconnaissance. The idea was that an aircraft could identify the storm center, report the attending winds, and return to base, while another flight left, took another reading of the center, and so on. After a few such flights, meteorologists would have a series of data points from which they could derive a running track of the storm's course and from which they could extrapolate a future track. There seemed every reason to make the practice of reconnoitering the eye a standard procedure. But as the conference wore on, the participants became aware of a rather serious technical problem.

Air crews had learned to find the hurricane eye by using their compass and dead reckoning, by using previous estimates of its position, and by following the pressure altimeter. But once they were inside the eye, there was no sure way to determine their own position—and more importantly the *eye's* position—with regard to anywhere else. A sextant fix on stars was unlikely as no one thought it wise to fly a penetration mission at night. In daylight hours, getting a fix on the sun—visible only occasionally and against no real horizon—was difficult at best.

During the first years of hurricane reconnaissance, many techniques were attempted, but even eleven years after the Washington conference, no one had found a single foolproof means to determine the position of the eye. By 1955 there were, however, a set of partial solutions: astrodome, loran, radar, and the three instruments of dead reckoning—compass, airspeed indicator, and driftmeter.

It is ironic that Crew Five's navigators, the ones who had stations near no port or window, were the crewmen who were expected to know the plane's position at all times. Even if they had a view, they probably would have had no time to enjoy it. Greaney and Morgan were working continually, and their work was tremendously important. If the navigators did not know exactly where Snowcloud Five was, then when they located Janet's eye, they could not tell the staff in Miami exactly where *it* was, and in some part the mission would have failed.

There was another reason for Greaney and Morgan to be good at their work, a reason none of the crew cared to think about. If they had to ditch, the navigators would want to give Combs a chance to transmit as good a fix on their position as possible.

13

Approach

7:30 A.M. EST / 1230 Zulu

Snowcloud Five was over open ocean about an hour out from Gitmo. Jamaica was already behind them. Sitting at the radio station just aft the wing root, Joseph F. Combs, Aviation Electronics Man First Class, radioed the first position report.

If Windham and Herlong wanted to communicate with a tower themselves, they could select their own frequencies, and if they ran into interference, they might use the interphone to call back to Combs for another frequency. Once Snowcloud Five was airborne, though, signals came directly from Combs. Greaney and Morgan would give him position reports, which he transmitted to the Fleet Air Wing Eleven station in Jax. At regular intervals Buck would send a page of coded weather data through a messenger tube/clothesline rig. Combs would pull the tube from the line, open it, and then transmit the data to the Hurricane Forecast Center in Miami. Combs made both types of transmissions in Morse code, a method preferred over voice radio for two reasons: First, it was a faster way to transmit what the radiomen called "nonidiomatic character groupings"—that is, numbers and letters. Second, if the frequency shifted during a voice transmission, the words would be slurred and unintelligible, but key clicks could still get through.

A thick-set man in his thirties, Joe Combs was a likeable, friendly sort. His eyes bulged out a little, and people said he looked remarkably like the actor Ernest Borgnine. He and a sailor named Don James used to do a little freshwater fishing on weekends, mostly on the St. Johns River, near Jacksonville. It was a fitting avocation for a man who was nothing if not relaxed. Combs had a penchant for catching naps at every available opportunity, and crews took to calling him "Sleepy." The predisposition was far from unique, but Combs went one better. He did not need the wing root—he could nap sitting right at his station. Not that anyone ever suggested the habit interfered with his work; quite the contrary, he was regarded as a very good radioman, and he had managed to integrate the naps into his duties. Much as most people can hear their own name spoken softly against a solid wall of background noise, Combs could sleep right through all sorts of radio traffic, but when he heard his aircraft's call sign in the headphones—this was "5U93"—he would open his eyes, clear his throat, lean forward, and tap out the aircraft's position and heading.

Combs had flown with VP-23 in Miami, on PB4Y-2s, and had become the regular radioman with Bud Shipman when they commissioned VJ-2 in Jacksonville in 1952—the season of Hurricanes Baker, Charlie, and Fox. He was an old hand at hurricane hunting, and familiar with the difficulties of communication in the vicinity of violent weather.

In headphones *precipitation static* was a kind of white noise, and often it would increase until it drowned out all other sound. There was also a type of static caused by electrical phenomena like lightning strikes. It was atmospherics, the same phenomena that meteorologists once believed might allow them to track a storm. These caused the staccato bursts that the radiomen called "cracks." There were also silences—"nulls." The cracking, popping, and long silences could go on for more than an hour, and during that time all Combs could do was send transmissions and hope that somebody was receiving. Sometimes his only choice was to delay a transmission until static cleared, but on weather reconnaissance this solution was less than satisfactory. Hurricanes had been known to change course and intensity in a matter of hours, and the Hurricane Forecast Center in Miami needed to issue warnings as soon as possible. Every minute of delaying that transmission eroded its worth, and data sent hours after it was collected might well have been sent too late to do any good.

As long as a plane was in stable air, the radioman had no difficulty sending a message. But when the plane started bouncing, the vibrations caused variations in transmitter voltage. This was a real worry, as on VHF a drop below a certain voltage could render the radio inoperative. There was another difficulty. A radioman could have a hard time keying the message because his arm was shaking along with the aircraft. To steady his hand, one operator strapped his arm to the desk. Another radioman, informed of the solution, said he needed both arms just to hold on. An Army Air Force radio operator named Robert Matzke described his practical problems on a 1945 mission. He said, "No sooner [had we] left the ground when we encountered rain and turbulence." The receivers were noisy as the flight began, and he knew he would have to send transmissions blindly. As they neared the storm, the rain increased and the interior was getting "damp." There was a leak right over his table, a steady downpour of water, and he wrote with the log tablet braced against his knee to keep it from getting wet.

In 1955 reconnaissance aircraft were struck by lightning three times. Generally, aircraft are hit by a specific sort of lightning called a *cloud-to-cloud discharge*. The most frequent path is through one of the aircraft's long axes, from nose to tail or from wingtip to wingtip, and in most cases crews are at no risk, not directly at least. But there are indirect dangers, and one was of particular concern to Combs. Radio antennas can get damaged. It was true that the P2V had a great deal of built-in redundancy—there were several radios and several antennas—but a sufficiently powerful strike could render all of them inoperative, putting Combs out of work for the duration of the mission.

Although the crew was tired this morning, the mission was in daylight and they would encounter Janet within the hour. No one, not even Combs, was in the mood to sleep. Soon he was picking reports from Buck off the clothesline rig, and every few minutes there would be another.

In twenty or thirty minutes they could expect to feel her winds.

After Halsey's typhoon, Nimitz demanded that airborne hurricane reconnaissance begin immediately. Fortunately, the Navy had already had plans in the works that had grown out of the Washington conference. Beginning in June 1945 Navy crews flew weather reconnaissance daily, twice daily for typhoons. They called the missions "recco flights" or "reccos." From June through September 1945, the Navy flew one hundred such missions, an average of ten hours each. When the program began, no one was sure it would succeed, and for this reason, the hundredth mission was cause for some celebration. Perhaps it was best that they enjoyed success while they could. The next day—it was October 1—a recco flight departed for a typhoon over the South China Sea. It never returned.

Meanwhile, by war's end all the ground gained in weather reconnaissance was in danger of being lost. With the demobilization, pilots with hard experience flying through hurricanes, the *only* pilots with such experience, were returning to civilian life. The changes threatened to end reconnaissance of tropical storms in both the Pacific and the Atlantic. But the Navy acted swiftly, formalizing the training of pilots in weather reconnaissance. In 1945 a Hurricane Hunter school was established at Camp Kearney, California. The same year, the first tropical weather reconnaissance by aircraft started on a regular basis.

A patrol squadron operating from Naval Air Station Miami had nine PB4Y-2M's, and its primary mission had been tracking German submarines. Now it was given a secondary mission of hurricane reconnaissance, and for the first time such work was part of a squadron's ongoing duties. For half the year they patrolled waters off the coast for submarines. Then, a few weeks before hurricane season, maintenance crews spent a few days working over the planes. They pulled the two upper-deck turrets, removed armor plating and electronic countermeasures equipment, and in their place installed aerological instruments.

Meanwhile, the Navy worked to define the role of weather reconnaissance more precisely. There were many questions as to type of and number of missions, whether they should be coordinated with related duties, and so forth. There were reassignments of personnel and shifting of responsibilities. Finally, there was also the not-insignificant matter of names. Between 1945 and 1955, the squadron would be redesignated six times.[8] In 1952 the squadron was renamed Airborne Early Warning Squadron Four. It would be the last change. With this designation, 109 enlisted men, seven officers, and four aircraft were relocated from Miami, 300 miles north along the coast, to Naval Air Station Jacksonville.

Because two branches of the military had undertaken a duty

---

8. In 1945 the squadron was redesignated as Weather Reconnaissance Squadron Three (VPW-3), then in 1946 as Meteorological Squadron Three (VPM-3), and then Heavy Land Based Patrol Bomber Squadron Three (VP-HL3). By 1949 the squadron had become Patrol Squadron Twenty-three and had been relocated from Patuxent River, Maryland, to Naval Air Station Miami. By 1952, Patrol Squadron Twenty-Three was relieved of hurricane-hunting duties, and the weather personnel remaining at Naval Air Station Miami were made the core of a wholly new unit, Weather Squadron Two.

that overlapped, some conflict was inevitable. On September 18, 1947, an Air Force plane out of Bermuda penetrated the eye of a hurricane moving west-northwest to the south of the island. When they were in clear air, the crew saw a Navy Privateer circling the center, on its own reconnaissance. Shortly after, the Air Force made an official protest to the Joint Chiefs of Staff that said, "There is not sufficient room for two airplanes in the eye of the same hurricane." The chiefs agreed, and immediately there were new attempts to coordinate missions and divide responsibilities.

From 1945 to 1948 the methods of reconnaissance, for Navy and Air Force both, evolved considerably. The first crews did not follow Duckworth's example of careful entry into the storm. Their method was to fly straight in, and when turbulence became too severe, to turn 180 degrees and head out. More or less following Wood's recommendation to approach "gingerly," they would re-enter again and again at points around the periphery of the hurricane. They did not know that such missions were unnecessarily difficult, that they were flying in the most turbulent air. But those same missions found areas of milder winds. On one side of any given hurricane the strongest winds might lie in a belt perhaps 30 miles wide, and on the side opposite, in a belt perhaps only 10 miles wide. Crews began to call this the "soft spot." In the Northern Hemisphere the soft spot was the trailing left quadrant, and for a hurricane that was moving due west, it was also the southeast quadrant. The discovery was fortunate, especially because the policy of both the Air Force and the Navy, recognizing that a reasonably accurate fix of the hurricane's position could come only by locating the eye itself, required full penetrations. For the first Navy missions, the reconnaissance technique was "low-level penetration" at 200 to 800 feet over the water.

Within hurricanes winds circle the center at different speeds. The area of the winds was judged to be important, and in 1948 the policy was modified slightly. Some flights circumnavigated the storm in a counterclockwise direction on the 74-mile-an-hour wind circle, trying to define the outer fringes of the band of hurricane-force winds.

By 1950 the Navy had refined the technique into a standard flight profile. Their PB4Y-2 Privateers proceeded to and from the area of the hurricane at normal flight altitudes. The Hurricane Forecast Center sometimes asked them to observe specific areas around the storm, a developing low, for instance. When they encountered the hurricane itself, they circumnavigated it, either completely or partially, at the 74-mile-an-hour wind circle. Then they entered the storm through the trailing left quadrant.

The altitude of that entry was a matter of some concern. Turbulence below 300 feet could get bad enough to slam a plane into the sea. But a hurricane's rain bands began above 700 feet, and a crew flying through them would have difficulty seeing the water below. Reliable radar altimeters would not be available for several years, and a crew needed to see the water in order to avoid flying into it. So they flew in the clear air at an intermediate altitude. Once they had gained the eye, they circled at a few hundred feet, for as long as it took the aerologist to obtain his data. They exited in roughly the same direction they had entered, give or take a few degrees. Then they made their way out through the back side of the storm, keeping the wind on the starboard beam until they were clear of the worst of it.

The Air Force developed a slightly different technique, suited to its concern with conditions aloft. Their B-25s entered and departed the eye at about 8,000 feet and rarely descended below 2,000 feet. They entered from the trailing left quadrant, and maintaining the same heading, they flew directly through the eye and into the leading right quadrant. When they reached the storm's periphery, they turned left, flew counterclockwise along its leading edge for about 45 degrees (it was a slow turn a few hundred miles long), then turned left again and flew into the storm, straight through the eye and out through the rain bands again to the storm's trailing edge. They called it "slicing the pie," and they might do it six or seven times at 8,000 feet and six or seven more at 14,000 feet. An overhead diagram of their paths would look like the outline of a three-leaf clover.

In the years when hurricane reconnaissance became routine, there had been considerable advances in tropical climatology and specific developments in the field of *cyclogenesis*—that is, how a hurricane is formed. The meteorologists who had advocated the existence of a "tropical front" had seen their ideas overturned. They had asserted that the tropical front appeared in the boundary between the trade winds and the wide belt of air currents around the equator, called the *Intertropical Convergence Zone.* But Herbert Riehl and others at the Institute of Tropical Meteorology observed that many tropical storms began farther north, in the latitudes of the trade winds. Advocates of the so-called tropical front had modeled it on the temperate fronts discovered by Vilhelm Bjerknes. The problem was that Bjerknes's fronts marked boundaries between two masses of air that had different temperatures, pressures, and moisture content. But the tropical fronts separated nothing like this. In fact, there was nothing to separate, as the Intertropical Convergence Zone and the trade winds were essentially the same great mass of air.

The belief in the existence of tropical fronts was born of a misconception, and it had serious consequences. Some claimed that the reason Halsey's typhoon went unnoticed is that Kosco was trained to look for fronts and so did not recognize that tropical cyclogenesis observed different rules. In 1945 a standard meteorological handbook was revised to include the caveat "Although organized systems of bad weather in the tropics resemble the fronts of the temperate zone (marked by rain, wind shifts, cloud sequences, and sometimes temperature oscillations), they behave in a manner quite unpredictable by the usual rules for high-latitude forecasting."

By the 1950s meteorologists knew that tropical fronts, as such, did not exist. There were, however, other signs of developing storms. The best indicators were the phenomena called *easterly waves*. Early in his career Gordon Dunn had noticed a series of areas of falling and rising atmospheric pressure moving east to west. He found that almost every day from June through September a great trough of low pressure moved slowly across some part of the Caribbean. The eastern Caribbean could expect two waves to pass every week.

A lot of flights during the early 1950s were "investigative" reconnaissance expeditions sent to look for disturbances in easterly waves and associated indicators—squalls, a sufficient fall in pressure, and a certain type of cloud. Most rainfall in the tropics comes in the form of showers and scattered thundershowers from cumuliform clouds. When crews saw a variation in this pattern to, say, steady rainfall from solid altostratus or cirrostratus clouds, they had reason to suspect that a storm was already forming.

*

For several hundred years the Spanish named Caribbean hurricanes after the saint's day on which the hurricane occurred—the "Santa Ana" hurricane of 1825, the "San Felipe" of 1876, and so on. Because it was rare for two hurricanes to present a threat simultaneously, no one thought it necessary to name a hurricane during its existence. The only ones who needed to differentiate among storms were historians. However, on Labor Day Weekend of 1950, three storms were on the map at once—two in the Atlantic, one in the eastern Gulf of Mexico. The first to name them were the first to see them—the reconnaissance crews. They called the smallest one the "Baby." It was a hurricane that crossed western Cuba and moved up the west coast of Florida. They called the larger one the "Great Atlantic Hurricane," because it was discovered in that ocean and no one thought there was any danger of confusing it with the storm of 1944. They called the third hurricane "Crew Six's storm" after the crew that was working it out of Guantánamo Bay. The designations were ad hoc and seemed workable in the short term. But because the names would make little sense to anyone outside the small community of weather reconnaissance crews, meteorologists identified the same storms by their position. Of course, those positions were changing. In the days that followed there was considerable confusion among pilots, forecasters, and those issuing public advisories. Clearly there was a problem.

The agencies involved met in early 1951 to develop a common system of naming. Some thought was given to using numbers or letters, but both were deigned too confusing, and in voice communications the sounds of letters could be difficult to distinguish. Besides, it had been tried. In the early twentieth century some meteorologists identified storms by the latitude and longitude at which they were first reported. The practice had confused matters by adding numbers to reports already full of numbers, and was judged a failure. So in 1951 the agencies decided to adopt the military's phonetic alphabet—Able, Baker, Charlie, and so on. It worked and was used again for the 1952 season. By that time though, a new international alphabet (Alfa, Bravo, Coca, and so on) had come into widespread use, and some agencies used the new alphabet, while others continued to use the old one. Once again, concerned parties met. They decided that for the 1953 season, they would adopt an entirely new system.

No one was quite sure where the idea of using women's names originated, but there were several precedents. In the last years of the nineteenth century, Australians were educated and amused by the antics of a meteorologist named Clement Wragge. He was a popular speaker who would arrive at lecture halls so well lubricated that some began to call him "Inclement." Wragge began a practice of naming mid-latitude storms after politicians who had earned his disfavor. He might say, "Nasty weather expected from this one," and describe another as "wandering aimlessly in mid-ocean." But he reserved women's names for hurricanes or, as the storms are termed in the antipodes, *willy-nillys*. In the 1930s a meteorologist for Pan-Am followed Wragge's lead and named a typhoon "Chloe." In George R. Stewart's 1941 novel *Storm,* a forecaster names a hurricane "Maria," and during World War II, some Air Force and Navy meteorologists stationed in the Pacific named typhoons after their girlfriends and wives.

Whatever its origin, the use of women's names seemed eminently reasonable. They were easily pronounced, easily understood, and easily remembered. But the practice was not without controversy even in 1955, and when forecasters were called on it, they responded that like women, every hurricane is different, they are generally unpredictable, and they can make men feel small and inconsequential.[9]

For most Americans, the whole business was the stuff of a few short newspaper "filler" pieces, and that was it. But for the weather reconnaissance squadron at Jax, the new nomenclature changed the way men talked about missions. It was a place and a time where discussions of gender could be less than delicate. In 1950, some men had grumbled that there were lots of things they would rather penetrate than a hurricane, but it ended there. The phonetic alphabet of 1951 and 1952 did little to alter the discussion, as no one wanted to say, for instance, he had "penetrated Charlie." But the same verb juxtaposed to a woman's name changed everything. Suddenly, squadron comedians had before them a world of possibilities.

In those years, crews saw a number of severe storms, and there was a whole repertoire of stories—dramatic, humorous, and bizarre—enough to fill a bookshelf.

---

9. Names of particularly devastating hurricanes—1954's Carol, Edna, and Hazel—were retired. In 1979 the World Meteorological Association began naming hurricanes after men as well.

Most people have never heard of some of the worst storms because they never hit land. The only ones who knew they existed at all were a few meteorologists and the hurricane reconnaissance crews. In 1952 Bud Shipman had flown a Privateer into Hurricane Fox. It was a small storm, only 5 miles across the eye—it seemed to him almost an oversized tornado. When the aircraft broke into the eye, the crew saw birds, thousands of them. Seagulls had been known to stay within the eye for the entire life of a hurricane, and certain tropical species had ridden the air within that oasis for a thousand miles, finding themselves becalmed, a week after they began their unwilling trip, in the cold air off Newfoundland. But no one had seen numbers like this. Birds were hitting the airplane. Shipman decided it was too dangerous and to get out before the reconnaissance was complete. They made it through the eyewall again, but by then a bird had been pulled into the air intake. To a man, they believed they were lucky to have made it back. It was, Shipman said, a "helluva ride."

In the third week of October 1950, a hurricane was tracking north to Miami. Its maximum winds were clocked at 105 miles an hour. Patrol Squadron Twenty-Three was there. The base commander decided to keep his planes, Privateers, where they were needed. The sky darkened, and the commander ordered that the planes stay grounded but that they be "weathervaned." Two-man crews boarded the aircraft, aimed them into the wind with engines running at full throttle, and rode the brakes. For three hours they sat in the cockpits while engines idled and control surfaces shook and strained against lashing wind and rain. Metal trash cans flew past, fallen power lines sparked, and the tower reported wind velocities of 90 miles per hour. The crews shouted jokes to each other about formation flying on the ground, but it was anything but easy. At any moment a sudden downdraft could push a wing against the tarmac or slam one plane into another. They needed to be far more alert than they would be at altitude. And so by midnight the men were near exhaustion and they were still "flying." Then, without warning, the wind died. Tired and wet, crews fell out of the planes and walked wearily into their barracks. Meanwhile, another group of pilots began the second watch. Everybody knew it was not over. Now they were in the eye of the storm, and when the winds returned they would be from the south, behind the Privateers. It was a long night. By morning most of the aircraft were so badly damaged as to be unflyable.

In those same years a sort of subculture developed among the men who hunted hurricanes. The crews themselves seemed to regard the missions casually, and they might have talked about a given hurricane season as though it were an ongoing game of pick-up basketball. The Navy and Air Force squadrons cultivated a healthy rivalry, much of which revolved around an old ice skating shoe bronzed and mounted on a small plaque. It was bestowed on the crew judged to have flown the fewest missions, and it was called the "Hans Brinker Award," a reference to their having "skated" through the season. The award was a joshing reminder to weather reconnaissance crews that through no cause of their own, the contingencies of fate and atmosphere had, this season, conspired to let them stay home. It was also a subtle reminder that others, not so blessed, would enjoy no recognition whatsoever.

In 1950 the Navy crews formed an organization they termed the "Century Club." Membership was granted to anyone who had been on an aircraft in a storm with winds of over 100 knots. The associated certificate was a piece of paper entitled "Not So Ancient Order of the Hurripooners," and it was full of ornate language, or at least some Navy copyrighter's idea of ornate language: "Know ye men by all these presents that [insert name of initiate] . . . is hereby designated a member of the honoured and illustrious group comprising this organization and is entitled to all the rights and privileges afforded to those aeronauts who repeatedly risk their lives that others may be forwarned." It was hand-lettered and framed by drawings resembling those on the borders of sixteenth-century engravings—clouds, mermaids, an angry-looking Aeolus or Boreas—intermingled with drawings of storm warning flags, a Super Connie, and a P2V.

The plaque and the skating shoe might be said to represent a small part of a whole secret history. There were drinking stories of crews too inebriated to fly, allowed to board their planes only after they were force-fed coffee and held in the propeller wash for an hour. There were stories of curious figures like Second Class Steward's Mate Walter Lee Sutton, who claimed to have seen action in half the major battles in the war and had talked his way into the good graces of admirals and heads of state alike. There were stories of crews returning from halfway across the Atlantic on one engine, of navigators or chief mechanics knocked unconscious, of broken arms wrapped in life jackets.

And so in the first half of the 1950s, weather reconnaissance missions took men close to death almost routinely, and in the service of citizens who knew very little about them. But nothing in the behavior of the crews suggested they considered themselves heroes. Quite the contrary, the skating shoe and the plaque had about them an air of self-mockery. It was an interesting attitude, well within the tradition of cultures confronted with regular and powerful storms. Boastfulness and pride tempt fate. Whatever their history, whatever their accomplishments, there would be no hubris within the ranks of weather reconnaissance.

14

The Law of Storms

Traditional weather forecasting—that is, all that happened before 1920—was in some ways subjective, and as far as many meteorologists were concerned, therein lay its failure. One of Vilhelm Bjerknes's great accomplishments was his realization that a more mathematical method was possible. But Bjerknes's own method was not *strictly* mathematical, as it employed graphical analysis. Some intuition, some subjectivity, was necessary to make the translation from raw data to weather chart. The first attempt to design a *purely* mathematical means of weather prediction was undertaken in the 1930s by an Englishman named Lewis Fry Richardson. In retrospect, that the first such effort would come from such a man is understandable. Anyone less eccentric might have known better than even to try.

Britain in the nineteenth century knew few scientists in the sense we understand the term today. Papers and conferences were written by gentlemen like William Redfield and James Espy who took up studies of natural phenomena in the interests of what was called "natural philosophy." By the second decade of the twentieth century, the generalist was a rare species, but by no means extinct. Lewis Richardson was one such person. Meteorology had long fascinated him, and for several years he corresponded with Bjerknes. Richardson believed that mathematical methods might be applied directly to the problem of weather prediction by a method called *numerical process*. There had been some recent developments in the field. A Swiss mathematician named Leonhard Euler, for instance, had derived a set of equations for wind velocity, pressure, and temperature.

By 1913 Richardson had secured a position as superintendent of a meteorological and magnetic observatory administered by the British Meteorological Office. In August 1914, he said he was "torn between an intense curiosity to see war at close quarters and an intense objection to killing people, both mixed with ideas of public duty [and] doubt as to whether I could endure danger." In May 1916, he joined the Friends' Ambulance Unit. The physical inconveniences of war did little to deter him from developing his ideas on paper. Often, he would work nights "on a heap of hay in a cold wet rest billet." Although Richardson took great care to protect a lengthening manuscript, for several months it was lost. Almost by chance it was found under a pile of coal near an encampment in Belgium and returned to him. In 1922 Cambridge University Press published it as *Weather Prediction by Numerical Process*.

The experiment the book described began with the most complete meteorological record that existed. It involved a set of conditions for May 20, 1910, at 6 A.M. EDT, described in Bjerknes's *Dynamical Meteorology and Hydrology*. From this record Richardson formulated a six-hour ex post facto prediction for a part of Western Europe, then compared that prediction to records of the weather that had actually transpired.

His forecasting method was to lay an imaginary grid over a map of Western Europe and the British Isles. Its squares were about 100 miles on a side. Each square represented a "cell" of five layers of atmosphere. For each layer of each cell he developed algorithms that accounted for solar radiation, cloud cover, evaporation of ocean water, falling and rising air masses, wind, and Coriolis forces. He also accounted for effects on adjacent cells. Calculating the effects of all these measurements would be an almost impossibly complex task—beyond the abilities of six thousand human computers, by his own estimate. So he simplified matters by reducing the initial grid from an area stretching from the Mediterranean nearly to the Arctic Circle to a region that covered only Germany and part of Switzerland. Moreover, he chose to predict only two characteristics: momentum and atmospheric pressure for two adjacent cells. But even this represented a great deal of work, and two months later he had formulated a prediction of wind speed for one region and atmospheric pressure for a region immediately to its south. At the centers of half the cells, Richardson recorded measurements of temperature, air pressure, and humidity. At the centers of the rest, he recorded "components of momentum"—that is, overall mass and velocity of the air masses. He began with the data for a large area, and at each time step he narrowed the area of inference to two adjoining cells.

Richardson's after-the-fact six-hour forecast had predicted a number of changes, the most dramatic of which was an increase in atmospheric pressure: an improbable 145 millibars. The forecast was at striking variance from the record: in actual fact, during those six hours there was practically no change in atmospheric pressure. Richardson acknowledged the error but determined that there would have *been* no change except for the presence of an unusual convergence of high-altitude winds in a region from which no measurements had been taken. In the 1920s weather balloons and cloud movements offered some sense of wind speed and direction at altitudes, but of all the characteristics of the cells in question, Richardson could be certain only of atmospheric pressure. The limits of his knowledge were determined not by mathematics or even technology, but by a relative paucity of initial data.

Despite the obvious failure of the exercise it described, *Weather Prediction by Numerical Process* was well received. At the time many publications in natural science posited theories or collected observations of specific phenomena. Here was something so different as to be nearly a shock. No rough theory, this was something closer to a manual for weather prediction, with supporting rationale and—most astonishingly—a detailed model. The book was admired for the audacity and diligence of its author, and for its frank self-evaluation. It was admired as well for a calculus that tolerated approximations, its assertion that numerical prediction was possible, and a conclusion that significant improvements in forecasting could not come without better initial measurements. More than half a century later, meteorologist Philip Duncan Thompson would call Richardson's work a "glorious failure."

Richardson himself was quite aware of the absence of any means by which useful predictions might be made. With tongue at least partly in cheek, he described a rather grandiose vision: a "weather factory," an enormous organization of specialized human computers working in a great amphitheater and directed by a conductor who sat on a raised pulpit, directing procedures and communicating information by telegraph, pneumatic tubes, and flashing red and blue lights.[10]

---

10. Richardson's description of the imagined place, included in *Weather Prediction by Numerical Process*, is astonishingly detailed:

A large hall like a theatre, except the circles and galleries go right round through the space usually occupied by the stage. The walls of this chamber are painted to form a map of the globe. The ceiling represents the north polar regions, England is in the gallery, the tropics in the upper circle. . . . A myriad of computers are at work upon the weather part of the map where each sits, but each computer attends only to one equation or part of an equation. The work of each region is coordinated by an official of higher rank. Numerous little "night signs" display the instantaneous values so that neighboring computers can read them. Each number is thus displayed in three adjacent zones so as to maintain communication to the North and South on the map. From the floor of the pit a tall pillar rises to half the

Richardson would continue to perform meteorological research, especially in the area of turbulence. In some ways he understood that his work was ahead of his time. His introduction to *Weather Prediction by Numerical Process* defined the book as a prelude, and offered a wistful prediction: "Perhaps some day in the dim future it will be possible to advance the computation faster than the weather advances and at a cost less than the saving to mankind due to the information gained. But that is a dream." The dream was not as distant as he might have suspected. But its ultimate realization would arise from a different realm of human endeavor entirely.

In 1837 Joseph Henry was first secretary of the Smithsonian Institution and overseer of the Smithsonian Meteorological Project. He had participated in the storm controversy in the 1830s as an outspoken supporter of James Espy. In the 1830s and 1840s, he was one of several American meteorologists who visited Europe to exchange and promote ideas. During a two-month visit in the spring of 1837, he visited Charles Babbage. Babbage was the Lucasian professor of mathematics at the University of Cambridge. He had drawn up schematics with which he hoped to construct a mechanical calculator.

---

height of the hall. It carries a large pulpit on its top. In this sits the man in charge of the whole theatre; he is surrounded by several assistants and messengers. One of his duties is to maintain a uniform speed of progress in all parts of the globe. In this respect he is like the conductor of an orchestra in which the instruments are slide-rules and calculating machines. But instead of waving a baton he turns a beam of rosy light upon any region that is running ahead of the rest, and a beam of blue light upon those who are behindhand.

Four senior clerks in the central pulpit are collecting the future weather as fast as it is being computed, and dispatching it by pneumatic carrier to a quiet room. There it will be coded and telephoned to the radio transmitting station.

In a neighboring building there is a research department, where they invent improvements. But there is much experimenting on a small scale before any change is made in the complex routine of the computing theatre. In a basement an enthusiast is observing eddies in the liquid lining of a large bowl, but so far the arithmetic proves the better way. In another building are all the financial, correspondence and administrative offices. Outside are playing fields, houses, mountains and lakes, for it was thought that those who compute the weather should breathe of it freely.

Even in the first half of the nineteenth century, mechanical calculators were nothing new. In fact, they had a surprisingly long history. In 1623 Wilhelm Schickard of Tubingen produced a set of drawings for a wooden device he called a "calculating clock." Blaise Pascal built the first mechanical adding machine in 1642, and it was based on a design described by Hero of Alexandria. (The basic principle is used today in water meters and odometers.) And in 1673 German mathematician Gottfried Wilhelm Liebniz built a "stepped reckoner" that could add, subtract, multiply, and divide. By the early 1800s many designs had become copied and embellished.

But Babbage's design represented a leap far beyond any of them. He realized that many long computations consisted of operations that were repeated regularly. His design was for a machine that would do these operations automatically. He called it the "Difference Engine" because it would compute tables of numbers according to the method of finite differences. With funding from the British government, Babbage produced a prototype of the machine in 1822, and in the following year he started work on the full machine, with a twenty-decimal capacity designed to compute tables. It was intended to be steam-powered.

During the mid-1830s Babbage abandoned the uncompleted Difference Engine and developed plans for an improved version. He called it the "Analytical Engine." It would perform any arithmetical operation on the basis of instructions from punched cards, a memory unit, and sequential control. It was more than a mere calculator; it was a true computer. A calculator can tell you what *is*—that two plus two equals four. But a computer can tell you what, under certain conditions, *would* be—that if x is 1, y is 2, but if x is 3, then y is 4. A computer, in other words, can accommodate conditional elements and branching paths.

Although Babbage constructed prototypes and assembled parts for the machine, its actual construction was prohibitively expensive, and the British government refused to continue

Babbage's funding. Finally, neither of Babbage's machines were built, and the designs themselves were forgotten until Babbage's unpublished notebooks were discovered in 1937.

But in 1837 Babbage showed Joseph Henry the completed part of the Difference Engine. Henry imagined an application to the understanding of weather, noting, "It will also be of great use in calculating the mean results of astronomical and meteorological observations." At least momentarily, Henry glimpsed a world in which mechanical calculations were called into the service of weather forecasting. His notion, if it was even that, was stillborn. It would be more than a hundred years before anyone would seriously consider the possibility again.

By the 1930s there were great advances in calculating machines, much of it in the United States. Vannevar Bush at MIT had designed the "Difference Analyzer," a machine the size of a large table, composed of levers and gears. It was the first analogue computer, a machine that could solve equations with up to eighteen variables. In some sense it was the realization of Babbage's Analytical Engine. It was designed, in fact, to solve differential equations—that is, equations with two variables, the second dependent on the first.

The Difference Analyzer could create models of many physical phenomena, among them, the flight characteristics of projectiles. During World War II these characteristics were of tremendous practical importance. A long-range gunner could not see what he was firing at. To aim a gun, he depended on "firing tables," a set of numbers determined by wind speed and direction, humidity, and atmospheric pressure. Tables were developed for every new gun and every new shell, and a gun was next to useless without them. A single set of tables for a given gun might take months to develop. Most of the work for the Army's firing tables—test-firings and formulae—was performed at the Ballistics Research Laboratory at the Army's Aberdeen Proving Ground in Maryland. A team of civil service employees called "computers" used mechanical desk calculators—large machines with typewriter keys and a crank handle to pull after each operation.

In 1943 Aberdeen was falling behind. Firing tables were not being prepared fast enough, and guns could not be aimed. More employees were hired, and still they were behind. Meanwhile, two professors of engineering, John Mauchly and Presper Eckert, had a better idea. They wanted to make the Difference Analyzer electronic, replacing its gears with counters driven with electrical pulses. To Lieutenant Herman Goldstine, it seemed the solution, and on April 9, 1943, Mauchly, Eckert, and Goldstine delivered a formal proposal to the directors of the Army's Ballistics Research Laboratory. They told the committee that mechanical calculating machines were slow, that a single misaligned gear was likely to render the results inaccurate. The computer they imagined would use electrical pulses. They argued that the concept of an electronic computer was not particularly radical, merely a logical and modest development of existing technology.

The men were never allowed to finish their presentation—not because it had been unpersuasive, but because in the opinion of the committee they were wasting time selling the idea when they should be building the machine. Mauchly and Eckert were awarded a contract of $61,700 for the construction of an "Electric Numerical Integrator." In time the words "and Computer" would be appended to that name, and even before construction was begun, the Army began to call it ENIAC. The machine's vitals were impressive. It was housed in forty cabinets, each 9 feet tall. Together they weighed 30 tons and occupied nearly 1,800 square feet. They contained several miles of wiring, and required 174 kilowatts of power to operate. But they worked, and for the Army's purposes, worked extremely well. A human required twenty hours to calculate a missile trajectory, and the Differential Analyzer took fifteen minutes. But ENIAC needed only thirty seconds. Unfortunately for the Army's purposes, it was not ready before the war's end.

What John Mauchly did not mention during his proposal in 1943 was that he was interested in possibilities he considered far more interesting than firing tables. Mauchly had developed a theory that rainfall occurred at regular, or at least predictable, intervals and amounts. But there were so many rainfall reports and water tables—in short, so much raw data—that workers using desk calculators would take months just to organize them. He had realized years earlier that a machine like ENIAC might be used to do exactly that.

Quite independently of Mauchly, by 1946 another scientist had become interested in numerical weather prediction, and he was a scientist with far more political influence. John von Neumann had been a professor of mathematics at the Institute for Advanced Study in Princeton, New Jersey, since 1933. In 1937 he was a consultant to the Ballistics Research Laboratory. Von Neumann had no inherent fascination with rain and wind. Rather, he was interested in weather prediction as a mathematical challenge. It was the most complex, interactive nonlinear problem imaginable, and it had the added virtue of being real. On May 8, 1946, he wrote a proposal to the Navy's Office of Research and Inventions for "an investigation of the theory of dynamic meteorology in order to make it accessible to high-speed, electronic, digital, automatic computing, of a type which is beginning to be available." Under grants from the Weather Bureau, the Navy, and the Air Force, he assembled a group of theoretical meteorologists at the Institute for Advanced Study. If regional weather prediction proved feasible, von Neumann planned to move on to the extremely ambitious problem of simulating the entire atmosphere. This, in turn, would allow the modeling of climate.

Lewis Richardson's dream of numerical weather forecasting was actually within reach. But there were practical problems. In the fall of 1949, the machine the group intended to use—what they were calling the "Princeton Machine"—was far from operational.

With von Neumann's influence, they gained access to ENIAC. The group's model, like Richardson's, divided the atmosphere into a set of grid cells and employed finite difference methods to solve differential equations numerically. The forecasts, covering North America, used a two-dimensional grid with 270 points, the distance between each point representing 1,100 miles. In March 1950 the programming began. They operated the machine manually, using a plugboard and a bank of keys. They worked in shifts, twenty-four hours a day for thirty-three days. In April 1950 the first work was finished, and the results looked good. They had made two separate twenty-four-hour forecasts. The second especially was better than they had expected. It had been made from a synoptic map of the Northern Hemisphere on January 31, 1949, and the "large-scale features" were forecast correctly. But they had some distance to go before they could put the program to actual use. The program had made a twenty-four-hour prediction, and it had taken exactly twenty-four hours to run.

The calculations fed to ENIAC had been based on a model with several deficiencies, two of which were especially worrisome: the model did not allow for the intensification of circulation centers, and it did not allow for centers to form where none had existed. For these reasons there was a rush to develop "baroclinic" models—that is, models whose vertical structure was simple enough that equations could be solved without overtaxing the computers, but sophisticated enough that they could simulate the intensification and birth of circulation centers. Between 1951 and 1953 six such models were proposed, and two were tested against real cases, with mixed results. There was a general expectation that better models and more computational power would be available soon. By 1952 four research groups were giving attention to the subject.

In April 1953, Reichelderfer, still the Weather Bureau chief, submitted a paper to the Joint Meteorological Committee outlining a plan by which numerical methods could be applied. On July 1, 1954, the Joint Numerical Weather Prediction Unit was established, and true to its name, it was jointly staffed, financed, and supported by the Weather Bureau and the forecasting agencies of the Air Force and Navy. In 1954 the code used to program the models for forecasting was written for and tested on an IBM-701 at IBM's New York headquarters. The machine had an electrostatic memory of 2,048 words of 36 binary bits each. It had an addition time of 60 microseconds, a multiplication time of 456 microseconds, and it could make 10,000 numerical operations every second. A simple weather prediction required 72,000 arithmetic operations per "time step"—that is, for every one-hour advance of the clock. A twelve-hour prediction, requiring 864,000 operations, could be accomplished in 35 seconds.

The first machine-run forecasts were made on May 6, 1955. The programmers began with simplified atmospheric models much like those Richardson had used. The forecasts were made on pressure charts for three levels of the atmosphere, predicted forty-eight hours in advance. Routine numerical prediction began on May 15. The results were decidedly mixed: the accuracy was little better than that of subjective forecasts. It had become clear that the longer the forecast period, the less the computer model resembled the atmosphere it purported to represent. The reason, most believed, was that the data grid was "coarse." It simply could not model the smaller influences. They had been stopped by the same problem that had bedeviled Tannehill and Richardson—a paucity of initial data, especially at higher altitudes.

Meteorologists work with two types of errors. Every meteorological instrument is accurate within a certain tolerance called the *instrument error*, a result of the design and of the conditions in which it operates. A mercury barometer for surface pressure measurements has an expected instrument error of about 0.25 millibars for a single reading, due to the effects of ambient temperature and wind. There is another type of error, in some ways more difficult to correct. It is called the error of *representativeness*. Any observation network is composed of stations at spaced intervals. If a storm lies between stations, it will be invisible to the network. If it lies directly over a station, it will be mistaken as a larger phenomenon than it actually is.

In 1955 several meteorologists were beginning to suspect that Bjerknes and Richardson were wrong, or at least that their faith in numerical processes was misplaced. They thought that the atmosphere was a system too vast and too complex to be quantified and modeled, that the error of representativeness would ensure that meteorological predictions would always fall short. Imagine meteorographs able to measure pressure, humidity, wind speed, and direction. Place them on the nodes of a grid, a foot apart. Spread the grid over the earth, from pole to pole, over continents and oceans alike. Extend it upward into the third dimension for 50 or 60 miles, all the way to the edge of the stratosphere. Now, imagine a computer that could understand and interpret data from all the meteorographs simultaneously, and then use it to create models of future behavior. Together, this would seem to be a system that could predict weather reliably and accurately. But it would be imperfect for the simple reason that the resulting data grid would be too "coarse." In the cubic foot of air between the meteorographs, slight fluctuations in temperature, air pressure, and humidity would develop and grow. In a few days phenomena that the system could not have predicted—a current of air, a temperature difference between air masses—would appear. These would in turn generate larger effects—a breeze, a small cloud—which in turn would produce still larger effects—a low-pressure area over the Indian Ocean, a snowstorm over western Canada—until, two weeks later, the weather map of the entire earth would bear no resemblance to the original prediction. So although a kind of crude long-range forecasting would be feasible—the location of the jet stream a month in advance, for instance—it would forever be impossible to predict weather more than a few days ahead.

Among those who posited a limit to weather predictability was a meteorologist named Jules Charney. Charney was something of a visionary, and he was one of the team that had worked on ENIAC's weather forecasting program. Like the others who suspected a limit, he attributed it to lack of data, an error of *representativeness*. But Charney described the problem with a different vocabulary. He said that weather prediction posed difficulties in the "parameterization of turbulent processes."

By evoking the phenomenon of turbulence, Charney had recast the problem in a rather different light, one that brought its inherent problems into sharp relief. Quantifying and even defining turbulence was famously difficult. The physicist Richard Feynman called turbulence "the most important unsolved problem of classical physics." In 1932 the British physicist Horace Lamb, in an address to the British Association for the Advancement of Science, is reported to have remarked, "I am an old man now, and when I die and go to heaven there are two matters on which I hope for enlightenment. One is quantum electrodynamics, and the other is the turbulent motion of fluids. About the former I am rather optimistic."

The study of turbulence is part of the larger field of fluid dynamics, the study of the motion of all liquids and gases. Turbulence is made of eddies, areas of swirling fluid continually forming and breaking down, moving randomly within the fluid's overall direction of motion. Turbulence is everywhere in daily experience and fascinates scientists and nonscientists alike, yet it is notoriously difficult to predict or quantify. Some of its characteristics are obvious. Generally speaking, eddies or whirls are formed easily in a less viscous, "thinner" medium and are inhibited by a more viscous, "thicker" medium.

Suppose we could stir a variety of fluids with precisely the same amount of force—for instance, using a set of kitchen blenders on the same setting. Suppose too that we had a way to make the eddies within those fluids visible, perhaps by using a "tracer" of suspended dark particles that moved with the fluid. We would see that a given volume of lightweight oil shows more eddies than does the same volume of water. The water, in turn, shows more eddies than does honey. Each of these fluids would show eddies on several scales, and the lower limit, the size of the smallest eddies, would be determined by the fluid's thickness. Lewis Richardson, in a summary of his 1920 article "The Supply of Energy from and to Atmospheric Eddies," put it more lyrically:

> *Big[ger] whirls have little whirls,*
> *That feed on their velocity;*
> *And little whirls have lesser whirls,*
> *And so on to viscosity.*

The single feature of turbulence that is striking even to the casual observer is that its onset is not gradual but sudden. As water emerges from the tap, the flow is smooth and more or less straight (*laminar*, in the language of fluid dynamics). One might expect that there would be a little turbulence, then farther along a bit more, still farther along a bit more—a kind of gradual and steady increase. But turbulence does not happen this way. Instead, the flow begins straight, but a few inches farther along its path, quite suddenly, it becomes very confused. Likewise, a stream of smoke rising from a smoldering match into still air is, for a short distance of a foot or two above the match, steady and straight. Then rather suddenly the flow becomes wildly turbulent. The reason is that at low speeds, viscous forces inhibit a fluid's tendency toward turbulence, but when fluid exceeds a certain speed—call it a *threshold speed*—its momentum overcomes the inhibiting forces.

What, we may ask, determines this speed? Put another way, why does the flow of water become turbulent at that precise distance from the tap? Why does the stream of smoke break suddenly into whirls and eddies at that particular height? These are fairly difficult questions, and they are answered by a set of equations that were discovered independently, more than 150 years ago, by a French engineer named Claude Navier and an Irish mathematician named George Stokes. The equations are called, logically enough, the Navier-Stokes equations. They predict and explain the onset of turbulence. They also make clear the relationships among a tremendously complicated set of unknowns—a fluid's velocity, pressure, density, and viscosity. Yet for all their explanatory power, the equations are models of brevity and symmetry, possessed of a quality mathematicians call "elegant."

The Navier-Stokes equations are especially useful to designers and builders of aircraft. In theory, the equations can predict the velocity and pressure of air at any point on an aircraft surface as it is moving. The problem presented by the Navier-Stokes equations is that they are "nonlinear." An equation is called linear because the relation between its variables can be plotted as a straight line on a graph. Equations of this type appear in introductory algebra. In a linear equation the relation between x and y, for instance, is strictly proportional. Apply force to a hockey puck on a frictionless ice, and its speed will increase in direct proportion to that force. If we know the amount of force applied to that hockey puck, we can always determine its speed; contrarily, if we know its speed, we can always determine force applied. Every linear equation is solvable.

What makes the Navier-Stokes equations so difficult is that the variables are maddeningly interdependent. A fluid's velocity, for instance, depends to some degree on its pressure, and its pressure depends on its velocity. Moreover, pressure and velocity at any given point will depend on pressures and velocities at other points.

An aeronautical engineer trying to solve Navier-Stokes equations over the surface of an entire aircraft would face a difficult if not impossible task. He would have to resolve the equation for the smallest, nearly microscopic eddies; he would also have to account for the largest eddies, some of them several feet across. Finally, he would have to resolve the equation for all the eddies between, in the space around the whole aircraft, a volume of several thousands of cubic feet. An engineer who wanted not a perfect but merely a "good" simulation of turbulence would have to make measurements at about 10 quadrillion points, a number which, written out, would appear as a 10 followed by sixteen zeros. Even a supercomputer that could perform a trillion operations per second (ten times faster than the fastest one in existence as of this writing) would require several thousand years to compute the airflow for exactly one second of flight time.

Fortunately, there is a tool that helps. It is called the *Reynolds number*. It is the namesake of British engineer Osborne Reynolds. For any given fluid this number represents the ratio of the inertial forces (the forces sustaining its motion) to its viscous forces (the forces inhibiting its motion). We might say that turbulence appears when the Reynolds number is greater than a given value. The Reynolds number for water flowing from a tap may be 10,000. The number increases dramatically as speed increases; the Reynolds number for air flowing across an aircraft wing is on the order of 100,000,000. Fortunately too, the engineer does not need a perfect prediction; an estimate is sufficient.

In short, aeronautical engineers simply cannot calculate each eddy, and they do not try. Rather, they observe the larger eddies and use a set of thumbnail rules (or what are termed *modeling processes*) to estimate the effects of the small eddies. Some of these processes are simple numbers; others are whole sets of equations. With them, engineers can average turbulence across the whole scale of eddies, and so derive a rough simulation of overall turbulent flow.

Herbert Riehl also suggested that the general unsteadiness of the atmosphere could be thought of as a kind of turbulence. It represented an enormously complicated problem, not unlike that confronted by aircraft engineers attempting to measure turbulence over a whole aircraft surface. Like the engineers, Riehl quickly surrendered the idea of working with every data point and instead sought larger patterns. He tried to discover the basic similarities of turbulent elements and to describe these elements in models. Then he tried to discover the parameters (that is, the variable or arbitrary constant) that determine the variations of those models. It was a means to refine a data grid without more measurements, a means to guess what was happening in the spaces between.

More than a century before, William Reid had included the phrase "law of storms" in titles of his works. It was in some ways a gesture of hope that meteorologists had discovered a pattern, a predictable behavior. What he could not know, but what meteorologists like Charney and Riehl were beginning to understand, was that at the most fundamental level, there was no law whatsoever.

15

Feeder Band

8:00 A.M. EST / 1300 Zulu

Cumulonimbi in tropical latitudes extend to greater altitudes than do their temperate counterparts. Snowcloud Five was still more than 100 miles from Janet, and already Buck and Cronk could see her upper levels above the southern horizon. The clouds were dark gray with an unnatural copper tint. As the plane approached, they could make out more detail. The storm was not a uniform dark cloud. Its edges were ragged, and against it they could see smaller, broken clouds. Buck watched the shapes of the bright cumuli sliding past. Whole mountains of clouds were rolling by them on either side. It was a mesmerizing sequence of sunshine, shadow, and sunshine. To port, they were looking at the dawn refracted through curtains of rain. Soon they were flying through showers—rain was hitting the Plexiglas. The winds from the southeast increased, and the plane was rocked by mild turbulence.

Soon nimbus clouds began to overrun the sky. There seemed to be an inexhaustible succession. They were flying through and beneath those clouds, and there were more rain showers. Against the aluminum skin the rain was louder even than the sound of engines.

Buck and his guest witnessed a peculiar phenomenon in physics. The airflow across the Plexiglas pushed the rain water smoothly back along its surface in such a way that on each side of the dome, next to the fuselage, there appeared a whirlpool of water about the size of a silver dollar. The one on the port side spun counterclockwise, and the one on the starboard side spun clockwise. Buck had seen them a few times before when he and Jim Meyer had ridden in the bubble together. It was like watching a hurricane in miniature.

Meanwhile, things were getting busy in the cockpit. Windham would "lead" the storm, flying ahead of it and around its forward edges. He would begin at the outer edge of the leading right quadrant, fly a curving southward course along that edge, staying in the 74-mile-an-hour wind circle. The partial circumnavigation would take ten or fifteen minutes, and for most of it the crew would see the storm as a dark bar of clouds on their port side. At some point in the leading left quadrant, Windham would turn to port, put the wind on his port wingtip and fly inward toward the eye. Janet was 200 miles in diameter, and her eye was only ten or fifteen miles wide, yet it was easier for Windham to find the eye than it was for the navigators to find their position. Hurricane winds move counterclockwise around its center. As long as Windham kept those winds on his port wingtip, simple geometry ensured that sooner or later, they would hit the eye.

Windham knew that it might take twenty or thirty minutes to fly from the periphery into the eye, and in that time winds could push the aircraft around it, probably into another quadrant. Such sideways motion is called *drift*, and drift in a hurricane is likely to be considerable. So pilot and navigator coordinated to effect an entry into the leading left quadrant, and by the time they were halfway to the eye, they anticipated that drift would have carried the aircraft 40 or 50 degrees counterclockwise around the hurricane, into the trailing left quadrant, the soft spot. They would make most of the entry in the area where the relative wind speed was least.

There was a narrow window of opportunity. If Windham entered the hurricane's circulation too soon, that would mean spending most of the entry in the leading left quadrant—not the area of strongest winds, but not the weakest either. If he hesitated and began entry too late, he would risk the chance that by the time they had made it through the outer layers, they would have been carried around to the leading right quadrant, the most turbulent part of the storm. If by some extraordinarily bad luck or misreading of winds, Windham missed the window entirely, he could turn around inside the outer edges and try again. It was difficult, but at some point in their career most VW-4 pilots had done it. The commander of an Air Force mission in 1951 had no choice: "Flight departed Ramey AFB, P.R., at dawn, and in a little more than an hour we were in hurricane winds and commenced circumnavigation, keeping an average distance of 70 miles from the center. On reaching the northwest quadrant, commenced gradual penetration until due west of the center, then put the wind on the port wing and probed until winds reached 125 knots and plane became almost uncontrollable. At this point radar showed edge of core to be 8 miles east. Unable to continue further, were forced to slide southward, eventually leaving storm."

No pilot wanted to retreat, and if Windham turned the plane around, they would have to circumnavigate again, and it might be another hour before they would be in position to effect a second penetration. The Hurricane Forecast Center in Miami issued an advisory to the public every six hours. They requested that crews be in the eye one hour before advisory time, to give themselves time to analyze data and ensure their warnings were current. If

Windham delayed his entry, the forecasters would not be able to include their data in the latest advisory, and perhaps more worrisome, the crew would have lost some of its edge. A tired crew could make mistakes. And this crew was already tired.

⤙

Just aft the navigator's station sat Julius Mann, aviation electronics technician second class. For weather reconnaissance flights, that rating meant he would serve as a radar technician. He was twenty-two years old, from Canton, Ohio.

As they circumnavigated the storm, Mann watched the patterns on a device called the *Plan-Position Indicator*, or "PPI." It was the most common sort of radar scope used in weather reconnaissance, a circular dark screen divided into concentric circles that represented 50-mile intervals. A point of light traveled from the center of the scope to the outside edge, returned to the center, and repeated. The line it traced rotated clockwise around the screen, and allowed Mann to calculate the range to target and bearing. But the PPI was merely a kind of gauge. The radar system itself was a few feet beneath Mann's position, in the P2V's underbelly.

The idea of using radio signals and reflections of radio signals to detect objects—a technology called *radio detection and ranging*, or radar—had been developed in the 1930s. An ultrahigh-frequency pulsed radio signal would strike a target and be reflected back to the transmitter, where a receiver would detect it, amplify it, and display it as a visible echo. The time elapsed between transmission and reception was measured in microseconds, and the distance to the target could thereby be calculated. The technology seemed most useful for identifying enemy aircraft, and it was adopted for such use in World War II. At first, radar operators had been puzzled by "ghost echoes" far too large to be aircraft or even formations of aircraft. Soon they realized that these were rain clouds and that the radio waves were being reflected by water droplets. It was not long before Army and Navy meteorologists realized that radar could be used to detect storms.

Soon the technology revealed a natural phenomenon that no meteorologist and no theory of hurricanes had predicted. In 1944 the Great Atlantic Hurricane happened to pass near some Army radar equipment in Orlando, Florida. The system had an automatic camera set to photograph the radar scope every fifteen seconds. Until that moment, most meteorologists assumed that the inside of hurricanes was fairly homogeneous—rain, clouds, and winds all the way to the open space of the eye. They did not expect to see clear areas, and they certainly did not expect to see clear areas in a pattern. But that was exactly what the photographs showed. There were clouds radiating from the eye in a kind of spiral. Each arm was a few miles wide and hundreds of miles long. A few months later, the photographs were described in *The Journal of American Meteorology*: "The storm was seen to be in the shape of a figure six with clockwise spiraling 'tails.' At one time the scope recorded six distinct 'tails,' three of them detached, and moving northward of the storm's center."

For forecasters, radar was not only a way to see through clouds but also a way to see in the dark. In the years immediately following the war, the Navy considered night airborne reconnaissance both dangerous and impractical. The Air Force's 53rd required that all flights "depart storm area prior to sunset, regardless of the degree of completion of the mission." But limiting missions to daylight hours had distinct disadvantages, the most serious of which was a twelve-hour gap in tracking. One crew would end its reconnaissance at sunset, and a second crew would reconnoiter the hurricane at dawn, ten or twelve hours later, when it probably had evolved almost beyond recognition. Radar promised to change all that. After the war, crews based at Quonset Point, Rhode Island, experimented with an airborne system, and in 1947 they began a coordinated study with a meteorological squadron based at Naval

Air Station Patuxent River, Maryland. They installed radar equipment in a few B-17s and began to track hurricanes. That same year they flew six experimental flights, some night reconnaissance. All were judged successful.

By 1955, weather radar had been installed on all weather reconnaissance aircraft, and crews no longer had to guess the location of the cloud eye. But there were still problems. A radar signal attenuates with distance, and consequently a radar image may reveal only rain bands that are nearest the receiver. Moreover, because the earth curves and a radar beam travels in a straight line, with increasing distance the beam will overshoot raindrops beneath the horizon and intersect raindrops at higher and higher levels. Two hundred miles is the upper limit of radar's useful range, after which point the beam has passed beyond the troposphere. There was another difficulty. Water droplets near the radar can reflect waves that, had they been allowed to continue, might have revealed droplets at a greater distance. For all these reasons a radar image was likely to show only part of the hurricane. A lopsided radar image and a "false eye"—that is, an area of clear air within the rain bands—could give a dangerously inaccurate impression. A radar operator might mistaken a false eye for the real eye, and he might underestimate the extent of the rain bands on the side of the hurricane most distant from the radar. The only sure way to gain a complete view was to circumnavigate the whole storm.

This morning's mission would begin its first penetration without a complete circumnavigation, and Mann had to rely on experience and some knowledge of hurricane structure to understand what he was seeing on the scope, and to guess at everything it was not showing. Among his other duties Mann had a more specific navigational chore: he was to inform Morgan and Greaney (or Windham himself) of the location of the rain bands. Clear air was likely to be steady air, and the area of rain bands was the area of greatest turbulence.

It is difficult to exaggerate the amount of rain produced by a hurricane. In temperate latitudes 1 inch of rain in a twenty-four-hour period is considered a heavy downpour. Rainfall in some tropical cyclones exceeds that amount by whole orders of magnitude. Rains have been so heavy that on a level surface, with no run-off, evaporation, or seepage into the soil, the water after a storm would be nearly waist deep. And in the storm itself, some reconnaissance crews have said that there is more rain in the air than there is air. Even in 1955 there remained a danger that engines would cool to dangerously low temperatures. But there were other ways hurricane clouds could turn an ordinary mission into what pilots, with characteristic understatement, called "a bad day." One was supersaturated clouds.

The meteorologist who discovered the phenomenon was Robert Simpson, the man who suggested the "warm tongue" as a means to predict a hurricane path. Simpson was an interesting character. He was seven years old when the Gulf hurricane of 1919 hit Corpus Christi. He and his parents and grandparents were preparing to sit down to a Sunday chicken dinner when water began rising so fast that his father said they would be wise to postpone the meal. His mother wrapped the chicken with the rest of dinner and put it in a paper sack, and they all left the house. Getting to higher ground was not easy. Soon the water was waist deep, a circumstance that presented special difficulties because Simpson's grandmother was in a wheelchair. His father carried young Robert on his back, his mother went ahead, holding the paper sack above her head, and all of them, grandfather too, helped pull and push his grandmother. Although the flood caused great devastation in the city, the family survived. But the storm made a lasting impression on its youngest member. Even in adulthood, Simpson could recall the moment his mother grew too tired to hold the sack, and he watched it fall into the muddy water and sink out of sight.

Simpson had been with the Weather Bureau since 1940. Within the small community of tropical meteorologists, he was known as the one who was not satisfied with reading reports and papers. He caught rides with reconnaissance crews into hurricanes, where he performed a number of experiments of his own devising. By the 1950s Simpson had flown more weather reconnaissance flights than any other meteorologist. He had been with an Air Force crew reconnoitering Typhoon Marge in 1951, Hurricane Dolly in 1953, and Hurricane Edna in 1954. Among his schemes was a plan to release chaff in the eye, in an attempt to learn of air circulation. He was prepared to perform the first of the "chaff experiments" in Hurricane Edna in 1954, but when Edward Murrow arrived with three assistants and 1,500 pounds of camera equipment, the meteorologist was pushed to the back of the plane, his experiment postponed. Crews joked that he was almost an irritant. He couldn't care less. From June to November he was always packed and ready.

During a 1947 hurricane reconnaissance flight with an Air Force crew, Simpson discovered an unforeseen effect of moisture in hurricanes. They were in a WB-29, a version of the Boeing Superfortress, trying to enter the storm from above the clouds. They were climbing and expected to reach the top, where the textbooks said they would be, at 28,000 to 30,000 feet. But they had to climb almost to 40,000 feet before they found clear air. When they did, they realized the textbooks were wrong again. The clouds should have sloped downward toward the center. But in the direction of the eye, they saw cirrostrati rising steeply, far above the WB-29's operational ceiling. To get to the center they had no choice but to fly into it. When they did Simpson found something else he did not expect: "Through this fog of cirrostratus clouds in which we were travelling at 250 miles per hour there loomed from time to time ghost-like structures rising like huge white marble monuments. Each time we passed through one of these shafts the leading edge of the wing accumulated an amazing extra coating of ice. We were so close to the center of the storm by the time the icing was discovered that the shafts were too numerous to avoid."

At first Simpson did not know what these shafts were. Then he realized they were supersaturated clouds. A few months earlier Irving Langmuir, in his work on cloud seeding experiments, had shown that water vapor could be cooled to a temperature below freezing and remain a vapor. For Simpson it was one thing to know it had been done in a laboratory, quite another to see it here, in the unimaginably violent air within a hurricane. To freeze into a solid state, all the vapor needed was a slight shock, and a shock was exactly what the aircraft was providing. Simpson knew that snow and hail formed in exactly the same way. A small particle in saturated air became a nucleus for water molecules that attached themselves to it and to each other. But those particles moved through the air at relatively slow speeds, and layers of ice accumulated slowly. The aircraft in which Simpson was flying, on the other hand, was plowing through the vapor at more than 180 miles an hour and gaining fresh layers of ice with startling suddenness. Many aircraft were protected from ice accumulation by heated leading edges, but no such system had been installed on this particular WB-29. They kept flying through those pillars, and every time they emerged into clear air, Simpson could see a fresh rime of ice on the leading edges and a clear glassy sheet along the rest of the wing. As Simpson watched, the aircraft was turning into a very large hailstone.

An airplane flies because the wings and horizontal tail structure provide lift by virtue of the shape of their cross section: a flat underside and a curving upper surface. The particular danger ice presents to an aircraft is not that it adds weight. Within limits, a heavier aircraft may actually become more stable. Rather, the danger of ice is that it deforms the wing shape. Layers of ice accumulate, and a kind of ridge of ice grows all along the leading edge. Soon the wing can no longer offer lift, in essence ceasing to be a wing. At that moment one of two things happens: either the aircraft begins a flat descent that the pilot might at least partially control, or it dives uncontrollably, accelerating all the way down.

Three inches of ice is usually enough to cause worry, but before long there were six inches of ice on every exposed surface of the WB-29. The airspeed had dropped to 166 miles an hour, and at the altitude they were flying, the plane would stall at 163. The pilot was doing his best to avoid the shafts, but it was impossible—there were too many. It was obvious they would have to terminate the mission and get out. The pilot decided to remove the ice first. He began a long straight glide, seeking a lower altitude where the air was warm enough to melt the ice. It worked. The aircraft's surfaces warmed, and in a few minutes, to their relief, Simpson and the crew could see the ice begin to slide from the wings in great sheets.

Under Buck's seat in the observer's station was a loose-leaf binder of photographs of the ocean surface at different wind speeds—everything from a flat calm to hurricane force. Scientists call a wave "any periodic, vertical displacement of a surface." There are many kinds of waves. There are waves that are too long and low to see, and waves that travel on density interfaces beneath the surface. Most ocean waves are caused by wind. A wave is born when the frictional drag from air moving over water creates a ripple. Once a ripple appears, there is a steep side against which the wind can press directly, and energy can be transferred directly from the air to the water. The ripple grows into a wave, and the process begins to accelerate. As the surface facing the wind becomes higher and steeper, more surface area is available to absorb energy. But the process has a limit. The shape of any wave is determined by a specific ratio of height to length. A wave 7 feet long can be no greater than 1 foot high. When small steep waves exceed this limit, they break and create a sea surface of small breaking waves that mariners call "choppy." Because there are variations in the speed of air and pressure on the surface, wavelets of all sizes are created simultaneously, and new ripples and small waves continue to form on the slopes of existing waves. Heights of crests and troughs are irregular, and any single wave in a sea will have a different shape, a different speed, and a slightly different direction than the waves around it.

Buck had flown enough flights that he did not need the photographs. He did, however, need to be near enough to the surface to see it. The only way to get a reasonably accurate reading of wind speeds and directions near the ocean surface was to look at the whitecaps, and to see them he had to be no higher than 500 or 700 feet. What made such an altitude a risk was that in the eyewall, updrafts and downdrafts can push reconnaissance aircraft a thousand feet in a few seconds. In fact, a few days earlier a passenger plane on a New York to London flight met up with remnants of Janet's predecessor, Ione, which by then had passed over the eastern seaboard and returned to the North Atlantic. The plane had encountered an air pocket or downdraft that dropped it suddenly, exactly 700 feet.

The orders from Fleet Weather Central did not include a recommendation as to the altitude of entry, and that omission was deliberate. It was thought best to leave that decision to the man piloting the aircraft.

The pilot, second pilot, and navigators had pressure altimeters. But the only reliable measure of their altitude would come from Buck, because the only radar altimeter in the aircraft was in the observer's station. It was called the SCR-718; the letters stood for "Signal Corps Radio." It was a very reliable instrument, but too large to fit anywhere but the observer's station, and even if it were smaller there was no easy way to install it into a cockpit instrument panel. So it was left for Buck in the observer's station to read altitude aloud into the interphone, and for Windham and Herlong in the cockpit and Morgan and Greaney in mid deck to listen, and then to adjust their barometric altimeters. The arrangement made Buck, at least for the entry, probably the second most important crewman after the commander. He would be calling out altitude all the way in.

In 1955 the relationship between aviators and meteorologists already boasted a complex history. It was not always amenable. Although the Weather Bureau took some pride in the fact that Orville Wright consulted them before the first powered airplane flight, few early pilots returned the appreciation. In 1921 a Weather Bureau employee had written that many aviators were of a type "characteristically daring and aggressive; they enjoy to a degree the obstacles presented by difficult weather." Further, he said, "Some aviators feel that meteorological advice deprives flying of some of its sporting chances and of its gameness, and consistently will not avail themselves of the assistance of the aerologist." Duckworth's flight into a hurricane was a new chapter in this alliance—the aviator given the chance to go where none had gone, the meteorologist grateful (and a little surprised) that somebody was offering a ride in that direction. And by 1955 at least among weather reconnaissance crews, the 1921 description of the relation had been almost exactly reversed. The pilot depended quite directly and openly on the aerologist to tell him the plane's altitude, and the aerologist was asking the pilot to deliver him to the proximity of a meteorological phenomenon that posed hazards to him, his crew, and his aircraft. In 1955 it was the pilot's job to follow the aerologist's instructions, bound by limits of operational safety and standard procedures. It was the pilot's job, in other words, to say no.

Among pilots and crews, "I trust him" was highest praise. Indeed, trust was necessary to the completion of any mission. The pilot depended on the navigator to tell him where he was, and the navigator depended on the aerographer to monitor the altimeter and the crew chief to monitor the engines. They in turn depended on nearly two hundred men on the ground—the planners in operations, the paper pushers in administration, the grease monkeys who inspected and maintained and repaired the engines and airframes, the electronics boys who pulled apart the radios and put them back together. It was a curious paradox that each crewman held a responsibility that felt more than anything like a small burden, a weight. Together they were held aloft by nine separate, private weights.

Windham pushed forward gently on the yoke, and they descended to 700 feet. He called into the interphone for the crew to buckle in and stow the breakables. They were punching through. Buck looked at the seas below and checked again the radar altimeter. And at the radio station, Combs managed to send a transmission. A few seconds later, a teletypewriter 700 miles away at the Hurricane Forecast Center in Miami tapped out a report. It was code, a long string of letters and numbers. But Gordon Dunn, Walter Davis, and everyone else in that room could translate:

NAVY RECONAISSANCE FLIGHT 5U93, OBSERVATION NUMBER FIVE, AT 1330 GMT (8:30 AM EST), MONDAY, LOCATED AT LATITUDE 15.4 DEGREES N, LONGITUDE 78.2 DEGREES W. OBLIQUE AND HORIZONTAL VISIBILITY 3-10 MILES, ALTITUDE 700 FEET, FLIGHT WIND 050 DEGREES (NE), 45 KNOTS (52 MPH). PRESENT WEATHER LIGHT INTERMITTENT SHOWERS, PAST WEATHER SAME, OVERCAST AND SOME SCUD BELOW, SURFACE PRESSURE 1,003 MILLIBARS (29.62 INCHES), SURFACE WIND 050 DEGREES (NE). 45 KNOTS (52 MPH).

The last few signals were two words in plain English: "Beginning penetration."

16

What They Knew

Janet was pulling warm, moist air from vast distances, and it spiraled inward along the storm's bottom strata. A slow force was taking hold of the plane and its crew with a complicated urgency, and there was a sense in which they were being pulled into something they could no longer avoid. The storm's winds began to buffet the plane from the south. Windham was not worried about horizontal wind speeds—his real concern was for updrafts and downdrafts. The plane began to lurch and buck.

The P2V was neither pressurized nor watertight, and rivulets of water appeared on the bulkheads. There were streams of water trickling down the sides of equipment, but by now most of the crew had too much to do to notice. In mid deck the astrodome leaked some, and Morgan and Greaney felt the water on their backs. Using the driftmeter was out of the question—even if Morgan could hold his eye to the eyepiece, the drift was so severe that it was off the scale. They were no longer giving Commander Windham advice. Rather he was navigating on his own, mostly by keeping the wind on his port beam. They were continuing to plot, of course, but they were "following" the plane, charting where it had been. Combs was sending data through the static, hoping that someone in Miami was receiving it. If he did not hear some acknowledgement, then when they reached the eye he would send the same data again. And at one of the aft stations, Clegg held on.

In the observer's station, the view below Buck and Cronk was sobering. They saw huge whitecaps, torn by long streamers of rain blown sideways. There were windstreaks—streamers hundreds of yards long, running upwind and downwind over the whitecaps. The spokes of a spinning bicycle wheel produce an optical illusion that make them seem to spin slowly backward. Buck and Cronk saw something similar. Whitecaps were falling forward with the wind, but because they were overrun by the waves, it was easy to imagine that the foam was sliding backward. Buck estimated that winds had reached 115 miles an hour. Every few seconds he glanced at the radar altimeter and called out altitude, wind direction and wind speed.

—

By 1955 Air Force and Navy crews had made more than a thousand missions into hurricanes and typhoons. Their findings enabled meteorologists to learn more about hurricanes in a matter of months than had been gained in the previous hundred years. But it had been an education of the most humbling sort. No one was sure of all the elements required for hurricanes to form, and most of what they *did* know, or at least what they knew with certainty, could be summarized on a few pages.

Meteorologists knew the hurricane required inflowing air near the ocean surface, or "low-level convergence," and that this inflow needed to be strong enough to dissipate the trade-wind inversion and lift the moist layer. They knew that at higher altitudes it needed outflowing air, part of a process they called "high-level divergence," which removed the air that had accumulated in the developing system and lowered air pressure near the surface. They knew the circulation needed enough energy to sustain itself. They knew that hurricanes could originate in easterly waves, in the Intertropical Convergence Zone, and in the trailing southerly areas of polar troughs. They knew that hurricanes developed over warm water, 79° Fahrenheit and higher. And that was all.

What they did *not* know, on the other hand, could fill a small library.

A few suspected there must be a "main trigger," an event that somehow ignited all the necessary elements into forming a hurricane, but they had no idea what it might be. They did not know exactly what outside influence intensified the initial disturbance. Once hurricanes *had* formed, their growth seemed to follow a bewildering variety of paths. Some began with a tightly wrapped core of strong winds and build outward. Others seemed to grow from the outside in. More confusing still, this growth operated on wildly different time scales. One tropical depression could take six hours to become a full-fledged hurricane; another might require three days.

They were not sure why the air in the eye was warmer than the air in the clouds surrounding it. They did not understand exactly how a cold-core disturbance (a disturbance with a center colder than the air surrounding it at the same altitude) became a warm-core hurricane. Because condensation released latent heat, they expected that the most warming within the storm would occur in areas of greatest rainfall, but reconnaissance flights were showing that its warmest areas were elsewhere. They were having difficulty understanding interactions among the storm's components. They knew, for instance, that while moisture, heat, and momentum were affected by wind speed, they did not understand exactly how. And most believed that the hurricane was likely to hold a number of phenomena they had yet to discover. Robert Simpson, for one, suspected a kind of "internal" friction produced by the winds of hurricane working against each other and slowing each other.

There was something illusory about the storms. Like the familiar silhouette of the face that becomes a vase, some phenomena associated with the storms seemed to appear and disappear, depending on one's point of view. An aircraft flying at 35,000 feet could find everything to fit the standard model of hurricane formation: clockwise winds at flight level, counterclockwise winds at lower levels, clouds at the right altitudes. Yet surface ships directly below them might see only calm seas and light winds.

Once meteorologists began to examine details, the questions multiplied. As for what was occurring at certain specific levels within the storm, for instance, they might as well have been trying to determine the weather on Mars. (This question of the lowest levels in particular was more than merely academic. Civil engineers trying to design structures in regions visited by hurricanes wanted to know the wind speed through the lowest hundred feet above the surface, and that wind speed varied tremendously.) In 1955 meteorologists had read scores of written accounts of the storm wave or hurricane wave, but the physics of the phenomenon were poorly understood. The surge seemed to develop near the eye, but many surges had traveled far ahead of it. Some had been described as coming ashore as a single great "wall of water," and others seemed to be a series of waves.

The precise nature of the relation of hurricanes to the seas beneath them was a mystery, but hurricanes had been known to set up currents that were incredibly powerful. In August 1915 a hurricane off the Texas coast created a current that moved a buoy 10 miles westward. The buoy weighed 21,000 pounds and had been anchored in 42 feet of water with a 6,500-pound sinker and 252 feet of anchor chain.

There was ignorance on greater scales, too. Meteorologists did not understand which weather patterns were associated with

developing hurricanes. They did not know exactly how disturbances of the lower troposphere interacted with disturbances in
the upper troposphere, if indeed they interacted at all. Some suspected that the tropopause (the layer of air between the troposphere and the stratosphere) acted as a sort of boundary, but
exactly what it separated in a hurricane and how effective it was at
maintaining that separation, no one knew. They did not understand the exact nature of the relationship between the hurricane
and the steering current in which it lived. There seemed to be a
kind of reciprocation, some sort of feedback between the two, but
they did not know exactly how that feedback might operate or
exactly how important it might be.

In the late 1940s, radar showed that in well-developed hurricanes, the main concentration of rain bands in various quadrants
varied from day to day. It might be in the trailing right quadrant
one day, the leading right quadrant the next. It seemed the rain
bands rotated too, in a movement perhaps associated with the
winds, perhaps separate from them. Meteorologists did not know
whether the rain band rotation was clockwise or counterclockwise,
continuous or discontinuous. They were not entirely sure it existed
at all.

Indeed, meteorologists were having difficulty even defining a
"typical" hurricane. One meteorologist might say, for instance, that
wind speeds at such and such a quadrant and such and such an altitude were typical, and all he meant was that similar wind speeds
had been recorded in other hurricanes. Somebody else would
report a new phenomenon, and the definition of *typical* would be
stretched to include it. The weather reconnaissance flights
promised answers, yet it seemed every crew came back with new
data that only provoked new questions. No sooner would a meteorologist begin formulating a theory of say, mid-altitude winds, than
a flight would return with observations that undermined it completely. There were mysteries inside mysteries.

In hurricane science there was a single nagging problem that suggested something fundamental had been overlooked. The number of hurricanes in any given season was curiously small, especially compared to the incidence of other storms. At mid latitudes, say, the latitudes of Western Europe, on any given day there might be twenty or thirty storms scattered across the globe. But in an entire year the Northern Hemisphere might experience only about fifty tropical storms. This infrequency was difficult to explain, among other reasons, because hurricanes seemed much simpler than mid-latitude storms. They were something physicists called "heat engines." They gained heat input from the warm, humid air over the tropical ocean, released it through the condensation into the thunderstorms of the eyewall and rain bands, and gave off a relatively cold exhaust in the upper levels of the troposphere. Interrupt or decrease the flow of heat into the eye and the whole engine would sputter or stall. The mechanism itself was that simple, and the conditions that made it possible appeared with astonishing regularity. From June through September all the factors known to generate hurricanes—temperatures, moisture, wind speeds, and easterly waves—appeared somewhere in the tropics, simultaneously, as often as every day. From June to November there should be a hundred hurricanes. Yet an average season might produce only ten.

In sum, meteorologists knew when a hurricane was likely to form, and once it formed, they knew at least in a general way what it was likely to do. But they understood almost nothing of hurricane structures and life cycles, and even less of their development. They had few answers to how it moved or how its internal circulation operated. Each hurricane showed them something new. Gordon Dunn would say that any student of hurricanes became impressed with their individuality.

Lieutenant William Buck knew that Janet was different not only from other hurricanes but also from herself as she had been only a few hours earlier. And there were still unknowns. As he checked the radar altimeter, he knew that before the day was over, in all likelihood he would see something that he had never seen before.

17

Wall

8:45 A.M. EST / 1345 Zulu

Through the outer layers they had seen clear areas below and less often, clear spaces above them. Now Windham and Herlong could see nothing. The windshield wipers beat furiously. There were patterns of raindrops and rivulets on the windscreen, and outside were brighter and darker patches of cloud and wisps of vapor, but mostly it was a gray featureless wall. The eye strained to make out detail, but it was impossible to tell whether one was seeing for inches or thousands of feet. It was likewise impossible to tell whether some features were a mere play of light or a trick of the eye. The plane was bucking, thrashing. They were falling through the air: lifted gently, pushed down violently and forcibly, pulled upward for a moment, pushed down again. It felt as though they were riding in a truck without shock absorbers, bumping down a gravel road, every few seconds hitting a rock or a pothole and lurching into the air.

In the observer's station, Buck and Cronk held on and strained to see. A scud cloud would obscure the view, and in a moment they would break into clear air and look below at a sheet of blowing white spray. Buck could no longer estimate the wind speed, and he did not try. For the first time in more than an hour, he had little to do. So he simply held on, shouted a joke to Cronk, and every few seconds looked at the radar altimeter and called out an altitude reading.

✦

Human physiology reacts to wind. Metabolism increases, blood vessels dilate, pupils widen. One study of general blood-vessel disorders found that fully half of all myocardial infarctions and strokes occurred when the wind was blowing at force four or five. If there is an evolutionary advantage to such sensitivity, perhaps it is that windy days were inherently more dangerous— destroying shelters, masking sounds of predators, blowing branches down, and in all ways making the world less predictable. And yet for some, wind seems to increase powers of concentration. Ivan Tannehill was astonished at the abilities of meteorologists to take notes as waters rose around them and as the roofs of their stations blew off. He would know that a certain person was nearly drowned or that someone in the station with him was killed, but the notes might make no mention of those events, the only indication of difficulty being a written apology for some water stains and the generally untidy appearance of the report. This sort of focus was precisely what was expected of aerologists and navigators.

An Army Air Force navigator named James P. Dalton described his experience of navigating through Kappler's hurricane in September 1945. He said that one minute the plane seemed under the pilot's control but then would suddenly wrench itself free, throw itself into a vertical bank, and head straight down. Rain was so heavy, he said, it was as if they were flying through the sea, and navigation was practically impossible. They never seemed to fly in any single direction for more than a minute. At one time he recorded 28 degrees of drift. Two minutes later they were headed in the opposite direction and the wind was almost as strong. Dalton was able to record a wind of 125 miles an hour, and at one time the altimeter indicated 2,600 feet, owing to the drop in pressure, when they actually were at a mere 700 feet. Then, he said, "The bottom fell out." They went into a dive, and Dalton admitted, "Right then and there I prayed. I vouched if I could come out alive I would never fly again."

⤙

Snowcloud Five neared the eyewall of Janet, and on the PPI Mann saw a solid circle with the inner rain bands converging into it. The wall itself appeared as a hard, sharp, amber-colored arc. Meanwhile, the rain against the aluminum skin was deafening, and turbulence increased. The airspeed fluctuated and again the aircraft was pushed up and down. Windham and Herlong strained with the control yokes and rudder pedals; it took both to keep the plane straight and level.

They hit the wall.

The aircraft shuddered. The wind speed climbed rapidly, 85, 90, 100 miles per hour, howling at the airplane from the port side, and the plane began to buck. Windham jammed the power levers full forward, but it seemed to make no difference.

The plane was pushed and battered, and inside the men held on and were thrown sideways. In the cockpit Windham and Herlong gripped the yokes. It lasted only minutes—but they were very long minutes. They were battered again, and with each down-draft there was a fear that the plane would be damaged, or pushed lower and nearer to the churning seas beneath them. Most amazing was the rain. It was as though fire hoses were blasting the windows. Suddenly the plane lost altitude. It felt as though it was being forced down, and the crew was pushed upward against their safety harnesses. Windham compensated, pushing the throttle forward. The engines revved, and for a second the gray outside brightened to a lighter gray.

Then, without warning, they fell into sheer light and utterly transparent air.

18

Eye

In the observer's station the sudden sunlight was so bright as to be almost painful. The noise of rain had ceased, and Buck and Cronk could hear the engines again. Water leaking through down bulkheads slowed to a trickle. The air was calm and they were flying level. When Buck's eyes adjusted, it took a moment for his brain to register the scale. There was no detail on which to focus. He was looking at a vast amphitheater of clouds. The walls loomed tens of thousands of feet above them, gently curving outward to encircle a clear blue sky. Within the clouds were striations, a thousand shades of white and gray. There were small cumuli circling the inner edges. They had entered the eye from the southwest, with the sun behind them. Buck saw that the upper levels of the opposite wall were illuminated. They were as bright as snow at midday.

It seemed a realm of gods. Twelve miles away was the opposite wall, and the shapes of its clouds were visible with startling clarity.

He could see whole continents, long archipelagos of cloud shapes. At this distance and on this scale, it should have been impossible to discern movement, but the clouds were moving at 120 miles an hour, and Buck could see motion. It was like watching a film projection running at twice its normal speed.

Excepting a difference in altitude of 300 or 500 feet, what Buck saw was like what mariners had seen for centuries. In 1853 a British author named Alexander Bridport Becher published a rather sensational (and cautionary) description:

> *The focus of the hurricane is that special part of it which the seaman has to avoid, and knowing its bearing, sees how it is best avoided. It is there that a ship, after enduring all the severities of the first half of the hurricane, and having experienced the last few more rapid changes of the wind, near the margin of the mysterious circle, where electricity appears to be principally developed, is left by a terrific overpowering wind in a dead calm! where, above, all is peace and tranquillity, and below, a maddened sea raging in turmoil and confusion in huge pyramids, and in motion like a boiling cauldron.*

The hurricane eye is one of the strangest phenomena in meteorology. The diameter of the eye in a mature storm can be 15 miles, and in some typhoons it has been 40 miles. It may be perfectly circular or elongated, and its edges may be sharp or diffuse. It may even have a double structure—that is, there may be a false eye.

Robert Simpson was particularly interested in the eye. In 1953 he had begun to suspect that many witnesses exaggerated the contrast between the storm and the eye and reported that the eye was completely clear or completely calm. Simpson found this was seldom the case. Edna's eye, for instance, held a deck of stratocumuli some 6,000 or 7,000 feet above the sea surface. It was circular, 20 miles wide, and completely surrounded by towering nimbostrati. A mound of stratocumuli at the center rose to 8,000 feet and tapered near the walls. There were breaks through which they could glimpse the sea. It looked, Simpson said, like the hubcap of a giant rotating wheel. He did not know why such a structure appeared in some hurricanes and not in others, but he suspected that the surface layers accreted the mass of clouds through "gradual frictional transport" and fed a weak circulation in the eye itself.

Simpson noticed that the growth of one part of a rain band would create a fall in pressure near it. This in turn would deflect the steady circulation in the band to form an eddy, a kind of miniature eye that could "compete" with the true eye at the center, robbing and diverting its energy. It was a strange phenomenon—the hurricane fighting itself.

The water surface in some eyes is calm. In others it is extraordinarily violent. In an average hurricane, waves build to 35 or 40 feet, and in larger storms they build to 45 or 50 feet. Within the eye these waves move in all directions, as the winds creating them blow in a circle. Waves on open ocean have an upper limit because their tops are blown off by winds. But because waves in the eye develop beneath calm air, they may reach greater heights than waves in any other part of the storm. In the China Sea on September 21, 1869, the *Idaho* passed through a typhoon's eye. In his *Handbook of Cyclonic Storms of the Bay of Bengal,* John Eliot described the passage:

> *Till then the sea had been beaten down by wind, and only boarded the vessel when it became completely unmanageable; but now the waters, relieved from all restraint (in the calm center), rose in their own might. Ghastly beams of lightning revealed them piled up on every side in rough, pyramidal masses, mountain high—the revolving circle of the wind, which everywhere enclosed them, causing them to boil and tumble as though they were being stirred in*

some mighty cauldron. The ship, no longer blown over on her side, rolled and pitched, and was tossed about like a cork. The sea rose, toppled over, and fell with crushing force upon her decks. Once she shipped immense bodies of water over both her bows, both quarters, and the starboard gangway at the same moment. Her seams opened fore and aft. Both above and below the men were pitched about the decks and many of them injured.

The *Idaho* was "tossed about like a cork" because she was fortunate enough to be in waves that were not breaking. There is a vast difference in the destructive power of breaking and nonbreaking waves. When wind blows a crest off a wave, the blown water moves faster than the waveform itself, and a ship unlucky enough to be in its path will meet with disaster. But a ship in nonbreaking waves behaves like a cork in a small basin of agitated water. It displaces a given volume of water and makes the same motion as the water it displaces; there is little *relative* motion between the ship and the water around it. For this reason, although the experience of being aboard a ship in heavy nonbreaking waves may be uncomfortable, it is not especially dangerous. Waves within a hurricane's eye may be higher than waves in the eyewall, they are likely to be nonbreaking. And a ship caught in a hurricane's eye, so long as it remains in the eye, is relatively safe.

The center of a hurricane can be a place of startling and awesome beauty. Murrow described Hurricane Edna's eyewall as follows: "Calm air, flat sea below, a great amphitheater, round as a dollar, with white clouds sloping up to 25,000 or 30,000 feet. The water looked like a blue alpine lake with snow-clad mountains coming right down to the water's edge. A great bowl of sunshine." It was in the eye that Murrow's commentary grew quiet and contemplative. "The eye of a hurricane," he said, "is an excellent place to reflect upon the puniness of man and his works. If an adequate definition of humility is ever written, it's likely to be done in the eye of a hurricane."Alexander Bridport Becher described a similar scene: "In this magic circle the glorious sun may be pouring forth his splendour on the shattered vessel, whitening the foaming sea." He imagined that the eye would have a renewing effect, "cheering the worn-out crew to fresh exertion in clearing the wreck, and repairing as well as they can the damages sustained, before the second part of the gale comes on."

Although Crew Five probably made no repairs, Buck may well have welcomed the calm air so he might take and record measurements more easily. Combs may have needed clear air to transmit. So now they began the work they came for. Morgan asked Buck for advice on wind speed and direction. Buck gave Windham and Herlong a heading across the eye. They were trying to locate the epicenter of the eye, the center of the center. They searched out the lowest barometric reading, and Buck called out small navigational adjustments. There would be another indication: the wind would shift direction. So Buck also called out the ever-decreasing wind speed and direction. His work became more difficult. He held a clipboard on his knee, and on it he had a page of columns, into which he entered figures from code tables. There were numbers for flying conditions, time, position, cloud types, altitudes of cloud bases, turbulence, temperature, pressure, altitude, and "unusual phenomena"—every conceivable scrap of meteorological data. The operation was all but continuous. He would finish a form with all the boxes checked, roll it up, and slide it into the message tube. Barely did he put one report in the message tube, tug on the line to let Combs know it was coming, before he began another.

19

Human Factors

In the cockpit Windham relaxed a bit. Perhaps he allowed Herlong to take the controls and while he had the chance, took time to admire the view. No doubt he would have welcomed the break from his duties. As patrol plane commander, he ensured a thorough inspection of the airplane and all equipment. He oversaw planning. He supervised the preparation of the flight plan drawn up by Greaney and Morgan. He coordinated the crew members during flight planning and preparation. He ensured that Tate and Cronk had been briefed in the use of emergency equipment and were familiar with emergency signals and exits. He determined when the safety of the crew outweighed the needs of Aerologist Buck and the Hurricane Forecast Center. Finally, he flew the aircraft.

Navy aviators were assigned to weather reconnaissance as they were to any post. There were no specific requirements or qualifications beyond proficiency in a basic flight specialty—navigation, twin-engine, and so forth. Nonetheless, it was clear that the men who flew weather reconnaissance were an interesting group. They flew on a regular basis into unpredictable circumstances, and they flew in airplanes not particularly suited to heavy weather. From a certain point of view, one might have said that the Hurricane Hunters were materially deprived. Ideally, a plane that flies into hurricanes would have engines that would not stall in the walls of rain, and superstructures that were specially reinforced. But the aircraft supplied to weather reconnaissance crews—the PBM Mariner seaplane, the PB4Y Privateer, and the Lockheed P2V Neptune—were seconds, hand-me-downs. Even the Super Connies had been originally designed for surveillance. For any other group the situation would have been cause for bravado, complaint, or both. But the Hurricane Hunters made no claim to being a superior breed (at least not within the already superior breed the Navy claimed for its aviators), and neither did they grumble about second-hand aircraft. Most thought of themselves merely as pilots in another squadron at Jax, although they would admit that their day-to-day duties, compared with those of other squadrons, were slightly more interesting.

The danger a VW-4 mission presented even a seasoned aviator was evident to pilots who rode as guests. Every now and then an officer on leave from another assignment would hitch a ride out of curiosity. When the mission was over, and the plane had touched down and rolled to a stop, he would drop out of the forward hatch with the rest of the crew. Then he would walk a little unsteadily to the crew quarters. Somebody would observe that he seemed quieter than he had been before the mission. And later, at the little bar just off base, somebody else would overhear him admit he was as frightened as he had ever been in an airplane, that all things being equal, he would rather fly combat missions.

In fact, combat pilots had a ready means to identify the relative danger of any given mission upon its completion: simply count the bullet holes or examine damage from shrapnel or flak. Similarly, for test pilots there were rather clear and identifiable gradations of achievement: a higher altitude, a greater speed, a new aircraft, and so on. The exploits of the weather reconnaissance pilots enjoyed no such clarity. No instrument could measure a storm's danger, no gauge could calibrate risk to the crews, and there was no way to say with certainty whether any given storm was more dangerous than another. The reason was that wind speeds are averages or approximations, and the devil is in the small scale. Within the storms were eddies, currents, downdrafts, gusts. It was not unusual for a plane entering a hurricane with reported 80-miles-per-hour winds to experience a rougher flight than another plane flying at the same altitude and with relative bearings into a hurricane with winds that were far stronger.

On November 4, 1948, Captain Louis J. Desando and his crew struck the winds of the typhoon known as "Vulture-Charlie." He said they hit heavy rain, when suddenly the airspeed and rate of climb began to increase "alarmingly." They accelerated to 260 miles per hour and were climbing 4,000 feet per minute. When the plane broke out of a thunderhead, they felt a "terrific bump," the airspeed decreased to 130 miles per hour in a few seconds, and the crew were momentarily suspended in air. Desando's feet came up off the rudder pedals. The engineer, sitting on the nose-wheel door, rose slowly into the air. A coffee cup on the back of the commander's instrument panel floated to the ceiling and landed on the weather observer's table. The left wing dropped slightly, and Desando shoved the nose down to regain airspeed. They fell out of the sky for 2,600 feet—two thirds of their altitude—before they recovered.

In December 1948 a WB-29 Superfortress crew under the command of David Lykins reconnoitered Typhoon Beverly. Captain Lykins was no novice. He had taught instrument flying in the states and flown combat missions in rough weather out of England. After the war he spent thirty months with the 524th Reconnaissance Squadron, much of that time on weather missions. But he said that none of that prepared him for the flight out of Beverly. Sometimes the updrafts pushed him down in his seat. Other times he was thrown against his safety belt so hard that he could not move his arms to reach the controls and could barely life his head enough to see the instruments. Lykins and his copilot could not control their altitude; they could only hold the airspeed within limits to keep the airplane from tearing up from too much speed or from stalling out from too little. The third pilot had no safety belt, and he was tossed all over the flight deck. Lykins said, "It is almost impossible for me to describe accurately or to exaggerate the severity of the turbulence we encountered."

If hurricane winds were uniform and steady, then flying through them would be considerably easier. But a hurricane's winds are not steady. There are gusts, and they may exceed wind speeds by as much as 50 percent. Gusts represent a tremendously destructive force, especially when one appreciates that wind increases its pressure on an object with the square of its velocity. A wind that doubles its speed quadruples its force. If a 60-mile-an-hour wind exerts 15 pounds per square foot, a 125-mile-an-hour wind exerts 78 pounds. The dangers that gusts pose to an aircraft are compounded by the fact that air passing across a complex shape will develop positive and negative forces—a frontal force and a suction force—and in certain parts of an aircraft surface those forces may be in proximity. Ground crews for Lykins' WB-29 required no physics class to appreciate the effects of that proximity. The condition of the plane upon its return was testimony enough: a bent vertical fin, warped flaps, tears along the fairing joining the wing and fuselage, shorn rivets on all parts, a twisted fuselage, and a part of the bomb bay torn from its mounting.

Flying through a hurricane required particular skills and imposed its own rather specialized set of risks. Zero visibility

required that the pilot take three gauges as the only reliable mea-
sures of the aircraft's relation to the earth or sea. These were the
bank indicator, the artificial horizon, and the altimeter. So long as a
pilot or copilot did not rely exclusively on his own instruments, and
so long as he regularly and continually checked them against the
instruments of the other, there was nothing particularly dangerous
about flying on instruments. But a hurricane presented specific and
unique dangers. The first crews who flew into hurricanes relied on
the altimeter as they would if they were flying through heavy cloud.
Although they understood that pressure decreased in a hurricane,
they seldom appreciated how *much* it decreased. Aircraft air-pres-
sure altimeters were calibrated on the runway before takeoff, and as
the crews flew into high- or low-pressure areas, that calibration lost
effectiveness, and changes in air temperature could compound the
error. Again and again crews would break into clear air, see an angry
white ocean below, and realize with a shock that they were 300 or
400 feet lower than they thought they were.

Even a radar altimeter did not ensure safety. Sooner or later,
anyone flying in hurricanes would encounter conditions that pre-
vented him from reading instruments for long moments. Buffeting
from hurricane winds could make the aircraft vibrate so severely
that instruments became a blur, and lightning flashes could
momentarily cause the pupil to contract. In either case a pilot
might be sightless for a fraction of a second, and his brain would
be forced to work with the instrument readings he saw last. Such a
situation would be especially dangerous during a bank.

A *bank* can be defined as the lateral tilting of an aircraft during
a turn. An aircraft cannot turn without banking and cannot bank
without turning. Contrary to the beliefs of many nonaviators, a
shallow bank—say, of 30 degrees or less—cannot be felt. The g-load
increases imperceptibly, and unless one has a view to the outside or
a bank-and-turn indicator, one will not know that a plane is banking. A bank of 30 degrees produces an increased g-load of only

1.15*g.* It would be barely noticeable even to an otherwise unoccupied passenger, certainly unnoticeable to a pilot giving attention to other matters. An especially fatigued pilot, momentarily unable to read the bank-and-turn indicator, might revert to his own sense of equilibrium, a course of action that could be misleading and even fatal. It is quite possible to be in a shallow bank and not realize it.

As the angle of bank increases, the aircraft in the turn accelerates. As the bank steepens, the aircraft might lose altitude, and at very steep bank angles, most aircraft begin to descend. As it begins to bank, the plane tends to lower its nose and accelerate. Then begins a snowballing effect. The acceleration tightens the turn, which increases the bank angle, which in turn causes further acceleration. The airplane may bank straight down in a spiral dive, spinning into tighter and tighter circles. Recovery at this point is unlikely. The aircraft either breaks apart in midair from stresses or hits the ground or the ocean.

Now the work became more relaxed, but only slightly so. Buck coded his observation, made a comment to Cronk nearby, put the forms in the tube, and tugged the clothesline. Crew Chief Windham watched the engines. In mid deck Greaney leaned over his small writing space and figured the position of the eye and computed a double drift for wind. Aft the wing root, Combs pulled Buck's messages off the clothesline, and sent the tube back the same way. He tapped out messages that had accumulated during entry and had been unable to penetrate the atmosferics. Clegg was in the rear, unused to the camera and a bit unsteady, waiting for clear air so he could get a good shot of the surface. Tate, sitting opposite, scribbled notes on a yellow pad that had been dampened a few times by rain leaking through seams in the aircraft's skin.

The day was far from over. They would have to exit through the wall again, then circumnavigate the storm. In early afternoon, they would perform a second penetration at an altitude that would allow Buck to gather another kind of data.

The aerologist had a second station in the aft section of the plane, where there was more equipment, dropsonde racks, and a pressurized dropsonde chamber. Buck would pull one of the dropsondes from the rack. It was a cardboard box, and inside were a battery and an antenna. It weighed about 2 pounds. He would slip it into the pressurized dropsonde chamber and screw down the lid. Then, receiving the signal from Morgan, he would pull the release that dropped it from the plane. The dropsonde was attached to a small paper parachute that popped out—the dropsonde would slow, swinging a little. It would radio weather data as it fell to the water. During its descent it would measure barometric pressure, temperature, and humidity and transmit the data to a recorder in the aircraft. Buck would have a vertical cross section of weather information from flight altitude to surface. But that would be later. At the moment it was time to leave the eye, to get back on the railroad tracks.

On the interphone Windham told Morgan and Greaney they were getting out and called for an exit course. In a moment Morgan's voice responded, saying the best route was south by southwest and advising a heading of 120 degrees. Windham made one last turn inside the eye and told the crew to buckle in and stow the breakables. He felt the muscles in his shoulders tighten, braced his feet against the rudder pedals, gripped the yoke. He brought the plane around. Herlong gripped the yoke at his station too. In all likelihood it would take both of them to control the aircraft. Directly ahead they saw the wall. The shadings and shadows of the clouds stood in sharp relief. And it came nearer and nearer.

There was sudden darkness, a hammering of rain, and immediately the plane bucked. Windham did not have to call for interior lights. Mann had turned them on. Again, the view out the forward windscreens was a gray wall. Immediately they were shaken violently. The windscreen was hit with torrents of rain.

20

The Devil and the Deep Blue Sea

In 1909 London's *Daily Mail* offered £1,000 for the first crossing of the English Channel in a powered aircraft. A number of aeronauts took up the challenge, and on July 19, a Frenchman named Hubert Latham launched his monoplane from the French coast at Sangatte. He gained about 900 feet of altitude, circled once near the shore, and began out across the channel. After 8 miles his engine stopped, and after a series of long glides he put "Antoinette" down safely on the water. The tug that came to his rescue found him sitting on the floating fuselage. He was disappointed, but otherwise a perfect model of *sang-froid*, calmly smoking a cigarette. The prize for crossing the channel would go to Louis Blériot a few days later. Although few realized it at the time, Latham had made a different, if less notable, kind of history. He had become the first pilot to make a controlled landing in open water. He was the first pilot to ditch an aircraft.

In the years between 1909 and 1940, all types of lifesaving equipment—parachutes, inflatable life vests, collapsible boats, and inflatable rafts—were designed and developed. One might have expected the survival rates of pilots abandoning and ditching aircraft to have increased measurably over the same period, but such was not the case. The simple reason was that although the equipment was effective, too often there was no time to use it. As the lifesaving equipment was refined, aircraft had become heavier, with higher wing loadings and faster landing speeds. Consequently, they were hitting water with greater force, and once down they tended to sink quickly, sometimes in a matter of seconds. Moreover, because crews were flying over greater stretches of open water, wherever they ditched they were likely to be farther from rescue.

For the first four decades of the twentieth century the U.S. military saw little reason to give attention to strategies for bailout and ditching. But in World War II the Ferrying Command and the Air Transport Command extended flight routes across oceans, aerial combat was for the first time waged over large expanses of water, and the long neglect was exacting its price. In the first half of 1942, only 6 percent of American aircrews downed on water were recovered. The Army Air Force worked to improve the situation, and they did. They looked to the example of the British Air/Sea Rescue Service and began training in ditching and survival. They established the position of personal equipment officer, whose duties were to ensure that crews had life jackets and a raft. The changes had positive effects. From March 1943 through March 1944, out of a total of 2,130 Americans who ditched, more than half—1,169—were saved.

Although records of pilots abandoning aircraft over water and aircraft ditching on water existed as far back as 1918, no one had conducted a thorough study of the experience. Many assumed the sequence of events in ditchings was more or less what had been described in the training manuals. The second-to-second particulars of *actual* ditching was a subject few had bothered to think about. But a man named George Llano suspected that the situations described in manuals were polite fictions, and the realities of bailout and ditching were far more dangerous. In the early 1950s he undertook an exhaustive program of research. Llano was hardly a library sort of scholar. During the war he had conducted field tests of sea survival equipment and life rafts for the U.S. Air Force Air Proving Ground Command, and he tested equipment himself. Llano reviewed 1,500 cases of bailouts and ditching that had occurred during World War Two. In 1956 he published a complete report. It began with rather direct advice: "The swiftness of a forced landing at sea leaves little time for orderly procedure, and nothing short of the reflex action of trained personnel and reliable automatic equipment can effect a successful change from airman to seaman. . . ."

All subjects in Llano's study had been faced with a simple decision: bail out before the aircraft hit the water, or ride it all the way down. It was a fairly straightforward problem, a choice, as the saying goes, between the devil and the deep blue sea. The paper enumerated a fearsome set of obstacles to orderly procedure: injuries, structural damage to the aircraft on impact, fire or explosion, high seas, and perhaps worst of all, "disorganization or panic."

Llano identified two categories of reasons for which crews chose to bail out. The first was to avoid immediate dangers: an aircraft out of control, fire, smoke, or potential for explosion. The second was to avoid anticipated dangers: for example, a crew knew that their plane was heavy and they expected it would sink quickly.

But a crew making the choice to bail immediately met another set of hazards. A pilot of a single-place aircraft was supposed to vault over the side of the cockpit, expect that the slipstream would push him back along the fuselage, and perform a shoulder roll off the wing. In practice the procedure was seldom that easy. Leg straps got tangled, chutes became caught in bucket seats, buckles and strap loops got fouled on narrow projections, feet became wedged under bent rudder pedals. Even the moments immediately *after* the egress were dangerous; many crew were killed when they struck a wing, engine cowling, or some other part of the aircraft. Of course, a great number survived egress, and quite a few survived by means not anticipated in the manual. The variety of ad hoc emergency exits that airmen choreographed during the war might have taxed the imagination of circus aerialists, trapeze artists, and Hollywood stuntmen alike. If the experience of aerial combat proved anything, it was that if there was a way for a man to leave an aircraft in midair, you could be sure that sometime during World War II, a man had done it.

As one pursuit pilot made his exit, the chute harness slipped off his shoulders and got tangled and caught on his feet. He fell away from the plane head first, but he managed to contort himself upward and pull the ripcord in time. He survived the descent with only a twisted knee and strap burns. There was the crew member who, falling without a parachute, struck another, clutched his legs, and held on until they touched down together, awkwardly, but safely. There was a B-24 turret gunner, attempting to bail from the cramped quarters of the turret. He wedged his legs and was caught halfway out, his upper body pummeled in the slipstream as the now pilotless plane screamed through lower and lower levels of atmosphere. He could barely breathe but realized that if he pulled his ripcord and the parachute deployed, it might pull him forcibly from the plane. He knew there was a very good chance he would lose his legs, but he pulled the ripcord anyway. He blacked out from the concussion—and a few minutes later, he came to consciousness lying on the ground, his parachute near him. To his surprise, his legs were still attached to his body.

Even when a bailout was effected properly, the jolt of the parachute opening could cause momentary shock and loss of consciousness. And even the man who rode a chute all the way to the water and managed to stay conscious could have problems. The parachute had a quick-release harness, but many reported difficulty forcing the mechanism underwater, and even in calm seas some found themselves tangled in lines and shrouds. If there was wind, a man in the water could be dragged by the still-airborne chute, in which case he was likely to be pulled by his legstraps, turned upside-down, and drowned.

Those who made a successful descent under an open canopy could expect further difficulties. Parachutists were instructed to release the chute sling at 10 to 15 feet over the water surface and so allow themselves to fall the remaining distance. But many misjudged their altitude, pulled the release too soon, and were injured or dazed by the fall. Those who released at the right moment sank beneath the surface 5 to 10 feet, and were momentarily disoriented. Many who were knocked unconscious at some stage of the bailout were revived by the water but were simply too exhausted to swim.

All factors being equal, any given crew stood a slightly better chance of survival by ditching. In debriefings, crews enumerated three specific circumstances in which they considered ditching the only choice: first, a pre-existing situation—injured men, malfunctioning exits or canopies, or a shortage of parachutes; second, an expectation that the aircraft could still perform within design parameters, and a reasonable chance that it could be ditched close to shore or sheltered waters; third, a belief in the value of communal survival—many crews expected that should they survive the ditching, they would be able to keep each other alive long enough to be rescued.

In the second half of World War II, the Army Air Force developed and disseminated ditching procedures. For all multiplace aircraft—whether bombers, reconnaissance, or cargo—the recommended courses of action were roughly similar. Pilot and copilot would fasten safety belts and safety harnesses to avoid crashing through the instrument board or Plexiglas. They would jettison excess fuel. Pilots over water would disregard the conventional wisdom to ditch upwind, and try to land parallel with the swell. Crew members would stow or toss out loose articles and open all exits. Using closed chutes for padding, they would brace for the shock of impact. Each man was to leave through a specified exit and take with him assigned survival gear. All these recommendations were sound, but they could not accommodate the unexpected, and there was a great deal that was unexpected.

During mass bomber raids with B-24s and B-25s, whole crews were lost. Teams investigating wreckage were baffled. They were finding something no one had expected and no one could explain. Bodies were at duty stations, nowhere near the exits. There seemed to have been no attempt to get out of the plane. What they were finding went against all logic and became cause for considerable consternation. But there were suspicions. Studies at the University of Southern California had already suggested that a crew under pressure of more than 2.5gs would simply be unable to move.

Accounts of ditchings in World War II describe the aircraft striking the water with at least two impacts before coming to rest. The first impact was a force as great as 8gs, severe enough to dislodge crew members from bracing positions. Momentarily, a 160-pound man would weigh 1,280 pounds. And the second impact was far worse. In a moment a healthy crew sustained enough injuries to fill a hospital ward. There were broken arms, dislocated shoulders, sprained backs, concussions, and skin lacerations.

The aircraft's fuel—gasoline or kerosene—added another danger. One B-29 pilot preparing to ditch dumped excess fuel as per recommendations, but some interplay of the slipstream and the plane's yaw caused it to vaporize in the bomb bay. It almost asphyxiated the crew, and when the plane hit the water, the fuel exploded. A PV-1 with a crew of six ditched 260 miles from Natal,

Brazil. When the plane struck the water, the main exit hatch blew open and the fuel tanks caught fire. The three in the rear compartment jumped into the water, inflated their vests, and swam clear. The ocean rushed in through open ports in the forward section. The three men there were unable to move as quickly, but their wet clothes offered some protection and bought them enough time to get out. They rested for a moment in the water, holding onto a wing. Gasoline was burning on the water surface around much of the plane, and they knew they had little chance without a life raft and a few minutes at best to secure one. Two men were able to swim *under* the burning fuel to a point near the tail section, re-enter a rear hatch, and pull out a case that held a five-man life raft. Its covers were burning, so they flipped it into the water, dousing the flames. They jumped in after the raft and managed to inflate it. Then they climbed aboard, and in a few minutes found the paddles, negotiated themselves clear of the burning fuel, and pulled the other crewmen aboard. Shortly after, the six were clear of the flames and watched the aircraft sink and the last flames disappear. Every one of them had suffered serious burns. But every one of them survived.

Many planes built during World War II floated for at least long enough that the crew could escape into life rafts. In fact, it was not uncommon for ditched aircraft to float *too* well. Some became shipping hazards and had to be sunk by artillery. One such plane was the B-17 Flying Fortress. Of 112 ditched during the war, 85 floated for more than one minute and 59 for more than five minutes. But other aircraft were far less seaworthy, and some designs had made no provisions for forced water landings. Exit hatches in some aircraft were not in the ceiling but in the deck, making escape through the hatch impossible if the plane were sitting in the water. Some crews in ditched planes had to improvise hatches, breaking through windows and domes.

Until an aircraft of a given series had actually ditched, no one knew how long it would float. Reports from survivors and rescue teams suggested that certain bombers—the North American B-25 and the Martin B-26—had a tendency to sink rapidly. Most agreed that the plane that posed the gravest danger was Consolidated's B-24 Liberator. It had a fundamental design flaw. Under stress, the number six bulkhead would collapse under the weight of the turret, pinning and perhaps crushing anyone unlucky enough to be caught in the midsection. In three B-24J ditchings involving thirty-one men, all wearing safety belts, eighteen were killed. An analysis of ten B-24 water landings made in 1944 concluded that even in "normal" ditchings—that is, with wheels up and bomb bay closed—at least one man was likely to die.

A number of crews who had ditched reported surprise at how quickly water could flood an aircraft. A survivor of a PB4Y ditching reported, "Besides the sudden deceleration, the most noteworthy fact was the fast rush of water into the cockpit and flight deck. Almost the second the nose dug in, the water was above the pilot's shoulders and by the time safety belts and shoulder harnesses were off the water was level with the top escape hatch."

Men in the water tended to hold to wing and tail surfaces, but especially in waves of a few feet or more, the practice was danger-ous. A heavy sea would lift a wing or tail section for a moment, then it would slap it down on the water with great force. When it lifted again, they would be pulled beneath.

The most valuable equipment issued to aircrews was the jacket-type life preserver called the Mae West. It could be inflated by pulling toggles that released carbon dioxide from two pressur-ized cartridges. If the cartridge mechanism failed, the user could inflate the vest by blowing into a valve. Many rightly credited the vest with saving the lives of countless airmen by keeping them afloat. Fewer realized that it also helped them escape from sinking aircraft and brought them to the surface when they were too dis-oriented to know where the surface was. One pilot said, "I came to underwater, green all around me. Wondering where I was, I pulled the life jacket valve and shot up."

Many ditchings trapped men in the fuselage, but unless they were somehow pinned inside the wreckage or otherwise incapacitated, they were able to swim through an exit. Some pilots, knocked unconscious during the fall, sunk beneath the surface and awoke to see luminous instrument dials in pitch-dark water. They were able to save themselves simply by inflating the vest. A typical account: "The plane nosed over. I lost consciousness. When I came to I was under water and it was very dark, I must have been approximately 40 to 50 feet under, because after approximately 10 good strokes upward and still about 10 feet from the surface I saw a bright yellow glow above me. I knew there was a fire on the surface and headed for the edge of it."

The life vest's redundant design made it possible to work when only one of the two air chambers was filled. Still, things went wrong. Some life vests simply failed to inflate. Men who tried to re-enter the aircraft tore their vests on jagged metal. A few punctured their vests while attempting to cut themselves free from parachutes. A crewman who inflated the vest before unbuckling his parachute harness nearly suffocated from the pressure on his chest. In some cases men pulled the life jacket toggles only to realize that the carbon dioxide cartridges had already been discharged accidentally.

The standard life raft used by American forces, inflatable and rectangular, had proved more maneuverable than the circular type used by the British. But in the first years of war the American rafts were of poor quality. Seams and patches were cemented badly, and many had been allowed to deteriorate in storage. At least theoretically, all rafts were equipped with water and food rations, a first aid kit, signaling equipment, a hand pump, a sea anchor, a compass, and paddles, but as late as 1945 a shortage of accessories in life rafts had reached "serious proportions." One man said in debriefing, "We had no survival equipment in the life raft. It just wasn't there."

Combat aircraft life rafts were released from inside the fuselage by a hand release. It ejected the raft from compartments in the wing or fuselage and automatically inflated it. But here too, equipment did not always perform as advertised, and the men made ad hoc fixes. When releases did not eject life rafts properly, crews had to pull them from their compartments forcibly, by hand. Releases were fouled and damaged the raft. Most aircraft had several release mechanisms for the life rafts, one on the flight deck. But the B-24 had only a single release in midsection, and when crew near it were incapacitated, the rafts were simply inaccessible. In B-24 ditchings, crews were able to use the inside manual release only half the time. Large rafts stowed in the midsection were difficult to remove in all but the calmest seas. Often the bulky casing made it difficult to gain a handhold, or there were not enough handles, or the case was made more slippery by water, oil, or blood. And in many ditchings the B-29 standard-issue E-5 raft kit was left with the plane. Some crews abandoned life rafts because they could not remove the tight-fitting covers or could not find the safety wire holding the release toggle. There were cases of life rafts being inflated accidentally inside the aircraft, through force of impact or sheer confusion. An inflated raft was worse than useless—it was an actual impediment, simply too large to fit through the hatch. One crew, having snagged a raft half in and half out of the aircraft, punctured it with a knife, pushed it out the rest of the way, and abandoned it to the seas. Some crews deployed rafts successfully but tied them insecurely to the aircraft and then saw them blown away. A few crews tried to launch the raft on the windward side of the plane, where the raft was blown against the aircraft, fouled on the tail section or antenna, and threatened to be pulled under by the sinking plane. All life rafts were attached to the aircraft by lines designed to give way should the aircraft sink. Still, some lines had to be cut by hand. Crews who had managed to hold onto their knives were fortunate: one life raft tied to a door was held so tightly that the crew—lacking a knife—was forced to jettison the door and pull it into the raft with them.

Crews were unable to inflate rafts for any number of reasons— worn safety wire, faulty plunger pins, greasy valve knobs that could not be turned with wet hands, carbon dioxide cartridges that crews could not find because they had been packed improperly. Crews had difficulty finding the plunger pin, and when they did, it might be crushed or broken. One pilot opened the valve with his teeth; another crew pushed the pin into the cylinder with a pistol butt. A crew who could not inflate a raft from the carbon dioxide cartridges might hope the equipment officer had included hand pumps. But they were tied to the raft and were often lost when the raft was pushed into the water or inflated.

Almost all crews who ditched reported difficulties boarding the life raft. Men who were injured or exhausted managed to get aboard only with help from others. Many found that the Mae West impeded them. They had to deflate one or both chambers to get aboard, but first had to separate themselves from the parachute harness. Many were so exhausted by the effort of merely staying afloat and inflating the raft, that once it *was* inflated, they had no strength to climb in, and so they simply hung on to the sides. Those strong enough to board the raft had ample opportunity to make their situation worse. Many rafts were punctured by knives that had been improperly sheathed.

Once aboard the raft, men found other problems. Paddles were bound with twine, and the men who lost their knives during ditching found they had no way to cut it. They could not untie the knots because their fingers were wet and swollen and their finger-nails were water-softened. Some men chewed the knots apart with their teeth. Although the rectangular raft was more steerable, it was also more likely to capsize, and crews who managed to gain the raft in heavy seas reported being overturned again and again. Often a raft would be lifted to the crest of a wave, become flooded when the wave broke, and slide down into the trough, where it took on more water. It was easy to capsize. Winds of 40 miles an hour were enough to catch the exposed underside of a raft and flip it over. One survivor reported that a wave struck the under edge of the raft, and "the next instant we were in the water, the raft flying through the air over our heads."

Men had little training or experience in rafts. Ditched crews who had reached rafts discovered that they gained stability when they were lashed side by side. They also discovered that a raft awash—half filled with water—although uncomfortable, was relatively stable even in heavy seas.

Among the equipment packed with the raft was a sea anchor—a 3-foot canvas sheath held open at each end by hoops of wire, a line attached to the larger end. It was supposed to be towed in the water behind the raft to slow drift, prevent capsizing, and keep the raft headed into the wind. Crews who could not find the sea anchor improvised with parachutes, deflated life vests, or raft casings. Others, with no training and no understanding of its function, forgot about it altogether.

Most formal reports of survival neglected mental aspects. There were several reasons. Air Force records concentrated on aircraft malfunction, and medical records focused on physical injuries. Boards of inquiry were concerned mostly with physical aspects of emergencies. This emphasis was agreeable to most crews, who did not volunteer information on their mental states because they did not want a panel to suspect their sanity.

Many did not remember how they received their injuries. Indeed, memory loss could be so complete that some described the ditching along the following lines: "the commander gave the order to prepare to ditch and all of a sudden we were in the water." Most crews regained their senses when they gained the relative safety of the raft, but a rescue team reported finding one group of survivors so disoriented that they could not even tell the rescuers their names. Those whose recollections were intact found it difficult to speak about the experiences, particularly in cases where a crew member was killed. During World War II, First World War ace Edward "Eddie" Rickenbacker was serving on special assignment for the secretary of war when a plane on which he was a passenger ditched in the Pacific. He was adrift for twenty-three days, and he did not relish the memory. It was, he said, "like trying to remember being dead."

Nonetheless, many did recall and recount events, and it was possible for Llano to note behavioral and mental states of aircrews in situations of bailing out and ditching. He had expected psychological stress, but he had not suspected all its manifestations. Some crewmen, engaging in sober and orderly, step-by-step preparations and from all appearances quite calm and collected, were in fact severely disabled. One copilot, ordered to bail out, was preparing to leap from a rear hatch when he realized that he had time for a gesture of bonhomie, and he returned to the cockpit to offer a last handshake to the pilot. When he got there he noticed his parachute still sitting on his seat.

In 1946 a researcher named Hans Selye published a description of a theory for what he called the "general adaptation syndrome." He suggested that a person in a stressful situation is likely to undergo a sequence of three mental states. First is the "alarm reaction," in which the shock phase of lowered resistance is followed by countershock, when defense mechanisms become active. Then follows "resistance," the stage of maximum adaptation and successful return of equilibrium. But if the stressor continues or the defense somehow misfires, the subject will move to the third stage—exhaustion, when the adaptive mechanism collapses entirely. Indeed, the stress of ditching triggered profound exhaustion. The physiological and psychological stress was so great that many who managed to climb aboard life rafts simply collapsed and fell asleep immediately.

It became clear to Llano that a crew came to regard their aircraft as home and protector. Abandoning that aircraft demanded a sudden and radical shift in frame of reference, a shift some were simply unable to make. A crew in a life raft saw one of their own still standing on a wing, holding a flashlight. They called to him to jump and swim toward them. But he slowly turned away and disappeared again inside the aircraft. A few moments later it sank beneath the surface.

General Nathan Twining's B-17 was forced down in the Coral Sea in February 1943. Eight officers and seven noncommissioned officers spent five days and six nights adrift, surviving on a few tins of sardines and some chocolate bars. Twining reported that the first moments in the water were in many ways the worst: "Some of the boys were off their nuts, yelling at the top of their voices and striking out for Tokyo, swimming in all directions as fast as they could flail. We had to strike out after them and pull them aboard."

Many of those who survived had approached abandoning an aircraft as a problem solvable by forethought and an orderly approach. The pilot of a fighter reported: "Oddly enough, I never once became panicky or confused. I seemed to perform the jobs which had to be done as they required doing, and planned ahead as time permitted. I planned my water-entry procedure while still descending. I went through the whole experience more by cold calculating instinct than by conscious mental thought." In fact, there were instances of astonishing self-possession. One pursuit pilot, attempting a bailout, struck the canopy and severed a leg. Somehow he remained conscious, pulled his ripcord, and as he descended, he removed his belt and applied it as a tourniquet. He lost his belt upon hitting the water but managed to inflate his life vest and tighten his pants leg as a second tourniquet. He was rescued shortly thereafter.

But there were also cases in which a crew member found that the greatest danger was not the seas but one of his own. A crew of twelve bailed out of a B-29 just prior to ditching in the Bay of Bengal. One was a waist gunner. He inflated his life vest under water and rose to the surface, dazed and belching salt water. He heard a yell from the floating wreckage and hunted inside until he found the radar operator, clutching an oxygen cylinder. The man was unable to swim and complained of pain. The reason soon became clear: he had sustained a broken right arm, a broken hip, and a compound fracture of the left leg. Nonetheless, the waist gunner managed to get both of them from the wreck and inflate the other's life vest. They stayed alive through the night, but at one point the radar operator grew delirious, pulled a knife, and threatened to kill his companion. For a few moments they fought awkwardly for the knife. Finally it was dropped and lost. The next day both were reunited with the rest of the crew, adrift in rafts nearby, and all survived to be rescued.

As for the possibility of riding a life raft through a hurricane, there have been only two documented incidents, both mentioned in Llano's report. The crew of a ditched B-24 rode out a hurricane for three days before making land on the Irish coast, and an Air Force lieutenant lived through a 125-mile-an-hour typhoon in the Pacific. The submarine that rescued him reported that the surface was churning so violently that they had rolled 10 degrees when they were 200 feet below the surface.

Little information regarding these events survives, but certain aspects may be surmised. The conditions on the sea surface in a hurricane are unimaginably violent, with spray as high as 200 feet. Seas would overturn and toss a raft with such violence that a man would have only a vague sense of which way was up. To survive he would have to tie himself loosely to the raft, leaving enough line so that every time the raft is overturned he is not caught beneath, but not so much that he has to swim far to regain it. Certainly the air nearer the surface is so filled with water that he would somehow have to improvise a filter over his mouth and nose so he could breathe.

The twentieth century saw great improvements in survival materials and ditching skills, and yet in 1955 the chance of an aircrew surviving after a ditching was no better than that during any seven-year period since Latham's flight in 1909. The reasons had largely to do with the fact that aircraft had a lower weight to volume ratio—they were heavier. Studies showed that the crew's chance of survival occurs in the span of time between contact with the water and abandonment of the aircraft. In 1955 that span was short. Most ditched aircraft remained afloat only for about sixty seconds.

At Jax the safety program was among the responsibilities of the Operations Department, headed by Commander Ken Mackie in September 1955. Personnel were assigned specifically to stitching life rafts and packing parachutes. They spent a lot of time with glue pots and industrial sewing machines. They took the "Rigger's Pledge": "I will pack every parachute as though I am to jump with it myself, and will stand ready to jump with any parachute which I have certified as properly inspected and packed." So crew members had parachutes, but a parachute would not deploy easily in high winds, and a man hitting the water would likely become hopelessly entangled and drown in minutes. Hence, in the vicinity of the hurricane, the parachute was valuable only as what one aerographer's mate called "a pretty good seat cushion."

The VW-4 crew training syllabus called for ditching drills on a quarterly basis, and training flights practiced simulated emergencies that could progress to the point of preparation for ditching. There was no specific procedure for ditching in a hurricane. Perhaps the thinking was that no amount of instruction would avail a crew, because survival would be impossible.

21

Loss of Signal

10:15 A.M. EST / 1515 Zulu

The last certain radio contact with Crew Five was the message from the aircraft at 8:30 that ended, "Beginning penetration." At 10:15 A.M., the Hurricane Forecast Center in Miami received an unintelligible signal. It is possible that the crew was in the eye, and that atmospherics or precipitation static was interfering with the transmission. It is also possible that the signal was from another source. We can only speculate as to what actually happened. For this reason, the three sections that follow posit three possible courses of events. Although purely imaginary, all are based on eyewitness accounts and accident investigations of aircraft and aircraft crew in circumstances similar to those of Crew Five.

ONE

Inside is the relentless pummeling of the buckshot rain, the unsteady roar of the engines, the unintelligible shouts of crew, the headphone static. Then a new sound: a low groan of stressed metal. It is felt as much as heard, a shudder through the whole plane. Through a side port Clegg can see that near the wing root a section of fuselage is dented. There is a low creaking sound, and at the base of the left wing a small crack appears and widens. A second gust hits the aircraft. There is a shriek of metal and the wing and its engine are torn nearly off, blown back and slammed against the side of the fuselage and tail. For a moment the wing section is hanging by a few wing struts and electrical and hydraulic cables, and there is a terrific banging as it hammers against the fuselage, and the plane yaws to port. Then with a final loud crack it twists off and falls away. Immediately the plane loses all remaining aerodynamics—the aircraft yaws like a hockey player skidding sideways. Windham compensates instinctively, giving full right rudder and cutting power to the remaining engine. But already he knows. The P2V is an aircraft no longer. Now it is a child's broken toy, a length of aluminum pipe falling through the clouds. In the headphones he hears curses and confused scraps of prayer. He knows that the crew is going through the dutiful and ultimately pathetic actions of men trained to save themselves who know they cannot save themselves. He hears calls for tightened safety harnesses. In his mind he goes through the emergency checklist and hears himself shout to brace for the impact. Inside, equipment is shaken loose and slammed against bulkheads, there are unidentifiable shouts, and to his right he sees Herlong straining to read instruments.

They have surrendered themselves to the caprices of the storm and can only hope that they will be spared its worst fury. It should take seconds to fall from 1,000 feet, but the plane does not fall directly—perversely, it is blown sideways. Another gust from behind and it actually cartwheels—once, twice. Then the wind lessens and the plane falls. It slams, upside-down, into the side of a sea, and for a moment seems to find rest there. For what seems a long time it lists horribly, sickeningly. A wave washes over the aft section, and only the underside of the nose and forward crew cabin remain visible. Then from another direction comes a second, larger wave, and the plane disappears, leaving only foam, froth, and the rain-lashed seas.

TWO

A flash of light, the simultaneous crack of thunder. On the headset, Combs is saying that radar has shorted out. Windham calls into his mike.

Herlong tries to scan all the instruments, but the vibration makes them a blur. In his headphones Windham hears Buck tell him that they are at 500 feet. Windham had known pilots to speak of downdrafts, and he does not like the thought of the seas so near, so he tells Herlong they are going to 700 feet, and he and Herlong pull back on the yokes and the plane climbs for 200 more feet. The air seems a bit calmer. Buck tells him they are at 720 feet. But Windham trusts that number about halfway and begins to consider another change of altitude when suddenly the plane is pushed by a great updraft, explosive in its power. The crew are forced back against their seats. Upward acceleration is so fierce it is as though the air beneath them has simply ignited. For whole seconds they are thrust upward, and they strain to breathe. Then the plane slows, they feel the *g*-forces relax, and Windham brings them level. The rain has diminished enough so that they can listen to the engines again. Crew Chief Windham strains to hear. Now both engines are changing speed, and he thinks maybe the propellers are cavitating or maybe the *g*-forces have upset the flyweights. Then another flash of light, another crack of thunder. The aircraft shakes and suddenly it is like a roller-coaster car coming over the crest, and for a long moment they are utterly weightless. Loose objects—a clipboard, a flashlight—float upward in the cabin. Then, as suddenly, they are in a shallow dive. In the cockpit the clipboard and flashlight fall sideways, radios are jarred from their racks, and in mid deck, Morgan is thrown from his seat onto a place where the deck meets a bulkhead.

Outside, panels are ripped from the wing. Windham compensates with right rudder. The engines are still running—an astonishing fact, considering they are being flooded with torrential rain and Windham cannot close the cowl flaps for fear the water will build up inside them. Morgan pulls himself over the wing root and makes his way aft. In a moment he can see that matters there are no better. Clegg, Combs, and Tate had been thrown about. Clegg was struck with a toolbox and his wrist was broken.

Windham hopes to put the plane down on its belly, but Buck and Cronk are still in the observer's station, a dangerous place where the full force of the water will strike. Windham tells the aerologist and the photographer to get to a station in the rear. Cronk goes first. He pulls himself back and moves beneath the crawlspace beneath the cockpit, then makes his way to the right of the navigator station and then through the fuselage. The mood in the aft section is decidedly sober. Everyone—Tate and Cronk too—had been through training on ditching, had heard the lectures and run through the drills. They knew enough to know their odds were slim to nonexistent. There were stories of survival, mostly from World War II, of crews lasting for weeks in open ocean. Yet none of those crews had ditched in hurricanes.

Windham dumps the remaining fuel, knowing that empty tanks would be buoyant, maybe allowing them to float a few minutes more. Greaney comes on the interphone to give Combs their position, and immediately Combs sends it on all frequencies. He receives no response, switches channels, and sends it again. It is all he will do until they are down.

In the aft section, every instinct tells Morgan to maintain the integrity of the aircraft skin—to keep the storm *outside*. Yet he knows that when they ditch, the weight of the plane against the water will hold the hatch shut, so he holds the hatch lever and pushes the hatch with his shoulder. At once there is tremendous suction from outside, and with his free hand he jams a spare life jacket between the slightly opened hatch and the frame, pulls the hatch inward, and wraps the ties of the life jacket twice around the lever. Now there is air and some spray whipping about inside the cabin. In the cockpit, mid deck, and the aft section, the crew tighten their harnesses and brace themselves. Now it is up to Windham and Herlong.

The Navy manual for ditching in high winds recommends "pancaking" the plane on the backside of a swell, the place that is most stable. Windham hopes he will be able to make out the white foam of the wave crests and be able to determine the direction of the waves. He switches on approach lights. He also turns on the searchlight in the starboard wing pod. The sudden view through the forward windscreen is eerie. The seas might be hills in a snowstorm. He knows that if he flies too low, a wingtip might catch a piece of water and the plane could cartwheel. But he needs to get nearer to the water to see, and he hopes that the winds there will be calmer. He strains to identify a swell with a whitecap crest and a trough, but he can make out nothing through the spray. Then he realizes that it's *all* foam and spray. It is impossible to tell the direction of the swells. He cuts power to the remaining engine, drops flaps, and the plane slows almost to stall speed. Again he strains to see. The illustration he remembers from the manual was a line drawing of a light aircraft putting down on an 8- or 10-foot wave, but now he is looking at seas that are three times as big.

They are flying very near the surface, maybe 50 feet above the crests. He can see along the sea. Suddenly they hit the crest of one wave and feel a jarring impact. Then for a second they are airborne again and they crash through a second crest. The plane's nose takes it hard. The observer's station is smashed, and the crew is thrust forward against their seat harnesses. The pilot's side windscreen is cracked, and water explodes into the cabin. There is a mild curse from Morgan, and now they slide over the wave and, nose first, almost fall into the trough behind it. There is more water in the cabin, sounds of wrenching metal, and again the crew is thrown forward against their harnesses. Windham feels the control yoke pulled from his grip, and for a dazed moment he watches it move about violently in all directions as the control surfaces are slapped by waves. The plane is skidding across the seas—lurching, careening. Finally it slows and rests.

They are down.

Windham is facing down a steep slope, half suspended from his seat and restrained only by the harness. It is dark—the electrical systems have shorted. There is no sound of engines, just incessant rain against the aluminum skin and now gushing water, and from somewhere else trickling water and sounds of straining metal and then a sharp crack. The whole fuselage is pitching downward at a steep angle, and it is flooding through the observation station. He calls out and pulls off his headset. There is a sudden flicker of sparks. For a second he sees Herlong held forward in his seat against the straps, eyes open, head bent sideways at an unnatural angle. Then dark again. He reaches across and touches the shoulder and then another lurching. They are listing, and he realizes the right wing must be under water. The increasing weight of the forward section is acting like a sea anchor, stabilizing them, but the cabin is flooding quickly and he guesses they have four or five seconds before they are under water. If they are struck by a wave, they have even less time—one or two seconds. He will have to exit through an aft hatch. To reach it he will have to half climb, half pull himself back through the fuselage. With one hand he braces himself against the instrument panel. He unbuckles his harness and pulls himself upward. Lodging himself between the panel and his own seat, he unstraps Herlong. Then he pulls Herlong's left arm over his shoulder and half pulls and half carries him. He can feel water to his knees—it is almost warm. It is rising and is now waist deep. It is impossible to move. Somewhere he is hung up. The water rises further, to his chest, and for a moment he thinks Herlong has stirred. The water buoys them, and then they are free of whatever was caught. He looks up into the rear and can see nothing—he thinks he can hear shouts. Then, suddenly, the plane shifts and the foam around him rises. He is caught unaware and inhales water and foam, coughing. Again it rises. Suddenly the water engulfs him. Now he releases Herlong and kicks against the backs of the seats, using both hands to climb to the rear of the cabin, trying to find the water surface.

He feels the pressure increasing, he can see only darkness, and he realizes that the plane is sinking quickly, and irretrievably. His final thoughts are muddled, but among them is a vague satisfaction at the knowledge that he will die with his crew.

THREE

The P2V has lost power to an engine, and Buck is in his ditching station near a hatch in the aft section. They had left the eye, but now he can see sunlight through the port, and the plane is flying level. He realizes that Windham and Herlong managed to turn the plane around, and they are in the eye again. It must have been a conscious decision. At least a hundred miles of wind and rough seas separated them from the outer edges of the storm, and the pilots must have known they had a marginally better chance of survival if they ditched in the eye, where the winds were calm and the waves were nonbreaking. Buck senses the plane slowing, descending.

The P2V crashes nose first into the sea, Buck is pushed against his harness with tremendous jolt. He feels the plane yawing to port, and there is a second impact from starboard, and then the plane comes to rest. Buck thinks he is unhurt and he unbuckles his seat harness. He knows that whatever happens next will happen quickly. He prepares himself, and he thinks *Pull hard on the release of the life jacket. Don't do it until you're clear of the hatch. Take a few deep breaths before you jump. Don't hyperventilate. After that, try to stay conscious. Try to stay alive.* The plane is taking on water and it is growing dark. There are shouts behind him, and he thinks he can hear Combs. Buck climbs onto his seat, pulls the hatch release handle, and with his shoulder he pushes the hatch open and throws himself forward and at the same time releases his hold on the hatch. He falls awkwardly into the maelstrom.

His body strikes the side of a swell and he is pounded by an avalanche of green water. There is shock at the utter violence of it. Suddenly he is submerged, inside a wave, several feet under water. He cannot find the surface, but he manages to pull the cord that inflates his life jacket. The added buoyancy seems to count for nothing, yet somehow he is pushed to the surface, and he struggles to breathe. When he inhales, he feels a terrific pain. There is no air, just salt spray, and then for a moment the air is clear of spray and he can actually inhale. The wave carrying him lifts him above surrounding seas, and he gasps for breath. The fit of the life jacket makes it difficult to raise his head, but for a moment he has a view of the ring of storm clouds above. The wave drops Buck a tremendous distance, and he is deep in a wave trough. For a split second he glimpses a horizontal slice of the upper eyewall illuminated with direct sunlight, and he knows that the storm's leading edge is in that direction, and that the opposite wall is moving toward him at 12 miles an hour. Before he completes the thought he is lifted again, 40 feet above the surrounding seas, and then dropped 40 feet into a trough between them. He has difficulty breathing and thinks that he may have broken some ribs during the ditching. He considers that he may be in shock, but he does not know what shock feels like. When he is raised on the next wave, he begins to feel wind. He is dropped again into a trough, and now the water there is white foam. When he is raised yet again, it is all foam, and the blown spray makes it difficult to breathe. The eyewall is nearer.

Then he is in the trough of a sea and cannot see beyond the next crest. The winds are fierce, and before he can take a second full breath, another swell—as though with an actual malevolence—crashes over him. Again he is beneath the surface and again he sees only white foam. He is being beaten on all sides, and he kicks with both feet but there is nothing to kick against. He opens his eyes but there is nothing to see. He throws back his head, hoping he will throw it clear of the water, but it does not clear. He opens his eyes and closes his eyes, and still there is nothing to see. Then, suddenly he feels a wave lift him—his face feels clear of it—he is above water. He coughs, tries to inhale. His side aches. He blinks at the salt spray and again he tries to inhale. But before he can take a full breath, another swell washes over him and again he is in a chaos of foam and ocean. He did not get enough breath and now again he cannot find the surface. Again he pushes with his feet and there is nothing to push against. The jacket should buoy him but here there is only a surging chaos and foam and he kicks against nothing. Then suddenly he feels air on his face. He blinks and he gulps air, but it is thick with spray and he coughs. A sudden flash of lightning illuminates everything and for a moment he can see seas like small hills—it is a frozen image of a giant's world, an enormous stage set—and every detail of foam and froth is unnaturally clear. There is another flash of lightning—the hills have changed places. A sea comes over him.

This time he does not struggle. He can still think, and he knows that unless he can get a full breath soon will begin the wild hysteria of wanting to breathe and being unable to breathe and finally surrendering to the primal, vital imperatives of throat and lungs. He knows that when the time comes, he will let them inhale even if it is water they will inhale. But the time has not come. Suddenly he realizes that again his face is in air. He coughs and gasps and now he tries to see. The others should have followed him into the water. He thought Combs was behind him and he tries to see a life jacket flashlight. The sea comes again.

Buck knows something of the appearance of waves from altitude, but now he is learning about them on terms most intimate. And his thoughts, now slowed by exhaustion, begin to take strange turns. He considers that the period—the interval between the crests—is five or six seconds. Five or six seconds to breathe. Each sea was submerging him for—*how to know?*—perhaps forty seconds. He is becoming accustomed to the rhythm of it: immersion, emergence, immersion again. Live for six seconds. Die for forty. This is the existence given him now, and these are its conditions. And to his dimming awareness, it seems a way of being that a man could get used to. It reminds him of something, but he cannot think what.

He is lifted to the surface again, and again his face is in air and he inhales. He cannot be sure, but through the rain and spray he thinks he sees the tail section of the plane. About 30 feet of it—the rudder, the aerodynamic "stinger" are out of the water. It is not moving—it seems almost to be poised, balanced. He is dumbly amazed at the sight, and he watches it with detached interest. Somehow he knows it should be important, and he cannot remember why. Then, as if by a magician's trick, it simply disappears.

The sea comes again and he feels his consciousness beginning to fade, and he does not fight. Now comes a feeling that is not so much acceptance and resignation as it is a sense of calm. He thinks that he is becoming a part of the sea, needing air and breath no more than a fish or a current does. There is nothing it can do to him now. In his mind the day runs backwards: the jump into the maelstrom, the shouts of the others, the rain against the skin of the plane, the alternating sun and shadow, the takeoff from Gitmo, runway lights glowing red against the lightening horizon. It is all a life so far away it might belong to someone else.

And his last thought is a vague hope that he might awaken.

22

Base

On the morning of September 26, Aerographer's Mate Jim Meyer was working in the Aerology Office at Jax. He was tracking the position using the radio reports, interpolating between reported positions, and drawing a series of x's along an invisible line curving southward from Cuba toward the center of the Caribbean.

The flight had commenced from Gitmo at 1133 Zulu, 6:33 A.M. EST. There had been three position reports: 7:30, 7:45, 8:00. The last certain transmission from Snowcloud Five had been at 8:30, at the moment of penetration. There was a signal at 10:15, but they could not be sure of its origin. Crew Five was expected to return at 4:30 that afternoon. They would have departed the vicinity of the hurricane at approximately 2:30.

After penetration a crew may transmit weather reports almost continually, so long as there is a clear signal. At this stage of the mission there was considerable flexibility, and so for those on base, a great deal of uncertainty. They had had no radio contact with Crew Five for an hour. At some point the mood shifted almost imperceptibly from mere awareness to concern. At 2:30, whatever happened, they should be clear of atmosferics and precipitation static and on their way home. And yet 2:30 had passed and there had been no report. By afternoon, eight Navy planes and two ships began the search.

⤙

When Nan got home from school on September 26 the house was filled with people, men from the base and their wives. Her mother took her aside and told her that her father's airplane was lost, but that she should not worry. The radio in the plane had broken, so it was the Navy that did not know where her father was, but he certainly did and he would be coming home soon. Nan thought a little about this, then at her mother's suggestion she went outside to play. She noticed that cars were parked all along the street, on both sides for several blocks. And she could not help but observe that more cars were arriving, and more people were walking up their front steps and knocking politely and being shown inside. Soon she went back into the house through the back door and snuck into the living room. No one seemed to notice. Her mother was sitting in the big chair near the fireplace. Nan crept behind the chair, waited, and listened.

The visitors would be there all day, and they would stay very late, until after her bedtime. They would come again early in the morning, and her mother would take up her station in the big chair. The doorbell would ring again and someone, not her mother but one of the "guests," would answer. As Monday gave way to Tuesday and Tuesday to Wednesday, there were more and more people, and the talking became more hushed. Her mother was ever polite and gracious. She seemed never to leave that chair.

 ⤚

Thc plane was "officially" missing at 11 P.M. on September 26. At the base a few hours later, a man in the administration office began a particularly unwelcome duty. He typed the following:

A Navy Hurricane Hunter plane with 9 Jacksonville Naval Air Station men aboard and 2 news men has disappeared while probing the 110-mile-an-hour winds of Hurricane Janet. Cmdr E. L. Foster, Commanding Officer of VW-4 at NAS, said the ship was operating out of NAS Guantánamo Bay, Cuba and has been overdue since 6:30 p.m., yesterday. He said the ship had enough fuel to last until about 10:30 last night. An air-sea rescue team has been alerted and will begin combing the Caribbean area at dawn today if no word of the missing plane has been received.

Capt. Frederick Davison of the Navy's Weather Central in Miami said planes and ships from San Juan, Puerto Rico, and Panama have been alerted.

Comdr. Foster, who said a communications alert for the plane was ordered at noon yesterday, said he did not know of any field in the area large enough to accommodate the P2V "Neptune" bomber "with which we are not in communication." He said it was possible, however, that the plane may have landed somewhere else under emergency conditions. A liaison officer at the Miami station, Capt. David Rudle, said a communication from the plane about 8:30 a.m. indicated the pilot intended to make a penetration into the storm.

Among members of the press, Commander Foster's suggestion that the plane may have landed somewhere else was cause for some confusion. It was difficult to know where he might mean. They had been 200 miles from the nearest land in any direction.

The search was conducted by Fleet Weather Central. Captain

Davison said that aircraft and ships were moving as close as possible to the fringes of the hurricane. Janet was still tracking westward at 13 miles an hour. That meant that she would soon leave the area in which Crew Five had ditched, if indeed they had ditched. No one yet cared to utter words for the alternative.

The fact that the signal faded and was lost was nothing new. That in and of itself was no cause for concern. Many crews were out of contact for hours and still returned safely. Likewise, it was impossible to say with any certainty how long after the 8:30 transmission the crew might have continued their mission uneventfully. It was entirely possible they had made a complete reconnaissance of the eye, and that the unintelligible transmission received at 10:15 had indeed been sent by Combs. On the other hand, that signal may have originated from elsewhere, and Crew Five may have begun preparations to ditch only moments after that first penetration.

Wind speed in Janet at the time of Crew Five's disappearance was between 140 and 150 miles an hour. Gusts, therefore, may well have been as high as 225 miles an hour. Forces on the aircraft structure would have been tremendous.

The search and rescue crews knew Crew Five had entered Janet in the trailing left quadrant. If they had managed a complete reconnaissance of the eye, and left it along the same path they entered but in the opposite direction, the search could be restricted to a relatively narrow corridor. The problem was that if Windham and Herlong had somehow miscalculated their point of entry or exit, they may have been swept around the storm's periphery for a considerable distance. Thus the search area was an expanse of ocean 300 miles long and 250 miles wide.

For VW-4's officers, visiting the missing crews' families—the Windhams or the Bucks or the Morgans or the Greaneys—became a duty like any other. They might spend an hour at the Bucks, or the Greaneys. They were Navy officers and practiced in "officer and a gentleman" politesse. They would get the right words in the right places. They could offer a few words of hope, a platitude. But it was difficult. There was no news from the base, and after a while they had nothing to say. In truth, most would have preferred being assigned a search and rescue or a reconnaissance mission. Still, when they were off duty, they went.

Because Tate and Cronk were aboard, there were some international relations matters to deal with, and the unenviable job was given to a Captain G. R. Selby, an information officer at the Pentagon. He notified the *Toronto Daily Star* that Tate and Cronk were aboard the plane. He said, "There is a good chance they may be found. The Neptune was superbly equipped with emergency life-saving gear." (That the Neptune's equipment was "superb" was a matter of opinion; there were standard life jackets and two life rafts.) He told the *Star*, "We have picked up plenty of others in the same circumstances, who have been able to get out their life rafts. The question is whether the crew had time enough to get out the emergency gear and get free of the plane before it came down." It was not the only question. Lieutenant Commander O. B. Adams was better informed and voiced the hopes of the search crews. "We're hoping they cleared the area of violent wind before they had to ditch."

This, indeed, was the best chance. That Crew Five completed its mission and had made it back out through the eyewall and the worst parts of the storm. That whatever happened—engine failure, structural failure, or something else—the pilot and second pilot had retained control and power long enough to manage a ditching. Further, that whatever happened had happened near enough the periphery of the storm that they had a chance to get out of it, and if they had managed to ditch, it was not in 40-foot seas and driving spray.

A mind looks for numbers, examples, odds. The crew had parachutes. No one believed they could be used in a hurricane. They might, though, be used *outside* a hurricane. There were several situations that might put a plane in jeopardy yet allow a pilot to keep it airborne long enough for a crew to bail out. In the case of an engine fire and an imminent explosion, for instance, Windham would have ordered the crew to bail out fast. There were several means to exit the P2V—the forward hatch and aft belly hatch and the windows at the observer stations. There were also less conventional routes—the astrodome and the hinged windows of the cockpit canopy—although these would be inadvisable means to exit for a man with a parachute, as the slipstream was likely to pull him into an aircraft surface. Nonetheless, crews of B-17s had made less probable escapes during the war. And if the cases studied by George Llano had demonstrated anything, it was that the range of possible escapes from aircraft was great.

It was possible that there had been no radio transmission because lightning had struck the plane or because vibrations had caused the VHS transmitter to drop below a voltage at which it could function. Perhaps Combs was otherwise occupied or incapacitated. Perhaps he was injured or unconscious, or perhaps he was assisting Clegg or Tate. It was possible that the plane was lost, but that the crew or at least some of the crew had survived, in life vests or even a life raft, and were drifting somewhere in the waters the hurricane had recently passed over.

If they ditched outside the hurricane, there was a chance. The P2V was a coastal patrol craft designed for overwater missions. Assuming no major ruptures in the hull, in relatively calm seas like those outside a hurricane, it could float for at least a minute. And if Windham thought the way most pilots thought—that is, as someone who considers every available option—then he would have tried to ditch. They would have hit hard. They would have sustained some injuries, and there may have been serious injury or even fatality. But they would have managed to get the life rafts through the hatches. And a few minutes later, when the P2V had sunk out of sight, they would still be there in rafts or life vests, wait-

ing in relatively calm seas and hot sunshine, and every twenty seconds or so riding a swell. They would take comfort in the knowledge that Janet was moving farther from them with every passing
minute. They would make a few jokes. In due time the rescue plane
would circle overhead and radio their position, and a few hours
later a ship would be there to retrieve them. They would be back
at Gitmo by early afternoon. There would be a debriefing, a lot of
forms to fill out, and some bad cases of sunburn.

But imagine the worst. Imagine that they had to ditch in the
storm. Men had been flying into hurricanes for twelve years, and
every one with a view had looked down at the seas in the eye and
imagined, for a moment, what it might be like to be aboard a plane
that was falling into it. Most assumed that death would come
quickly, probably on impact. There would be an initial crash as the
plane touched the surface obliquely, and then a second more violent one, as the plane's forward momentum suddenly diminished,
and its belly slapped into the trough of a sea or the face of a wave.
Lieutenant Edward Bourdet had served as weather officer with Air
Force reconnaissance crews in the 1940s. He said a crew who
ditched in a storm "would not have a chance of getting out alive."
If they were not killed in the force of the ditching, then they would
die by drowning almost immediately thereafter. As to how long the
P2V might stay above the surface in seas like that was a guess, but
it could not have been more than a few seconds. And if they did
not die in a sinking aircraft, then they would suffocate trying to
breathe air so thick with spray that, in the words of one aerologist,
"a fish would drown."

Still, a pilot is no fatalist. Bud Shipman could recall one
instance when his aircraft was out of control and falling out of the
sky. He was over rugged terrain in Wales and was certain he was
about to die. But he kept working and gained control and managed to level out at 800 feet. Pilot and aviation writer William
Langwiesche wrote of another pilot seeing "God is My Copilot"

stenciled on an aircraft, and remarking, "Any son of a bitch who needs God to fly beside him oughta stay on the god-damned ground."

Indeed, Windham and Herlong were a pilot and a copilot with no particular wish to end their own lives, a pilot and copilot responsible for the lives of seven crewmen and two passengers. Probably they did not know that at least two men had lived through hurricanes in life rafts, but certainly they knew that aviation history was full of stories of men who had bailed out of aircraft in improbable circumstances. If there were a chance in a million, Windham and Herlong would have tried. It was true that a successful ditching in a hurricane was unlikely in the extreme, and it was true that there was no record of any such ditching, but it was also true that ditching in a hurricane was not, in the absolute strictest sense of the word, *impossible*. With luck and skill, a lot of both, it could be done.

Grover Windham had seen accidents at sea. He had seen men in shock, and the bodies of the men taken from the *Portland*—he had known the slowing of time. He had also known the feeling of quick adjustments to circumstances and the narrowing range of choices. Perhaps once again, he saw before him a quickly narrowing set of choices—one after the other falling away, until before him was only the final thought and the final acceptance: *We're going to ditch. Okay, then. We're going to ditch.*

It was, she realized, a deathwatch. But she would behave with graciousness and strength. All the new friends so familiar from Saturday nights at the officers' club came to visit. And every time they came, they brought food. People from the base kept coming too, and they all seemed to bring food. The kitchen was full of cakes and covered dishes. It was in the refrigerator, on the countertops. Soon there was nowhere left to put it.

As the wife of a naval aviator, Nancy Windham was conditioned to become a rigorous pragmatist, and in the face of possible death she became almost legalistic in a demand for "ocular evidence." Until remains are located and identified beyond any doubt, he was still out there somewhere, alive. He would return.

There would be a phone call from the base. A few hours later he would be standing in the front hallway. She would cry, she would feel shock, then a sudden and luxurious flood of relief. Certainly there would be a story, and in the days and weeks that followed she would hear him tell it over and over again. He would tell it at home with friends and later he would tell it again at the officers' club. She would hear it so much she would grow tired of it. And when she could bear it no more, she would allow herself to show anger, and one evening she and Grover would go into the bedroom and close the door and begin a "discussion." She would look him in the eye and say that she was worried, that he was unfair and selfish, that she had no desire to be a widow, and that she wanted her children to know their father when they grew older. And he would answer her point by point. He would say that the circumstances that contributed to the accident were unusual and unlikely to be repeated. He would say that their life in Jacksonville was good. He would say that he would be more careful in the future. And somehow they would resolve the matter. They would stay at Jax, or they would request a new billet, or they would quit the Navy altogether. But he would return, and soon enough, life would be normal again.

He would be back. It had happened often enough. He had, after all, survived the worst. He had lived through Guadalcanal.

In one analysis of 607 incidents of water survival, the time downed crews spent awaiting rescue ranged from five minutes to forty-eight days. Most recoveries—68 percent—were made within the first twenty-four hours. Twenty percent of the men were recovered between the second and fifth days, 4 percent on days six through eight, and the remaining 8 percent in the six weeks following. Obviously, the chances of recovery diminished rapidly with time. But rescuers may have found cause for hope in the fact that after the sharp dropoff after the first day, the falloff becomes more gradual. It is easier to stay alive after the second day than it is between the first and second. So there was cause for hope.

By Wednesday, September 28, the search was expanded. Four planes from Jacksonville, two from Patrol Squadron Three and two from Patrol Squadron Five, were dispatched to Gitmo. There were already others—three PBM Mariners and three P5M Marlin seaplanes from the Canal Zone were criss-crossing that stretch of water in the middle of the Caribbean. Rescue reports collected during World War II demonstrated that the best altitude for sighting life rafts was 800 to 1,000 feet, and the best altitude for spotting a man afloat was about half that. Glare off the water made it difficult, and for this reason there would be a better chance of a sighting from multiplace aircraft, with spotters stationed at various ports and viewing the water from different angles with respect to the sun.

And then came the clearest reminder that pursuits of VW-4 were not merely scientific. Had missions been of mere scientific interest, the loss of a crew would have had an immediate effect on operations. Further missions would have been postponed at least until an investigation was begun or even completed. But hurricane season at Jax was something like a war. Hurricane Janet was still out there, and her winds were gaining strength. Even as search and rescue operations were underway, she was threatening the coast of the Yucatán Peninsula. And because her precise trajectory was in question, the need for VW-4 was as great as ever. So the squadron's work went on, still flying two missions a day, ten or twelve hours each. On schedule, another plane left Guantánamo Bay. The crew had orders to be on the watch for the missing aircraft, but their primary mission was to reconnoiter Janet. They flew a P2V-5JF, the advanced version of the Neptune with two Westinghouse jet engines. They made a low-level reconnaissance and penetrated the eye. They clocked winds at 135 miles per hour. The entry took its toll. The commander reported possible wing overstress and little to no aileron control. He called to request a return; it was granted immediately.

Janet's winds diminished only slightly. On September 27 at midday she approached the Swan Islands, where the U.S. Weather Bureau shared a station with Navy seismographers. There were eight men there. One was John Laban, who had dreamed a message was sent regarding his own death.

Laban prepared the Quonset building for the storm, cut off butane gas, went to the mess hall, and then the weather station. He wrote in the log, "Winds increasing, waves higher, a few coconut trees starting to uproot." Laban and his colleagues released a radiosonde that rose to 45,000 feet, where it found winds at gale force. A P2V made a low pass, within 100 feet of the ground, and the pilot said, "You boys have your hole ready? Better get into it." They covered transmitters and receivers with empty mailbags, abandoned the weather station, and took cover in the mess hall. At noon Laban estimated the wind was 150 miles an hour. A diesel tank near them burst, and they were soaked with the fuel, so they made a run for the concrete seismograph building, where they expected to wait the storm out. At 6 P.M. the winds and rain subsided, and they emerged. Laban wrote, "The sky is partly cloudy but the wind is still gale force. The island seems desolate—out of 10,000 coconut trees, only a few are still standing."

On the next day they began cleaning up and chlorinating water. Laban reported, "Isolated cattle, some beaches on SE side washed clean of all sand—other beaches piled with more sand—the woods and coconut groves almost impenetrable because of fallen trees and shrubs. . . . Preparations are going on to throw off debris from power shed to get at least one generator going. . . ."

Destruction was terrific, but Laban's premonition was wrong. He had survived.

Everything was conspiring to make Janet a storm to be feared. Her winds were increasing. It was near the autumnal equinox, a time of gravitational high tide. Moving almost directly west, all Janet needed to make the seas worse was a north-south coast and low-sloping land. A great deal of the coast in the direction she was headed fit that description. Some thought she might veer south slightly. But she stayed on a westward course, and on the twenty-eighth raked across the Yucatán Peninsula.

Aida Garcia was a housewife in Corozal, Belize. She went to the shelter with her husband Gregorio, four children, and two-month-old baby. Near midnight the ceiling of the shelter was ripped off. It was a rum distillery with large wooden vats. Her husband overturned one and put his wife and children inside. They spent the rest of the hurricane inside those vats and survived.

Maria Gomez was twelve years old and living in a two-story wooden building in Corozal. Her parents heard on the radio that Janet was approaching and took their family to the town hall. The wind became so strong that the walls began to crack. The wind finally stopped, and when the radio said they could leave their shelters, Maria's father told his wife to go home and make tea for everyone. When they reached their home, they saw it had been destroyed. Maria saw her father start to cry.

Janet tore across part of the Yucatán Peninsula and kept a steady westward course, entering the Bay of Campeche. The shrimp boat *Celestino Arias* out of Tampa had been working in the bay when it had suffered engine failure. Late on September 28 she was being towed by two sister ships. Gale-force winds snapped the two lines and the *Celestina Arias* began to take on water. A crewman named James Williams blacked out in a diabetic coma. The ship was sinking, and his crewmates strapped a life jacket around him and lowered him into the water. Captain Earl G. Millington retrieved Williams and swam with him to one of the sister ships, where crewmen pulled them aboard.

On September 29 Janet came ashore again in Veracruz. Her winds were undiminished. Once again she brought widespread destruction and death.

Meanwhile, throughout that long week there had been ten more reconnaissance flights of Janet. Each of those missions had orders to be on the alert for Windham's plane. None reported any sign of it. On Friday, September 30, airborne radar on a Super Connie had picked up an object in the storm's wake. Better identification was impossible, but the ships were sent to the area to investigate.

The search would last for four days and twenty hours. It would involve sixty aircraft, seven ships, and three thousand personnel. Ultimately, they would find nothing. Near the end of the week the search and rescue commander issued a "termination report" that stated in part, "It is believed that there is no chance of survival or rescue of personnel of the P2V."

⬩

On Saturday, a friend answered the door, and there they were, standing patiently on the steps outside: Commander Foster and two solemn-faced officers in dress uniform. The friend opened the door and stepped back. The three men walked slowly into the living room, eyes straight ahead. No one else moved. Nancy was sitting in the chair by the fireplace. They stopped on the carpet a few feet before her. Foster looked at Nancy, and she could see that his eyes were a little wet. He unfolded a letter. The two others stood on either side with hats held behind them and looked straight ahead. From where she sat, they seemed to be looking at the wall over her head. She did not need to hear the words, but in a quiet but steady voice, Foster began reading the letter: "The Secretary of the Navy has asked me to express his deepest regret that your husband Grover B. Windham was killed in action on September 26, 1955 while conducting reconnaissance on Hurricane Janet. The Secretary extends his deepest sympathy to you and your family in this tragic loss."

He folded the letter. Then she nodded and began to cry softly. She said she understood and appreciated all that had been done. There were sounds of quiet crying in the room. Then, suddenly, there was crying and then screaming from behind the chair. It was Nan. Someone tried to pick her up, but she broke free and ran back to her bedroom. She picked up a doll, a doll her father had given her, and she began to tear it apart. A few of the guests had run after her and could not understand her words for a moment. Then they realized that as she was pulling the doll apart, she was saying over and over again that this was what had happened to her daddy.

•

When Nan woke a few hours later, her mother was sitting next to the bed, and she talked very quietly and calmly. She told her that her father had died. They cried a long time. When they stopped, Nancy told Nan she needed to be strong for her brother, that she needed to be a good big sister. She said she was about to talk with Buz, and she would like Nan to be there with her. It was late afternoon, and the people were still in the house, talking quietly. Buz was outside with friends. Nancy called him in. There were people almost everywhere in the house, but the study was empty.

Nancy closed the door. She sat near Buz and told him that there had been an accident, and that Daddy would not be coming home. Buz said he did not understand. She said his father's plane had been lost in a storm. She waited and studied his face. Then she said that Daddy was now flying with God. Buz wanted to know *why*.

The particulars, the *hows* of it she could explain, but this was a question she could not answer even for herself, and so she began to cry. Buz began to cry, too.

Nan Windham knew that her mother depended on her, and she thought that she might say something, offer a change of subject. She looked at her mother and asked when they were going to get a dog. It made no sense. Her father had wanted a dog, and now he was gone, and her mother, who had *not* wanted a dog, was here—and yet Nan asked when they might get a dog. But suddenly Buz stopped crying. Nancy looked at Nan, and then looked at Buz, a little surprised. She swallowed once and blinked through her tears and said they would get a dog soon, perhaps the next time they went to their grandparents' house.

On Sunday, October 2, 1955, Commander Foster announced to the press that the search was being terminated. Ships and aircraft searching the several hundreds of square miles of open water south of Jamaica were recalled, and the Navy announced that while investigative flights would be made when floating debris was reported, it was ending its search for Windham and his crew. Foster said he had contacted families of the missing fliers personally, and as per Navy tradition, officers and men closest to the men and their families had been chosen to convey the decision to end the search.

Meanwhile, administration's work had ground on, and a list of promotions was released. Windham had been made a commander.

23

Aftermath

      Administration staff pulled records and located the "next of kin" as indicated on the forms. For Greaney it was a wife named Margaret in Jacksonville. For Buck a wife named Barbara in Jacksonville. For Morgan a wife Joan in Orange Park. For Mann a brother in Canton, Ohio. For JP Windham a wife Eloise in Jacksonville. For Combs a mother in Forest Port, New York. For Clegg a wife Joan in Cranston, Rhode Island. Seven times, three men in dress whites walked up front steps, removed their hats, knocked on a door or rang a doorbell, and waited to be shown inside. Then, while two stood at attention and looked straight ahead, the other read the letter.

      Newspapers wanted photographs, and the Public Information Office was expected to supply them. It was like the grim bureaucracy of war again. In personnel files there were glossies of officers in dress uniform, studio portraits made on the day they gained a promotion. The photographs of the enlisted men had been taken on base as per regulations, and some of their subjects were unkempt. They were not flattering photographs, but they were truthful. There was at least one image of all of them together— Windham, Herlong, Buck, and the rest. It was on the undeveloped roll of film in Doug Cronk's camera.

On Tuesday, October 4, 1955, services were held for six of the flyers and the newsmen at the Protestant chapel at 9 A.M.: Commander Grover Windham, Herlong, Buck, Morgan, Clegg, and JP Windham. A requiem high mass was sung an hour later in the Catholic chapel for Greaney, Combs, and Mann. All off-duty personnel of Squadron VW-4 were expected to attend both services.

Nancy had told her daughter and son that they were going to church to say good-bye to their father. She also asked them to be as quiet and still as possible. Their father would not like it if they caused a scene. They must be good soldiers to show him how much they loved him and to make him proud. So there they were, in a church full of people. Nan had never seen so many people in one place being so quiet. The three of them sat in the front pew. Through the whole ceremony Nancy and the children looked straight ahead at the chaplain and were very still.

When the service was over, the chaplain presented a folded American flag to Nancy. A bugler outside the building sounded "Taps." One bit of ceremony remained, and to witness it, they left the chapel and walked to the airfield. One of the squadron's Connies was being loaded with wreaths of flowers. It was headed for the last known position of Snowcloud Five, where its crew would drop the wreaths. The plane took off, circled once, and flew south by southeast. They watched until it was a dark speck on the horizon. They watched until they could no longer see it.

Then they went home, and again people were there, talking seriously and quietly. Nan wandered around the house, listening. Although she understood that her father was dead as much as any child could understand such a fact, she did not understand the particulars. Tearing apart the doll was a theory, something she had tried out. But she noticed that now they were using a new word. They were calling it the "accident." The word explained nothing. What happened—*exactly* what happened—was a mystery to her, and she sensed that these men in uniforms had solved it. She drifted among groups of officers and wives, listening intently. Sometimes when she came near, they stopped talking and looked at her and smiled. She asked the men in the uniforms, How could her father have been lost at sea if his job was the safest in the Navy? They would kneel, look at her with red-rimmed eyes, and hold her. They would say that things were going to be all right.

—◆—

Gradually the storm moved northward along the coast, wreaking devastation in a swath 80 miles wide. By the last days of September from all along the coast of Veracruz there were reports of hunger and sickness. By October 1 the death toll from Janet had reached two hundred.

For a few days the Associated Press reported on the hurricane and the devastation in parts of Mexico. In the United States there were other concerns. Eisenhower was recovering from a heart attack, and the Dodgers had won the World Series, the first team ever to win a best-of-seven series after losing the first two games. More and more, the stories related to Hurricane Janet were relegated to the back pages. The loss of Crew Five was mentioned in a few papers. The *New York Times* and of course the Jacksonville and Miami papers did several pieces that week. But neither *Time* nor *Newsweek* bothered to report the story.

And at Jax, there was speculation. Some said that Windham's showmanship had gotten the best of his better judgement, that perhaps he had flown lower than he should have to give Tate and Cronk a better look at the white seas. Jim Meyer would say it was unlikely, as no pilot took chances in a hurricane. Lieutenant John McTammay was a navigator who had flown into Janet with Crew Two. He told a reporter, "There's no way of guessing what happened."

A week later, Mexican customs officials spotted wreckage on a beach about 10 miles south of the mouth of the Rio Grande. It was a long way from the last known position, and no one thought the crew might have survived, but there was hope of finding at least a part of the plane. It was indeed aircraft wreckage, but not Snowcloud Five. It was an abandoned training plane that had been flown from Naval Air Station Corpus Christi and had made an emergency landing in a lagoon. A few days earlier its crew had been brought ashore by the Coast Guard.

At Jax a three-person board of investigation presented a report to the commander of Fleet Air Wing Eleven. Its findings were based on testimony from members of administration, operations, and maintenance, or in the words of the report, "those concerned with direction of missions, training of crews and maintenance of aircraft." It was a ten-page, single-spaced document that attempted to parse "findings of fact"—lists of ranks and service records, maintenance records, and so forth—from "opinions," the authors' own interpretation of events.

The report's conclusions were mostly about what was *not* the case. It maintained that the disappearance of Crew Five was "not due to the intent, fault, negligence or inefficiency of any person in the naval service." There was "no evidence of sabotage." It continued, "Pilot and copilot were in all respects physically and mentally qualified to perform their duties" and crew members were "sufficiently trained and qualified." The entire crew, officers and enlisted men, as well as the newsmen, had been "adequately checked out and drilled in emergency procedures." The report concluded, "Under the circumstances of sea and wind which reportedly prevail during hurricane penetrations, it is doubtful that a crew could survive a ditching." It did not entertain the possibility of extenuating circumstances—a ditching perhaps beyond the storm's outer edges. Neither did it speculate as to the nature of the accident that might have occurred.

On its tenth and final page, the report recommended an investigation of the "necessity of flying into the eye of a hurricane, or for circumnavigating the eye of the storm at low level, once the storm has been established as a hurricane." It recommended further that "the aircraft employed in hurricane penetration missions be equipped with at least four engines" and that "P2V aircraft employed should have two jet engines installed in addition to the two reciprocating engines. . . ."

At 11:45 A.M. on October 2, at Aberdeen Proving Ground, the power to ENIAC was removed. It was shut down and cooled, and dust began to settle on the cabinets. ENIAC had become obsolete. Coincidentally, it was the same day the search for Windham and his crew was officially ended.

Epilogue

It seemed that there was something changing in the weather. The U.S. Navy sponsored a study whose result was a publication called *Intensification of Tropical Cyclones, Atlantic and Pacific Areas.* In 1956 the U.S. Weather Bureau, in collaboration with the Navy, the Air Force, and the Army Corps of Engineers, organized a National Hurricane Research Project. It was Robert Simpson's design—the largest meteorological research project ever. It employed two WB-50s and one B-47 from the 55th Weather Reconnaissance Squadron. It also used photographs from rockets taken from altitudes of 50 miles. The study began to answer the old questions of rain bands, internal circulation, and the hurricane's origin. In spring of 1959 the National Hurricane Research Project was merged with the Hurricane Forecast Center in Miami to form the National Hurricane Center.

In 1962 the Navy and Weather Bureau began Project Stormfury, an experiment in controlling or at least reducing the destructive power of hurricanes. It would be accomplished by releasing freezing nuclei into the ring of clouds around the eye, in an attempt to lower the temperature gradients within the storm, thereby reducing pressure gradients and hence wind speeds. Crews may have had some success in affecting the development of Hurricane Debbie in August 1969, but no one could be sure the changes would not have occurred without their intervention. In subsequent years meteorologists became more concerned for unforeseen consequences and side effects, and the program was cancelled in 1983.

The ratio of property damage to number dead is a crude but illuminating means to demonstrate the effectiveness of warning services. Before the establishment of hurricane reconnaissance, for every $10 million dollars in property damage in the United States, about four hundred people lost their lives. By the late 1950s the second number was reduced to four.

VW-4 continued to add to its accomplishments. In 1959 the squadron recorded the entire life of Hurricane Gracie, taking more than 30,000 frames of radar photographs. During the 1960s the squadron actively assisted the tracking and recovery efforts of NASA's manned space program. In 1974 the concentric eyes of Hurricane Carmen were penetrated by a VW-4 aircraft under the command of a woman, Patrol Plane Commander Lieutenant Judy Neuffer.

On April 30, 1975, Weather Reconnaissance Squadron Four was decommissioned, ending thirty years of service. During their existence the Navy's Hurricane Hunters flew 2,119 missions and made 1,390 penetrations into 281 storms.

In the meantime, satellite technology allowed meteorologists to depend less on manned reconnaissance. It has yet to make such reconnaissance obsolete. For major hurricanes, the eye is well formed and easily monitored from satellites. But weak hurricanes or hurricanes in early stages are likely to have upper-level clouds that obscure their exact center. Flying into the storm's eye remains the best means to discover its exact location and direction. As of this writing, most hurricane reconnaissance is accomplished by the U.S. Air Force Reserve's 53rd Weather Reconnaissance Squadron, flying WC-130 turboprops. Its crews collect data on hurricanes in the Atlantic Ocean, Caribbean Sea, and Gulf of Mexico, and still radio the information to forecasters at the National Hurricane Center. If a hurricane is developing in the Atlantic or Caribbean, it is a good bet that a crew from the 53rd is flying reconnaissance on it. At present, the only other flights into storms are accomplished by the National Oceanic and Atmospheric Administration, which uses two WP-3D turboprops for scientific research.

Perhaps the Mexica were right in their belief that continued existence depends in part on destruction. For all their destructive force, hurricanes serve a kind of ecological function, acting as a thermostat, transporting heat from near the equator poleward. If for some reason hurricanes suddenly ceased to form, the consequences for the planet would be immediate and dire. The earth's tropical regions would become increasingly hotter and the poles colder. With no means to distribute excess heat, these trends would accelerate, and in a very short time the earth's climates would change radically.

The atmospheric warming detected in the 1950s by Roger Revelle and Jerome Namais seemed to slow and reverse itself—that is until the 1990s, when most atmospheric scientists concluded that warming was real and caused at least in part by human activities. Stanley B. Goldenberg and a group at the National Oceanic and Atmospheric Administration's Hurricane Research Division believe the waters of the North Atlantic Ocean have been warming in recent years, providing increased energy to fuel hurricanes.

In April 1957 a seventy-two-hour forecast by the Joint Meteorological Committee, using the IBM-701, was more accurate than its subjective counterpart. But computer modeling, it seemed, soon reached its theoretical limit. By the 1980s, many meteorologists began to suspect that atmospheric models were insufficient for predictions of more than two weeks. They had come to accept the validity of "sensitive dependence on initial conditions"—Edward Lorenz's "butterfly effect," the idea that small eddies of moving air created by the stroke of a butterfly's wings could grow, weeks later, into a tropical cyclone.

In the 1950s Jules Charney had an intuition that there was a limit to weather predictability, but he attributed the limit to a lack of data—the error of representativeness or a difficulty in the "parameterization of turbulent processes." Chaos theory, developed in the 1970s, suggested that the problem was deeper, a more fundamental property of natural systems.

Nonetheless, by the year 2000, the National Hurricane Center in Miami was using many computer models: nine for tracking a hurricane's course and four for predicting its intensity. Some were "simple statistical" models, others were "three-dimensional," and even the simplest was far more complex than that imagined by Lewis Richardson in the 1930s. In the views of some, the disadvantage of some models is that they are inherently "conservative." What meteorologists term *extreme events*, hurricanes among them, have been better explained by subjective analysis. The difficulty was that no one understood exactly why subjective analysis was better, in part because no one understood subjective analysis. (Robert Simpson once asked Grady Norton how he managed so many successful predictions of hurricane paths. Norton told him he stared at clouds sometimes, and the answer "just came.") Recently, though, some researchers have focused on parsing that activity. Certainly it involves rudimentary physics, experience, and memory. It seems that there is a quality of human intelligence that is as yet ill defined—some might call it intuition, others might term it unconscious pattern recognition.

➤

There is an old anonymous poem that is a litany of cause and effect and anticipates the butterfly effect by several hundred years: Because there was no nail to shoe a horse, they had no horse—and so lost a rider, a battle, a war, and finally a kingdom. The suggestion, of course, is that large effects derive from small causes. Perhaps more interestingly, it also suggests there are "nodes," points of instability, forks in the path of history. The idea seems reasonable and even intuitively obvious.

We might imagine many such nodes in the story of the mission of Windham and his crew. If Windham had stayed at a higher altitude, perhaps a certain downdraft would not have struck a wing. If Jim Meyer had flown, he would have died, but the newsmen would have lived. If another crew had been assigned, perhaps Crew Five would have lived to fly a search and rescue mission. Had ENIAC's development been speeded, forecasting models might have been developed to the point where reconnaissance might have been aided, and Crew Five might have avoided a certain part of the storm. Had Babbage's computer been funded, built, and put into use by the time Richardson began applying numerical forecasting, computer models might have made some reconnaissance flights unnecessary. Had William Redfield's understanding of cyclonic structure been developed and applied, there might have been incentive toward the development of Doppler radar. Had Henry Piddington's interests been carried out and acted on, more might have been understood of upper-level winds.

Each of these or all of these might be nodes at which events may have taken a different course. But chaos theory as it is understood by many suggests that such nodes are not discrete and intermittent. Rather, they occur at *every* moment, all points are equally unstable. Small matters and matters with no clear relation to a given outcome may affect it. A ten-year-old girl's misunderstood spelling lesson, a British numerical meteorologist dabbling in poetry—all of these events, in some subtle and perhaps unknowable way, influenced a larger history.

～

Many societies and cultures formalize the means to care for those members who have suffered loss. *Leviticus 25* says, "If brethren dwell together, and one of them die, and have no child, the wife of the dead shall not marry without unto a stranger: her husband's brother shall go in unto her, and take her to him to wife, and perform the duty of an husband's brother unto her." It is a precept advantageous to a people who wish to endure, explained in the next verse: "And it shall be, that the firstborn which she bareth shall succeed in the name of his brother which is dead, that his name be not put out of Israel." But it is also a kind of social welfare, a collective kindness. The Navy itself was and is a kind of family, and men who served as shipmates, perhaps especially those who saw combat, formed bonds as close or closer than brothers. In the years following the loss of Crew Five, John Haynie and Nancy Windham grew to know each other better. Haynie was under no obligation from the Navy, and in all likelihood was unaware of the biblical proscription. His offer of marriage no doubt had more complex motivations. At any rate, she accepted. Nan and Buz had known John Haynie as their father's friend. In time they grew to love him, and call him "Dad."

～

After World War II, psychologists began studies of trauma. Most of the subjects of these studies were prisoners of war or battlefield veterans, and the psychological effects of such experiences seemed to be of two types. There was a short-term trauma, its symptoms "normal stress reactions." Some of these were primarily emotional: shock, fear, anger, guilt, helplessness, and a sort of emotional numbness. Others might be categorized as cognitive: confusion, disorientation, fatigue, and insomnia. In most cases all symptoms disappeared by a month. But psychologists also identified a more serious trauma that could last far longer. Its victims had feelings of being outside themselves, a sense of living inside a dream. They suffered from nightmares, flashbacks, and panic attacks. Such symptoms, if they lasted long enough, could develop into a severe and prolonged depression.

Nan Windham did not suffer depression as such, but for a while she had blamed herself for her father's loss, using a sort of magical thinking. He had died and the plane had been lost because she had refused to hug and kiss him good-bye. It was another theory, an idea she took up for a while and forgot. In time, Nan stopped asking the men in uniforms to explain the loss of her father's plane. She realized they had no answer and could give her none. At least once, however, they tried.

The family had moved 50 or so miles inland, to Gainesville. It happened that a few weeks before his flight into Hurricane Janet her father had bought a great deal of life insurance, and her mother was able to buy a house for cash. She said that in some way he was still taking care of them.

By 1959, four years after her father's death, Nan and her mother and younger brother had adjusted, and Nan was living a mostly pleasant and unremarkable childhood. Friends and family had been on the lookout for a smallish dog that Nancy would feel comfortable with and that would satisfy Buz and Nan. A farmer in Millport, a friend of their grandparents, had one. She was a solid white, mixed-breed mutt they called Missy.

When Nan was in the seventh grade she entered the school science fair. She decided to make her project on hurricanes—how they developed, the destruction they could cause. It did not occur to her to make the project personal or otherwise mention that her father had been among those lost while performing storm reconnaissance. She had no plans to recount the pretend rides into hurricanes she had taken on her father's knee. She did intend, however, to acknowledge the work of the Navy weather reconnaissance squadrons. And although Nan started her research in the library, she realized she might gain much by a direct approach, and she wrote a short letter to the squadron in Jacksonville, telling them about her project, and asking if they might send her a few pictures of a hurricane. Again it did not occur to her to identify herself as anyone other than a junior high school student working on a science project. She expected they would send her perhaps five or six glossy photographs. But weeks passed without an answer, and she assumed her letter was lost or, more likely, discarded along with the hundreds of requests they received from seventh graders. She resigned herself to using only what she had found in the library.

Then, she came home from school one afternoon, and her mother said three sailors had driven over from Jacksonville. Missy had made quite a fuss, but they had been very polite, she said. They stayed only long enough to make sure they had the right address and to be assured that their delivery would get to the daughter of Lieutenant Commander Windham. Stacked against the wall in the kitchen were three large boxes.

The contents of those boxes would allow thirteen-year-old Nan Windham to win the school and county science fairs. She opened them carefully, one at a time. The first contained a complete history of the Navy Hurricane Hunters. The second was reams of scientific information and hurricane maps of the Atlantic Ocean and Caribbean Sea, showing the path of every hurricane on record. In the third box was something she had never seen before. It was several large pieces of pasteboard. One could unfold the pieces and fit them together to make a three-dimensional model cutout of a hurricane. All of this—the scientific papers, the history, the cardboard hurricane—was labeled as material from the VW-4 education office.

In the last box was a small strut to attach to the cardboard storm. There was something in the bottom of the box: the thing to attach to the other end of that strut. It was wrapped in cellophane, and somehow it looked impossibly fragile. She picked it up and held it to the light. It was a small model of an airplane.

Bibliography

Anderson, William C. *Hurricane Hunters; A Novel.* New York: Crown Publishers, 1972.

Bates, Charles C., and Fuller, John F. *America's Weather Warriors, 1814–1985.* College Station: Texas A&M University Press, 1986.

Battan, Louis J. *The Nature of Violent Storms.* Garden City, N.Y.: Anchor Books, 1961.

Becher, Alexander Bridport. *The Storm Compass, or Seaman's Hurricane Companion: Containing a Familiar Explanation of the Hurricane Theory.* London: Walter Spiers, 1853.

Berry, F. A., Bollay, E., and Beers, N. R. *Handbook of Meteorology.* New York: McGraw-Hill Book, 1945.

Bohun, R. (Ralph). *A Discourse Concerning the Origine and Properties of Wind: With an Historicall Account of Hurricanes and Other Tempestuous Winds.* Oxford: Printed by W. Hall for Tho. Bowman, 1671.

Brooks, C. F. *Why the Weather?* New York, 1924.

Buck, Robert N. "Hurricane—Inside." *Air Facts,* 1945.

Charney, J., Fjortoft, R., and von Neumann, J. "Numerical Integration of the Barotropic Vorticity Equation." *Tellus* 2: 237–254, 1950.

Cline, Isaac M. *Tropical Cyclones.* New York, 1926.

Clowes, Ernest S. *The Hurricane of 1938 on Eastern Long Island.* New York: Hampton Press, 1939.

Daley, Roger. *Atmospheric Data Analysis.* New York: Cambridge University Press, 1991.

DeBlieu, Jan. *Wind: How the Flow of Air Has Shaped Life, Myth, and the Land.* Boston: Houghton Mifflin, 1999.

Deppermann, C. E. *Outlines of Philippine Frontology.* Manila, 1936.

Dove, Heinrich Wilhelm. *The Law of Storms.* London, 1862.

Dunn, Gordon E., Davis, W. R., and Moore, P. L. "1955: Hurricanes of 1955." *Monthly Weather Review* 83: 315–326, 1956.

Dunn, Gordon E., and Miller, Banner I. *Atlantic Hurricanes.* Baton Rouge: Louisiana State University Press, 1964.

Eliot, John. *Handbook of Cyclonic Storms of the Bay of Bengal.* Calcutta, 1900.

Elsner, James B., and Kara, A. Birol. *Hurricanes of the North Atlantic: Climate and Society.* New York: Oxford University Press, 1999.

Engle, Eloise. *Escape, from the Air and from the Sea.* New York: John Day, 1963.

Espy, James P. *The Philosophy of Storms.* Boston: Charles C. Little and James Brown, 1841.

Fincher, Lew, and Read, Bill. "The 1943 'Surprise' Hurricane." Internet. City of Houston Office of Emergency Management.

Fishman, Jack, and Kalish, Robert. *The Weather Revolution.* New York: Plenum Press, 1994.

Fleming, James Roger. *Meteorology in America, 1800–1870.* Baltimore: Johns Hopkins University Press, 1990.

Fuller, John F. "Weatherman Third to Enter Hurricane's Eye." *AWS Observer* 25, no. 11, 1978.

Gleick, James. *Chaos: Making a New Science.* New York: Viking Penguin, 1987.

Grayson, Jack, et. al. "P2V 131442 Neptune Mishap Incident Report." Unpublished manuscript, Department of the Navy, 1955.

Greenfield, Stanley M., and Kellogg, William W. "Inquiry into the Feasibility of Weather Reconnaissance from a Satellite Vehicle." RAND report R-365, Santa Monica, Calif.: RAND Corp., April 1951.

Halacy, Daniel S., Jr. *The Weather Changers.* New York: Harper & Row, 1968.

Haurwitz, B. "The Height of Tropical Cyclones and the 'Eye' of the Storm." *Monthly Weather Review* 63, 1935.

Hyman, Anthony. *Charles Babbage: Pioneer of the Computer.* Princeton: Princeton University Press, 1982.

Joint Numerical Weather Prediction Unit Staff Members. "One Year of Operational Numerical Weather Prediction." *AMS Bulletin* 38, no. 5: 263–268, 1957.

Jordan, E. "An Observational Study of the Upper Wind Circulation around Tropical Storms." *Journal of Meteorology* 9: 340–346, 1952.

Kempf, Karl. "Electronic Computers within the Ordnance Corps." Aberdeen Proving Ground, Md.: Ballistics Research Laboratory, 1961.

Kinston, W., and Rosser, R. "Disaster: Effects on Mental and Physical State." *Journal of Psychosomatic Research* 18: 437, 1974.

Langwiesche, William. *Inside the Sky: A Meditation on Flight.* New York: Vintage Books, 1998.

Llano, George Albert. *Airmen against the Sea: An Analysis of Sea Survival Experiences.* Maxwell Air Force Base, Ala.: Research Studies Institute, 1956.

MacSparran, James. *America Dissected, Being a Full and True Account of All the American Colonies, Shewing the Intemperance of the Climates, Excessive Heat and Cold, and Sudden Violent Changes of Weather, Terrible and Mischievous Thunder and Lightning, Bad and Unwholesome Air, Destructive to Human Bodies, etc.* Dublin, 1753.

Markus, Rita M., Halbeisen, Nicholas F., and Fuller, John F. *Air Weather Service: Our Heritage 1937–1987.* Military Airlift Command, Scott Air Force Base, Ill., 1987.

McCartney, Scott. *ENIAC: The Triumphs and Tragedies of the World's First Computer.* New York: Walker, 1999.

Moin, Parviz, and Kim, John. "Tackling Turbulence with Supercomputers." *Scientific American* 276., no. 1: 62–68, 1997.

Monmonier, Mark. *Air Apparent: How Meteorologists Learned to Map, Predict, and Dramatize the Weather.* Chicago: University of Chicago Press, 1999.

Mutza, Wayne. *Lockheed P2V Neptune: An Illustrated History.* Atglen, Penn.: Schiffer Publishing, 1996.

Platzman, G. "The ENIAC Computations of 1950: Gateway to Numerical Weather Prediction." *AMS Bulletin* 60: 302–312, 1979.

Reclus, Élisée. *The Ocean, Atmosphere and Life.* New York, 1874.

Redfield, William C. "Observations on the Storm of December 15, 1839." *Transactions of the American Philosophical Society* 8, 1843.

Richardson, Lewis F. *Statistics of Deadly Quarrels.* Ed. Quincy Wright and C. C. Lienau. Pittsburgh: Boxwood Press, 1960.

Richardson, Lewis F. *Weather Prediction by Numerical Processes.* Cambridge: Cambridge University Press, 1922.

Riehl, H. *Tropical Meteorology.* New York: McGraw-Hill Book, 1954.

Saucier, W. *Principles of Meteorological Analysis.* Chicago: University of Chicago Press, 1955.

Schaefer, Vincent J. "Can We Do It Better?" *AMS Bulletin* 39, no. 1: 90–92, 1958.

Selye, Hans. "The General Adaptation Syndrome and the Disease of Adaptation." *Journal of Clinical Endocrinology* 6, 1946.

Simpson, Robert H. "Exploring the Eye of Typhoon Marge." *AMS Bulletin* 33, no. 7: 286–298, September 1952.

Soustelle, Jacques. *Daily Life of the Aztecs.* Stanford: Stanford University Press, 1961.

Spencer, Otha C. *Flying the Weather, The Story of Air Weather Reconnaissance.* Campbell, Tex.: The Country Studio, 1996.

Tannehill, Ivan Ray. *Hurricanes: Their Nature and History: Particularly Those of the West Indies and the Southern Coasts of the United States.* New York: Greenwood Press, 1938.

Tannehill, Ivan Ray. *The Hurricane Hunters.* New York: Dodd, Mead, 1956.

Thompson, Philip D. "A History of Numerical Weather Prediction in the United States." *AMS Bulletin* 64, no. 7: 755–769, 1983.

Toole, Wycliffe D. "The U.S. Navy's Hurricane Hunters." *U.S. Naval Institute Proceedings* 86, no. 9: 48–56, 1960.

U.S. Navy, Bureau of Aeronautics. *Intensification of Tropical Cyclones, Atlantic and Pacific Areas.* Fourth Research Project, Project AROWA, Norfolk, Va., 1956.

Viñes, B. *Cyclonic Circulation and Translatory Movement of West Indian Hurricanes.* Washington, 1898.

Walter, H. J. *Wind Chasers: The History of the U.S. Navy Hurricane Hunters.* Dallas: Taylor Publishing, 1992.

Watson, Lyall. *Heaven's Breath: A Natural History of the Wind.* New York: William Morrow, 1984.

Weiner, Earl J., and Nagel, David C., eds. *Human Factors in Aviation.* New York: Academic Press, 1988.

Whipple, Addison Beecher Colvin, and the editors of Time-Life Books. *Storm.* Alexandria, Va.: Time-Life Books, 1982.

Wood, Colonel F. B. "A Flight into the September, 1944, Hurricane off Cape Henry, Virginia." *AMS Bulletin* 26, no. 5: 153–156, 1945.

Index